Barbie III And Company

Lou Fulgaro

**Front And Back Cover Photos
By Leslie Hicks**

© 2003 by Lou Fulgaro. All rights reserved.

No part of this book may be reproduced, stored in a retrieval system, or transmitted by any means, electronic, mechanical, photocopying, recording, or otherwise, without written permission from the author.

ISBN: 1-4107-8707-9 (e-book)
ISBN: 1-4107-8706-0 (Paperback)
ISBN: 1-4107-8705-2 (Dust Jacket)

Library of Congress Control Number: 2003096115

This book is printed on acid free paper.

Printed in the United States of America
Bloomington, IN

1stBooks - rev. 11/14/03

DEDICATION

To all Weary Warriors, the sentinels of 43-4106. As keepers of the past you have unselfishly brought living history into the present. May those who follow have the resilience to bring her into the future.

IN MEMORY

Jerry Fencel
Ralph Quatrine
Walter Wild

```
NORTH AMERICAN-B_25_H
A.F. SERIAL NO.43_4106
MFG.SERIAL NO.178092
DATE OF MFG._1943
ENGINES_WRIGHT R 2600_29
```

Contents

A Long Time Ago 1
Barbie and Dora 5
Dream Come True 15
Enter the Museum 23
Enter the Pros 27
Preflight 33
First Try 37
Clow International Airport 43
One More Time 49
Enter the Author 55
Exit the Museum 63
Counting Beans 69
We Begin Again 77
The Fuel Cells 87
Thinking Positive 97
Live and Learn 101
A Real Experience 105
The Cannon Nose 115
Buyer Beware 121
Bingo a Couple of Times 133
Anybody for Paint 143
A New Shop Boss 149
Again the Fuel Cells 153
Off to a Good But Bad Start 159
We Hang an Engine and We Learn 163
Our First Air Show 173
Rain, Rain Go Away 185
Air Show Sunday 189
Odds and Ends 195
Pompous, Arrogant; 203
Wing and a Tail 209
Who? We Grow 223
Clear The Props 227
We Try Again 237
Bad Times 249

More Odds and Ends 255
From Bad to Worse 263
If It Was A Horse 267
Barbie III and Company 277
Retirement and the "Ding" 283
Barbie Waltzes With the Big Guys 289
Where Are They Now Year 2003 307

Acknowledgements

As I settle comfortably into my early seventies I have come to realize that women have been an incredibly positive influence on my life. Getting past the womb, my teachers, a patient wife, and three understanding daughters, there are many. From the receptionist and the office clerks, to the secretaries and those that were just friends, my sincere appreciation. You have supported me in my endeavors, comforted me during bad times, and guided me when I was troubled. I am sure there have been many times that I failed to say thank you. This acknowledgment is a way for me to do that. There are two women that are a direct link to my writing and I would like to acknowledge them. Carol Chamberlain the retired managing editor of my home town newspaper who fifteen years ago advised me to stop talking about writing and do it and edited my very first pages of prose; and Laura Reynolds, an ex-teacher who now serves as a municipal judge in Wisconsin who for years has been the final reader of my manuscripts, giving sound suggestions and ensuring reasonable grammatical correctness- many times over my objections.

Special Thanks

To Vic Tatelman pilot of Dirty Dora, R.T. Smith pilot of Barbie III, Mark Clark for the generous use of his equipment including the props on the wall, Tim McCarter for his caring and advice and all the other unknown, but not forgotten persons that were always there for us. Weary Warriors could not have completed our restoration of our B-25H serial number 43-4106 without you. On the behalf of all Weary Warriors, our sincere gratitude.

Introduction
World War II

After our sojourn into military history, you and I are going to skip ahead about forty years and, in the year 1981, are going to find a demilitarized B-25 with a long solid eight-gun-nose resting peacefully on a Midwest farm where she has slumbered for some ten years. She is intact, somewhat neglected, but all there. If everything worked, she would fly. Spring, summer and fall of 1981 would be spent preparing her for her maiden voyage to her new home and full restoration. Board her for that first, white-knuckled, teeth-clenching flight out of that farm pasture and, within four minutes, experience her first engine failure. A few days later, board her again and some twenty minutes into flight experience a second engine failure. Most pilots in their lifetime don't experience a sick engine, let alone an engine failure.

You will meet a unique group of real life characters and work alongside them removing frozen, rusty nuts and bolts, overhauling components and seeking parts and advice from around the world. Together, we will journey through gallons of burning paint stripper. Scrape, clean and then clean again. We will nurse cuts, burns and bruises; fight aluminum and wood slivers; and day-by-day, month-by-month and year-by-year, experience the joys and frustrations, the expense, the trials and tribulations as this warbird is dismantled and then reassembled. Every nut, bolt, washer, screw, cable, wire, hose, tube, switch, bracket, pulley and pipe will be removed. The smallest of components as well as the largest will be replaced, rebuilt, overhauled or remanufactured by skilled machinists. There will be no shortcuts; no paint applied over rust or corrosion; no imported substandard nuts or bolts. The journey from a standing derelict in 1981 to piles of steel and aluminum parts unloaded from two flatbed trucks and scattered gently across a hanger floor in 1984 to a pristine, airworthy, one-of-a-kind restoration in 1992. You will share the experience of sitting in the narrow cockpit between two thundering radial engines developing 3400 horsepower and feel the impact of spinning prop tips that beat the air a scant few feet from your head. All is graphically told and illustrated in the pages that follow.

Getting it right was not an easy task. I was not involved during the first year or so when the idea to "save" this B-25 was formed. While I was aware of the presence of this medium bomber (I lived some twenty miles from where it rested and had flown over it many times in my own plane). I was not aware that four men had formed an Illinois non-profit organization to rehabilitate the old bomber. As this plan progressed, I had to ask a lot of questions (who, what, where, when why and how), which was a relatively easy task. However, if I asked the same question of five or six people, sometimes I got five or six versions of the answer. The time "down on the farm" explained this dilemma to some extent, but it gives you a "peek through the window" at what it takes to prepare a warbird for flight and reflects the spirit of what happened and who did what. It is as close to correct as I can make it without giving you three or four versions. Once I became involved, I just took photos and made notes.

So —- let's get to the story.

A Long Time Ago

The famous Mitchell and the not-too-well-known cannon-nose version of this warbird entered the war with a tongue-in-cheek idea. It was born from one man's determination to put some real punch into the firepower of a B-25. The low level strafing role of this attack bomber had already been established in the South Pacific and, to many, the killing power was mediocre. In many of the strafing runs, the fifty-caliber slugs cut down Japanese personnel, demolished wood and tin buildings and tore wheeled vehicles in half. However, it fell far short when it came to steel, armor plate, dirt fortifications and cement pillboxes. Slab-sided supply barges, armored vehicles, tanks and ships simply shook off the impact and continued on.

Tiring of the lack of punch, one enterprising pilot traded a case of scotch whiskey to an artillery crew (who were being shipped out) for their 75MM cannon, which was a straightforward field artillery piece. With a lot of ingenuity and modification, the stripped-down cannon was bolted into the reinforced nose of a B-25. While some said a prayer, some did their beads and some crossed their fingers, the cannon worked. The B-25 bounced with the recoil but stayed together as the crew sent a few, let's-see-what-happens, rounds down the barrel. In the air, the cannon didn't perform any differently but some thought that the aircraft actually stopped flying as the airframe absorbed the recoil.

When it came to targeting, they came up with the simple solution of bore-sighting the cannon with the fixed nose machine guns and both were zeroed in at the same range. Once the machine gun projectiles found the target, the pilot would trigger off a cannon round or two during his strafing run. The designation "cannoneer" entered the crew tasks for the crewmember, many times also serving as flight engineer, who loaded and cleared the cannon.

North American heard about the modification, came for a look, liked what they saw, went back to the drawing board and soon produced one thousand cannon-nose B-25's designated as the "G" and, later, as the "H" models. This remarkable, though not well-known, cannon-nose version was the most heavily armed aircraft to see continuous service in World War II. With an unmuffled exhaust stack coupled to each massive engine cylinder, it also became the noisiest. The popping and crackling exhaust at idle and the brutal, earth-shaking blast at power was overwhelming and recognizable to all who came into contact with her.

The cannon-nose B-25H was nothing more than a short, blunt-nose killing machine. Its cannon, complemented by four, fifty caliber machine guns in the nose, with two more in side packs and two in the top turret, locked and facing forward provided an unheard-of concentration of forward firepower. Two more machine guns in the waist and two more in the tail made the "H" a formidable foe whether it was coming or going. Some Japanese defenders in Burma and the South Pacific called her the "Twin-Tailed Demon." She executed her savage mission of death and destruction at mast and treetop levels day after relentless day.

The impact of her incredible firepower could (and at times did) rip in half Japanese coastal supply ships up to and including gun ships and light destroyers. Supply tugs and their string of cumbersome barges caught scurrying out in open water from island to island would snap apart like plastic toys and disintegrate as the wall of searing projectiles found their mark. Large freighters and heavily armed cruisers fell prey to the relentless B-25's as they resorted to their fifty-feet-above-the-water, skip-bombing tactics. Carrying a total of three thousand pounds of bombs in their internal bomb bays, they could, with precision, deliver a five hundred-pound bomb with a one-and-a-half second delayed fuse. When the bomb found the frantically turning ship attempting to elude the deadly attack, it would penetrate deeply into the vital bowels of the enemy ship before exploding. In Burma, the railroad bridges fell like sticks of a child's toy set as the feared spike bombs bent rail tracks as if they were made of soft putty. From time to time, five-inch rockets were added, secured to hard points under the wings, making the strafing breathtakingly awesome.

The following story takes a unique approach to the small but decisive part played by the B-25 in the air war with Japan. It touches on the history from time to time but spends most of its pages telling a fascinating, true story of the discovery and restoration of a rare B-25H, fifty years after its manufacture and long after its deadly missions had ended.

Our cannon-nose B-25H, serial number 43-4106, was the second of its series to roll off the assembly line in 1943. The first H model, 43-4105 has disappeared into oblivion. Two other, non-airworthy, cannon-noses are known to exist in museums. For years, I referred to our warbird as "06" as she had no name or paint scheme during this period. We would eventually name her and decide on an authentic paint scheme as we neared a decade of meticulous restoration on this very rare B-25.

06 was rescued from an unknown fate on a farm in Northern Illinois where she had lain idle for years. She reposed on stubbles of green grass, her tires having worn depressions in the ground that had closed around them more tightly with each freeze and thaw cycle until they were held in a vice-like grip. Her odd paint job of red and white was scratched, faded and blotched and indicated that she had been put to civilian use after the war. The de-militarized interior, still decorated in musty olive drab, was stripped of its armament, worn from decades of use, stiff from years of inactivity but was, more or less, intact.

Occupation by generations of nesting birds and angry wasps, each determined to defend their sweltering summer home at all costs, made entry in the summer risky. The (original) olive drab paint was cracked and peeling, hanging from the sides and top of the interior like Spanish moss from a tree. Sagging cables and wires wove tortuous paths through the exposed framework that formed the bulkheads of the fuselage. Years of dust, debris, bird droppings, feathers and grassy nest materials littered every horizontal surface and had accumulated in every corner.

The double-rowed, fourteen cylinder Wright Cyclone R-2600-29 engines, their power silenced for years, sported rusty and unreadable engine manufacture plates. Oil that once oozed black through every opening in the engine cowling, showed its faint shadows of telltale stains. Traces of red hydraulic fluid, long ago dried up, left its pale imprint on the once-polished landing gear struts, now dulled by years of non-use. Tires were checked and sagged with age; antenna wires were missing; glass was flecked and yellow from the ravages of weather; zus fasteners and bolts were ringed with rust. But the neglected and forlorn Mitchell still reflected a haunting image of the energy and purpose of an era that has passed into history.

Standing next to this medium bomber, you could close your eyes and, with a vivid imagination, be taken back to the early 1940's. In the silence of early morning, you could hear the unmistakable deep rumble of her great engines. Your mind would see an olive drab B-25 banking steeply over an enemy-held island in the Pacific or a Japanese airbase, slashed into the deep, endless jungle of Burma. As it prepares to attack your heart beats faster with anticipation, fear and excitement as the B-25 now angles downward, throttles advanced to war emergency, it hurls itself toward the enemy. Your thoughts race with the Mitchell at your side.

You reach out and your fingers touch. Yes, she is there; she is real, she is awesome and you are insignificant alongside of her. She is the shadow of a time when the enemy was implacable but know, when boys became heroes as they grew to manhood and when a nation was called to come to the defense of a world that had not yet realized its potential.

With reluctance, you walk away. Your thoughts are yours, alone.

Barbie and Dora

They were two women, separated by thousands of miles with something in common. Their names graced the sides of two combat-weary B-25 medium bombers.

I had earned the price of admission to a movie theater by collecting scrap metal for the war effort, a common practice during the years of World War II. I was about twelve years old and was watching a black and white newsreel. As the news of our war with Japan flickered and flashed on the movie screen, an unknown voice described the action. I can remember palm trees in the background. As a line of glass-nosed B-25's taxied along a dusty dirt taxiway, a close-up of one of the B-25's fills the screen with the name "DIRTY DORA". The glass in the nose had been painted over and there were four machine guns protruding. The unknown voice named the B-25 and the named stayed with me.

Another theater of operation, Burma, unfamiliar to me, was on the same newsreel. This time, three short nosed B-25s were getting ready to take off. There was something said about "cannon-noses". They were too far away to make out any names, but the multiple stripes on the fuselage behind the wing were very evident. As they took off and flashed past the camera, I could see the Roman numeral I, painted on one of the stubby noses. The images of that day have stayed with me all my life. While I was not aware of it at the time, that day was the beginning of a love affair for me with a warbird called a B-25 named the Mitchell.

Some forty years later, I would be in my late fifties when, by pure chance, faith, and perhaps a smile from the Lord, I would come into contact with the pilots of those two aircraft and begin enduring friendships held together by the common thread called a B-25. The pilots were Victor Tatelman, the pilot of the glass four-gun-nosed DIRTY DORA and R.T. Smith, the pilot of the blunt cannon-nosed B-25 that sported the Roman numeral I and named BARBIE III. I would consider myself fortunate to be on a first-name basis with them. Both were real heroes. My stint in the Air Force during the Korean War pales when compared to these two very brave men.

There were two machine gun-nosed, non-cannoned B-25's, named Dirty Dora and Dirty Dora II. They were assigned to the 38th bomb group. In 1944, with sixty combat missions to her credit, Dirty Dora was transferred to the 345th Bomb Group of the Fifth Air Force. She flew with the 499th squadron of the famed Air Apaches.

In 1944, she was piloted by 1st Lt. Tatelman (who put another fifty missions on her) for about a year. Tatelman was transferred back to the states and Dirty Dora continued to play her role as a low-level attack bomber. A variety of pilots and crews flew an additional fifty or so missions, bringing her total combat mission up to over 160 missions. Finally, she became so worn out she was declared combat fatigued and was retired.

When the now Capt. Tatelman returned from his Search and Destroy tactical training stateside, there were no aircraft available on which to install his new, then state-of-the-art, equipment designed to ferret out Japanese radar signals. Resourceful and determined, he spent months in an island airplane "bone yard" and, from a variety of junked and wrecked B-25s, put one B-25 back together and installed his equipment. Thus did Dirty Dora II come to be. She was very successful in her role and, when hostilities ended in the South Pacific, Capt. Tatelman was still shooting up the Japanese war machine in Dirty Dora II.

Barbie III was a cannon-nosed H model B-25 assigned to the 1st Air Commando Group and piloted by Smith. The 5318th Air Unit was part of the 10th Air Force and lasted a few years. It consisted of twelve B-25H models, about twice as many early model P-51's and a few Spitfires. The 10th saw action in India and Burma. In China, Smith piloted a P-40 Warhawk with the Flying Tigers and reached the status of ace before the U.S. entered the war with Japan. When war was declared in December of 1941, the Flying Tiger pilots (some with reluctance) found themselves, amid considerable controversy, in the U.S. Army Air Force. Many Tiger pilots preferred flying as mercenaries and liked the pay even more.

Smith's hastily assembled outfit in Burma was completely out of whack with the typical chain of units, squadrons, groups, wings and etc. It was a short-lived, rag-tag mix of fighters, bombers, transports, gliders, liaison types and mules (the four-legged type) thrown in for good measure. What they all had in common was heat, humidity, rain, mud, insects, dysentery and malaria. Many pilots who were round pegs in square holes were assigned to this force just to get them out of the way. In later years, some referred to them as the "Black Sheep Squadron of Burma".

The pilots and crews raised all kinds of hell from rain-soaked, dirt airfields that had been carved out of the jungle. One was called Broadway after the famous street in New York. Some veterans claimed the airfields were actually behind enemy lines. All supplies had to be flown in and the injured, wounded and dying had to be flown out. Their low-level combat missions supported troops on the ground as they wrestled Burma from the Japanese. Many low-level combat missions penetrated deep into Burma. Their mission was to cut off vital military supplies. Smith's outfit tore up railroads and railroad bridges, sank barges on the many rivers, beat up airfields and destroyed truck convoys on the narrow, winding, mountain roads. The 75MM cannon mounted in the nose was unknown and shocked the enemy. To be on the receiving end of a searing cannon projectile was terrifying to the enemy. They could not understand or comprehend what was happening.

To many of the H crews, their biggest concern was whether their airfield would still be there when they returned. The front lines were fluid and without definition. The naked eye could only penetrate some five yards into the thick jungle undergrowth and the Japanese were masters of quiet, aggressive stealth through the steaming, insect-infested jungle. Many came to the conclusion that their most important piece of equipment was the mule. It was the only thing that could move and carry supplies during the months of rain when firm dirt had turned to thick soup.

The treetop level missions took place during some of the most vicious low-level air to ground combat of World War II. It was a time when the Japanese fighting man had a relentless hatred for the American Airman. This hatred was shared and paralleled by many civilians in the Japanese-occupied islands, especially in the South Pacific. During the sorties of the Air Apaches, death and destruction rained to earth with the accidental indiscriminate mixing of military and civilian targets. Civilians and soldiers lay dead or maimed alongside each other. Property damage was extensive, both civilian and military.

To the airmen of the Air Apaches, the end result of surviving the downing of their aircraft was capture (many times aided by civilians), torture, execution by beheading in some instances and, in some rare cases, cannibalism. Most airmen who went down over occupied islands did not survive the actual crash of their B-25.

Smith and his fellow airmen had it a little easier with the Burmese people but faced a vicious Japanese enemy as Tatelman did. They faced a different kind of enemy. While Tatelman could sight from island to island across the sea, Smith had hundreds of square miles of trackless jungle that, from the air, was an endless carpet of green.

At ground-level strafing heights, a fatal hit by enemy ground fire into the vital systems of a B-25 usually meant assured but delayed death to its hapless crew. There would be a flash, then a staggering shudder and perhaps a ball of flame as their aircraft became a mass of disintegrating metal with no place to go but down.

From the time when a B-25 was hit to the time it cartwheeled and impacted into a jungle-covered hill, many times inverted, minus wings, engines, and tails could be a matter of a few fleeting seconds. There was no time for the brave crew to do anything but hope the pilot could pull off a miracle and straighten out their sickening plunge to the terrain below, if not, they realized they were going to die. When a B-25 slammed into the ground, the brutal impact started a chain of events that was instantaneous and over in a microsecond. The bulkheads and skeletal frame, buckles, twists and collapses. The aluminum skin panels shear from the frame. Seats break away from their mounting points and the seated crew restrained or not are hurtled forward at the speed the aircraft struck the ground, many times in excess of 300 MPH. Their torsos and limbs collide with the naked frame members with such force the framework acts as blunt shears that instantaneously cuts through the mass of flesh, muscle and bone. Fuel and oil lines break from their brackets, fuel cells and oil tanks are split open spraying their deadly fluid from the ruptured tanks. The fiery explosion incinerates the body parts into ash that does not fully reflect the unimaginable death inflicted upon the young vulnerable crew.

If they were lucky, once the B-25 shook off the impact of the hit, it could continue on and the pilots might be able to coax and nurse their stricken aircraft home or to a safer place to go down —- which, in Tatelman's case would be the sea. The further from the landfall of the Japanese, the better the chance of rescue if they survived the impact into the sea. The air, like the sea, is terrible unforgiving of mistakes.

The young American airmen, hearing of the fate of their fallen comrades who were shot down —- or whose craft were lost because of mechanical problems, simple pilot error, or mid-air collisions —- swelled with compassion for their loss and went forward with a vengeance that was unstoppable. American airmen retaliated and strafing of Japanese sailors swimming away from their sinking ships became commonplace. The end result was that the crews of the B-25s took their knocks if they went down. They expected no mercy and they gave none in return.

Many years later some critics thought this type of tactic was most un-American. Such tactics were not becoming to American ideals. Most of these comments, however, came from people who were never in a cockpit of a combat B-25.

Back to Dirty Dora. Dora was a living, breathing woman of questionable reputation —- an Australian prostitute. From all indications, she impressed or endeared herself to many young American airmen. It was evident that the men of the 38th were impressed by her and named one of their B-25s in her honor. We do not know of Dora's fate or if she still lives.

We do know that Tatelman is alive and well, some sixty years after poking around in Dirty Dora, "the B-25." He is still tall, lean, has his wits about him and is of sound mind, with the tenacity and the eagerness of a young hunter. Today he is still a pilot, one of the few current, and rated to pilot a B-25. He cannot recall the name of the pilot from the 38th that named Dirty Dora. The pilot from the 38th introduced him to Dora and Tatelman remembers her as being in her twenties, dark-haired, and very refined. We will meet Tatelman later in this book when he reads about a crazy bunch in Illinois, calling themselves the Weary Warriors, who are restoring a B-25. Tatelman comes for a look, likes what he sees and joins to eventually become the group's chief pilot, a position he still holds, in his eighties as we enter the twenty-first century.

Barbie was named after Smith's wife, who was a Powers model. It was his third aircraft, thus the III was added after her name. If he recalled accurately, the Roman numeral I was for the First Air Commandos but at this late date, he was not sure why it had that designation. It had been a long time ago and his heart; memories and recall were with the Flying Tigers.

It was a dilemma in the late 1980s for the Weary Warriors as to the paint scheme of their B-25. They had to plan for the years ahead. They had a long eight-gun nose on their B-25. And they had Tatelman. Dirty Dora's scheme would be nice.

There were several long-eight-gunned-nose B-25s flying around. In fact, they were relatively common. On the other hand, there were no cannon-nose B-25's flying anywhere.

The B-25 that the Weary Warriors found was an H model. It was obvious they had a rare B-25 and, if they went with the cannon-nose, it would be the only one operational in the world. Once the decision was made, all Weary Warriors pulled together and went in that direction. In the year 2003, 06 still flies with the cannon-nose. The dust-covered eight-gun nose she came with rests on wood pallets and can be bolted on at any time.

South Pacific early 1940s. Dirty Dora and her engine maintenance crew, names unknown. If you look closely this is a glass nose B-25C with the glass painted over. Dirty Dora had ninety-six missions at the time of the photo, there would be more. She had four guns in her nose and four more in two side packs. Tatelman collection.

A very young Captain Victor Tatelman and Dirty Dora somewhere in the Pacific circa 1944. Tatelman collection.

Captain Victor Tatelman and the starboard side of the Dirty Dora. Note the very old design of the two-gun side pack. The line on the side of the fuselage above the machine gun barrels is the prop danger line and was in red. Tatelman collection.

Burma early 1940s. Left to right: LT. Wes Weber navigator, M/SGT. Chuck Baisden top turret gunner and LT. COL. Robert T. Smith pilot. Note the tape on the cockpit armor plate to prevent rust under the steel armor plate and the windshield armor plate. "—-Damn Lou, we had armor plate all over that thing except the belly, where all the bullets came from—-" R. T. Smith Photo from R. T. Smith collection.

Lou Fulgaro

Dream Come True
Winter 1981

The sun's reflection bounced off the polished side of the steel pick as Claude DeFacci held it momentarily over his head and then, with a grunt of determination, swung the pick at the frozen earth that had held 06's tires in a frozen grip all winter. Inflicting very little damage to the frozen earth, a few small crumbles of jagged earth were the result of his efforts. The chuckles and guffaws coming from his three partners, Mike, Walter, and Dick were ignored. Soon all hands gave it a try. Jackets and scarves were shed as they began to warm up from the physical exertion. Slowly the frozen earth was chipped away and a sloping trench was dug to all three tires.

A farm tractor in the capable hands of Dick Lambert was backed up to the nose of 06. The tow bar in place, and to shouts of encouragement and applause, 06 moved, shuddered ever so slightly, and groaned as the frozen Illinois prairie reluctantly gave her up. The short few hundred-foot trip to the south side of a well-kept farm building was accomplished without incident. Protected from the north winds, basking in the sun, and with the availability of electricity, this would be the new home for 06 for months to come.

The first order of business was a cleanup of the interior. The dauntless four would get together, usually on week ends, armed with a assortment of rags, worn brushes, brooms, a variety of ladders, tools, cleaners, and all those unwanted items that seem to accumulate in the corners of basements and garages. Debris was swept, shoveled, pushed, pulled, and vacuumed. The wasp's nests, with their dormant occupants, were gingerly removed. Sparrow nests were tossed. In between sneezing and flying dust, an occasional thunk-type clunk would be heard when someone hit his head on a bulkhead or perhaps tripped over one. As the weekends slipped by, the winding down of the shop vac seemed to say the interior was cleaned up. The four stepped back and admired their cleaning efforts. Their wives would have given them a "good try" mark.

Sagging rusty control cables of all types, pulleys, cams, hinges, levers, and all those mechanisms that pivot, slide, push, pull, and swing would be addressed next. This was more to their liking. It was man's work and being mechanical, something they were familiar with. The owners were becoming acquainted with 06. They hoped she would respond. Soon the groans, squeaks, and rubbing noises began to disappear. Elevator, rudder, and aileron hinges were cleaned, greased and oiled. Control wheel yokes and columns along with the rudder controls got the same treatment. They could be moved and all that could be heard was the odd occasional scrapping of a sagging control cable rubbing against a bulkhead. The hollow thumping of control surfaces hitting their travel stops meant only that when something was moved at one end, something moved at the other end —- which was good. Glances out the cockpit windows confirmed that the control services did move and appropriately in the proper direction.

Sitting on the mouse-chewed cushion on the pilot's seat, Walter Wild smiled and dusted off the instrument panel. There were a few gaping holes and they seemed to smile back. Walter wondered what instruments were missing and what happened to them. With the controls dusted off, cockpit windows washed and spider webs pulled free, the realization of the potential of 06 began to become a reality. Engine controls were not moved at this time. First, the engine cowlings would be removed and control rods and cables would be cleaned and receive the oil treatment.

As Walter vigorously scrubbed away at the bulkhead just behind the co-pilot's seat, a rather worn manufacturer's plate became readable. Everyone gathered in the cramped cockpit. Serial numbers, model numbers and dates were read off. Comments buzzed back and forth as the new find sparked excitement. All had assumed with the long eight-gun nose that 06 was a common J model but, with a little research, the four men soon discovered that they had a very rare H model.

Scrap lumber and clear plastic were accumulated (or perhaps the proper word would be scrounged) and put to use to form a shelter. It was flimsy but the two makeshift structures built around each engine provided refuge from the cold Illinois wind and let the warm sun radiate in. Warmth was still an elusive factor at this time of the year in northern Illinois.

With rusty zus fasteners squeaking in protest —- and with the usual profanity from the weekend mechanics —- the engine cowlings stubbornly resisted removal. Eventually the cowlings gave in and were removed and marked. The ever-present bird nests and accumulated matter were removed from around each cylinder of the huge double-rowed engine.

Each fourteen-cylinder engine was capable of developing over one thousand seven hundred-horse power and swung a three bladed prop with a twelve and one half-foot arc. Again, the cleaning rags and trusty oilcan went to work. Cowl flap rods, carburetor rods and all the related engine controls received the treatment. Anything in the engine compartment that moved back and forth or up and down was addressed with loving care. All engine controls were exercised from the cockpit with corresponding movement obediently taking place in the engine compartment firewall forward.

Next, the spark plugs were removed and a mystical formula of lubricating oil, transmission fluid, and rust inhibitor was generously poured into the top and side cylinders of the radial engines. The lower and up side down cylinders had to have the mixture sprayed through the two spark plug openings of each cylinder. With the spark plugs loosely replaced, Mike Butler did not have to count too hard to figure out that the massive cylinders taking two spark plugs each added up to fifty six spark plugs: at ten dollars each it was going to be a expensive plug replacement. The mystical oil solution would sit, soak, and penetrate for a week.

Early the following Saturday, with anticipation, Mike, Walter, and Claude drove to the farm to find a smiling Dick Lambert. To their joy, the oil had worked its way through the engine and some was dripping from the exhaust pipes and around the spark plugs of the lower cylinders. The oil put through the spark plug holes would make the top of the cylinders slippery.

Their concern was now the oil gallery in the center of the engine. Every moving part revolved and extended from what could be called a crankshaft. A small pump, a few pounds of pressure, would send the oil mixture to the bearings, which were the heart of the Wright Cyclone. The question was; should we or shouldn't we try and turn the engines?

Dick assures them the engines should and would rotate. Walter leans against one prop blade and it moves. Mike tugs at the prop blade of the other engine and the prop moves. Dick and Claude are smiling. Let's do it. With the spark plugs removed, eager hands pull and push at each prop as it nears the lower half of its rotation.

Blade after blade passes an imaginary point and with some unfamiliar interior metallic clicks and solid knocks, eight eager hands pull and push until every piston of every cylinder goes through a complete cycle of its intake, compression, power, and exhaust strokes. Oil gushes out of the spark plug holes and drips from the exhaust. On the intake strokes, the sucking of air can be heard. A good sign, the sound means that the engines are tight. More importantly, the big Wright Cyclones are not frozen.

The engine cowlings were installed and buttoned up. The marking of the look-alike engine cowlings made the chore easy and uncomplicated; it would have otherwise taken days to figure out the cowling placement. Some civilian odds and ends like the heater that was installed would have to be removed. There would be no room for such things in the restoration plan to bring 06 back to a military configuration.

As the simple, mundane work to be done was checked off, nagging questions began to become obvious. Was the Mitchell airworthy? If not, could it be made airworthy? Was there any hidden structural corrosion? Do we know what we are looking for and if we see it will we recognize it? Over the next few weeks, inspection plates and fairings would be removed and everyone took a look. Things looked okay. Will we truck it out? Fly it out? To restore it, 06 would have to have a hanger. What would be the hangar costs? What would be the restoration cost? What has to be done? Who do we know that can help? Someone would have to drop some names to get them started.

The four men relaxed under the wing of 06. She was indifferent to their discussion. Walter, in his sixties, was a somewhat-retired machinist. Walter loved the B-25 and was the person who got the idea of forming a not-for-profit corporation and restoring 06. He was a World War II Air Force vet and, at this time, was a student pilot. He would go on to get his ticket over the next two years. Mike Butler, the youngest of the four, owned his own machine shop and was a low-time pilot. Claude DeFacci was in the construction crane business and was also a student pilot. I got the impression that he was Walter's brother-in-law. Richard Lambert was a pilot and the original owner of the Mitchell and owned the farm were 06 now sat. He also had a private airstrip on the farm with a few light aircraft based there.

Dick was the most knowledgeable about the B-25. He had started it on many occasions and taxied it about his farm. He got it off the ground a few times for a hundred feet or so, but never really flew it. He had owned several warbirds and his farm once housed a rare P-38 Lighting, which he sold. When Walter and Dick got their heads together, they, by chance or plan, came up with a mechanism for a few partners to share the work and the expense. Short on knowledge and funds, with little experience on warbirds, they would go forward. They had the eagerness and camaraderie and they were warbird lovers. Now they had the opportunity of a lifetime and looked forward with anticipation to 06's restoration. It was rare that four would find each other and take on such a monumental task. As a rule there were two general types of warbird lovers. Those that dreamed about it and could afford them and those that dreamed about it and could not afford them.

Expense began to loom in the future. While they could do many manual mechanical tasks and were all inclined in this direction, they still needed expertise. How would they share expenses? Where do you find a round engine mechanic? In this day they were almost as rare as dinosaurs. What about an airframe mechanic? What are the regulations affecting this World War II medium bomber? Were there any mandatory directives that have to be complied with? If parts were needed where would they buy them? Some manuals were missing and they would need them all. The questions buzzed around in everyone's head but went unanswered. There was going to be much more to this project than just sitting in the cockpit and playing pilot.

The joys of being a warbird owner were being neutralized, and appropriately so, by the realization of their lack of knowledge and contacts. To add to their woes, the farm with the grass strip was sold and 06 would have to be moved. This recent development added more questions. Now that they knew "when", the "to where" and "how "became important.

With the warmth of spring, the discussion of their mission during their lunch breaks took on a cheery note that raised their hopes. Several nagging questions had been put to rest. They would endeavor to fly her out. A firm direction of their mission had been reached. They formed a not-for-profit corporation and named it The WEARY WARRIORS SQUADRON Inc. [most appropriately as you will find out later.] Simple by-laws one page long were agreed upon and written and officers were elected. A warbird expert was located to give them an appraisal of 06. She was in good shape, considering her age and lack of attention. It would take about four weeks to get her to the point where she could fly one time. If worked right, getting her ready for the ferry flight could and would be a step in getting licensed.

First on the list of things to consider would be the carburetors. They had been sitting for years and were all gummed and varnished up. Two carburetors with trade-ins and labor to install would cost over two thousand dollars. Weary Warriors swallowed hard and gasped for air. On the bright side, the warbird expert, who also sold warbird, offered to buy 06 —- which made them feel good. Most importantly, he began to drop names of people that were in the warbird loop that could help them.

They did, however, need a realistic number to get 06 off the ground one time. The man obliged and did not mince words. With Weary Warriors doing a lot of the grunt work, provided both engines worked, props were good and including fuel, oil and insurance for one flight; it would cost at least thirty thousand. The silence was awesome. The only sound heard was the expert's car door slamming shut as he left the farm after collecting his modest check.

Money. Where and how to get money. None were wealthy and, once they recovered from their money shock, Wild and Butler reached into their pockets and came up with $4,000 each. DeFacci had $3,800 and Lambert's contribution was the B-25. The corporation owned a non-flying medium bomber, had nothing to bomb, and had a little under twelve thousand dollars in the bank. Not too shabby. It would get them started.

They made phone calls, asked questions, and got acquainted. The most frequent question asked was, "how much?" Just to start, the engines needed new carburetors, fuel and oil filters and strainers, engine hoses and spark plugs, batteries and battery cables. The starters, generators, magnetos, relays would all have to be overhauled or replaced. Ignition harnesses and new engine wiring —- and don't forget the props. Add in oil and fuel they did not have enough money to certify the two massive engines.

The engines are worthless if the props are no good. Two props, overhauled hubs and six blades would cost $9,000-$12,000 - new blades would be $14,000 if they were needed. Weary Warriors would remove, deliver and install the props. Lambert felt the props would be okay and some of the engine accessories just needed cleaning up.

As they explored, probed, and obtained manuals, the secrets of 06 reluctantly and slowly revealed themselves. It was a delightful time for the group. They realized that, when North American and old man Wright got together, they had designed the oil system to neatly hold the contents of a thirty-seven gallon G.I. drum of oil, one drum per engine; that's 148 quarts of oil per engine. Wild learned that the engines worked just fine with thirty-three gallons each. Any more and the big Wrights just blew the oil out. Just to start the engines, they would have to drain and flush the two huge oil tanks that were separate from the engines. They would also need to flush and clean all strainers, oil coolers, lines, and the engines themselves.

Once that was done, new oil would be added and they would have to run the engines for at least five hours to make sure they would keep on running. Before flight they would have to dump the contaminated new oil and start all over again. They would need to buy four drums of oil. During that process, they would drain the fuel tanks, flush the tanks, [there are four of them], and clean all the strainers, fuel lines, and filters, work over the fuel pumps. Then they would add three hundred gallons of fresh fuel just for the engine run. The cost of all of this would exceed $20,000 without even considering the props.

But there was much more to 06 than the engines and props. They still had the airframe, controls, hydraulics, electrical, and the brakes just to name a few of the more important items.

While the determined four could dismantle, clean flush, and drain under the watchful eye of a certified mechanic, the precision work such as installing, adjusting, and testing had to be left to a mechanic. Once past that point, would the instruments work and would they be accurate? When the engines are on line would that be the time for liability insurance?

Time was running out. They had to move ahead —- and at a faster pace.

Lou Fulgaro

Enter the Museum

Word had spread about 06 and the "crazy guys" that were going to fly her out of a farmer's field. With the decision that 06 was going to go under her own power, a goal was set and each, in his own way, worked toward that goal. Tenacity could best describe their determination to go forward.

It was an old-fashioned, rural happening and people just showed up to take pictures and kill time. Visitors came, looked, and gave advice and words of encouragement. Some just shook their heads. None reached into their pockets. Many looked forward to the "When ya gonna fire her up?" date, which was very vague. There was the usual hanger advice, somewhat similar to that of a self-made jailhouse lawyer, well intended but misleading. Much of the advice was accompanied by a few war stories. At times, there were so many show-and-tells that work came to a standstill. Weary Warriors felt that they were in a zoo and, unfortunately, on the wrong side of the fence. One suggested they charge admission to build up their bank account.

They would persevere over the months. The warmer the weather, the more the people came and, much of the time, got in the way. Weary Warriors could never understand some of the negative comments that came from a few of the visitors. It was just bad manners. Some hated to see the landmark, clearly visible from the county road that passed the farm, disappear. Some felt possessive about it and had become attached to her. And some, if nothing else, resented "their" conversation piece being removed. After all, when uncle whoever came to visit next summer, they would not be able to point to the Mitchell and expound. Overall, though, there was mostly admiration with a little envy sprinkled in.

It was a mild day with a deep blue sky. The V-tailed Bonanza slowly circled the farm and its grass strip. Its four occupants viewed 06 for the first time. From the air, the few light aircraft parked nearby were dominated by the size of the medium bomber. The four occupants were officers and directors from a fledgling new museum. They were looking for a warbird project. The get together had been arranged by DeFacci in an attempt to solve their money problem.

While the four looked down, there were four looking up. Had their salvation arrived?

The Bonanza settled softly on the grass strip, taxied up to the Mitchell and shut down. The four occupants piled out and were greeted with open arms. There, in front of them, in her faded circus red paint sat a clean and not too shabby B-25, perhaps capable of flight. It provided a striking contrast to the one they had. Theirs, over the years before its acquisition, had been stripped of most of its parts and corrosion had set in to the extent that it could never fly. It had been used as a part hulk and nothing else. With the museum's B-25 supplying some parts, maybe, just maybe, there was a beginning. During the formalities of introductions, the visitors could not take their eyes off 06. There was much said, little heard during the first half-hour.

At this point, each group knew little of the other and, interestingly, both groups were composed of such novices, they did not dare admit it to the other. During the show-and-tell from Weary Warriors and the kicking of tires from the museum members it was obvious that the love of warbirds was the common bond —- or was it?

In reality, the museum viewed Weary Warriors as a donor of their Mitchell and as a source of cash. The opposite was true from the cash-poor Weary Warriors who sized up the museum as a supply of experts with the financial resources and manpower to get things done. Each group considered the other as an answer to their prayers. In reality there was very little money or expertise on either side.

The museum members were given the run of 06 and it appeared that one or two were aircraft mechanics. It was obvious the more they looked the more they liked. It was much more than they had hoped for. As they poked around, all the cleaning and oiling was paying off.

The serial number checked and documented through references. 06 was indeed a rare H model and the museum wanted her. After a few stories about the exploits of the cannon-nosed Mitchells, they all gathered in the bomb bay. There they were shown the dents on the sheet metal separating the cockpit area from the bomb bay. The half-moon dents were caused by expended 75MM casings striking the bulkhead sheeting when it was extracted from the cannon chamber then ejected from the cannon breech. The museum bunch were sold.

The cost estimates began to trickle in. To get 06 to a point were a ferry permit could be obtained was hovering at $40,000. The number was high but $10,000 could be shaved off with a lot of labor from the two groups. Phone calls and letters between the museum and Wild's bunch increased.

From the phone calls and letters, an agreement began to emerge. The museum would provide all the labor ("Don't worry, we have two mechanics on staff and a lot of skilled help"). It would be a ground up restoration. They would hanger 06 at their airport, pay for the insurance and come up with half the proposed cost to ferry 06. They would donate all the parts they could from their B-25. Wild's bunch would buy all the parts and have access to the Mitchell. The museum would own fifty percent. The agreement would be put in its legal form by attorneys from both groups and signed.

Weary Warriors were jubilant. They figured that they had gotten the monkey off their back. The museum shared the same exhilaration. They had a good B-25 and a rare one at that. Like most marriages, the honeymoon was fantastic. Both groups pitched in and worked well together while 06 sat on Lambert's farm.

It was now late summer and the deadline to move the Mitchell was drawing near. The museum mechanics brought 06 further along but, while aircraft mechanics abound in the Midwest, none could be found that were big military radial engine mechanics. Nor could they find an airframe mechanic that would know the systems. 06 may have just as well come from the moon.

As the saying goes, two heads are better than one. In California, someone found two men from a company called Aero Traders who did nothing but find, rebuild, and sell B-25s. Yes, they could come, yes; when the time came they could get two B-25 pilots that would take 06 to the museum. Yes, they could come now. Money was the highlight of the conversation. Details were hammered out. Things were looking good.

Well, almost good. The museum did not have $15,000 to match what Wild's group had in the bank and had spent cleaning 06 up. The museum, through one of its members, arranged for a $15,000 loan from a bank but Wild's bunch would not let the museum use 06 as collateral for the loan. Some of the museum's directors signed for the bank note and the money was deposited into Weary Warriors bank account. With buying power of $26,800 in the bank, the project gathered a head of steam and was on its way.

Carl and Tony, the boys from Aero Traders, loaded up their truck and trailer with specialized tools, parts, and all the conceivable odds and ends that only someone with B-25 savvy would know about and were on their way to Illinois.

There was much to do to prepare 06 for Carl and Tony, who would arrive in a few days; and their instructions were carried out to the letter. Labor was expensive and the more the they could do, the lower the total cost would be. All were aware the money in the bank might not be enough. Then what would they do?

Word spread very quickly that those guys with the B-25 would be starting those huge radial engines now referred to as "the -29's" (the correct model number was R 2600-29.) They liked how "29" rolled off the tongue and it sounded good.

It seemed that, at times, every pilot, would-be pilot, and World War II buff showed up. They brought their families, lawn chairs, cameras, lunch, and sound recording equipment. They waited and hoped the big day would come on a weekend so they could see and hear "the -29's" come to life. Soon the big radials and their thousands of long-silent horse power would once again awaken and drown the countryside with their deep, rumbling exhaust; a sound that, in 1981, few people had ever heard. It seemed more important to run the engines than fly the medium bomber.

When was the big event to be? It would bring back memories for some and be a new experience for others. Now Walter, Mike, Claude, and Richard were important to many people. They were no longer the crazy guys with the circus red and white B-25.

Enter the Pros

Carl Scholl and his partner Tony Ritzman from Aero Traders arrived. At long last there was someone on site who knew the medium bomber inside and out. The Weary Warriors were elated that anyone would drive thousands of miles to work on their Mitchell. Money was a consideration, but still, to drive a truck with a trailer that distance! Two men had arrived, perhaps the only two men in the world, that possessed the experience and knowledge to do what had to be done and do it the right way the first time. Carl and Tony, who were mesmerized by the medium bomber, considered the trip more like a Sunday morning trip to church. They had made many like it over the years.

The Illinois bunch eyed the truck and trailer piled high with an impressive array of boxes, crates, drums, barrels, equipment and tools strapped to the truck and trailer beds. Some of it was foreign to the boys that were going to pay the tab. Carl and Tony took a look at 06, decided she looked good and gave the boys a pat on the back. She should, if everything went well, be airborne in about three weeks.

It was a frustrating time for 06's owners as it relates to time spent. They all wanted to stay day after day, but some did have to work. Some arranged to take some vacation time. Not only did they want to pitch in and help or, as Walter called it, do the donkeywork; they wanted to learn. They could learn by asking, learn by watching, learn by listening and learn by doing. They had to learn and this would be their only chance.

Days disappeared and became history. Fuel and oil tanks were flushed and cleaned. Fuel, oil, hydraulic lines and hoses were flushed or replaced. Fuel and oil strainers, filters, and the hydraulic reservoir got the same treatment. Brakes removed, cleaned, serviced, and inspected. Hydraulic brake lines were bled and wheel bearings cleaned and packed. All hose clamps were replaced with new. Carburetors replaced with new modern ones. Mags were removed and worked over, as were the aged generators. Ignition wires were replaced, as were the spark plugs and more oil was poured into the engine. It was all there but time and weather had taken its toll and rendered much that was not brass, aluminum, or steel non-airworthy.

Rubber and manmade synthetics, such as were used on hoses, had to go.

Hydraulic systems pressured checked and, at long last, the pressure held. Aircraft jacks were carefully put in place. It would take three of them to hold up 06. Slowly 06 rose as all three jacks were worked at the same time. Soon her landing gear, along with her tires, was dangling about six inches or so off the ground. With her gear extended, she looked leggy. Every strut was coated with hydraulic fluid; every mechanism that hinged, rotated, pushed or pulled was oiled or greased. Everything was done to make every moving part as slippery as could be.

In the cockpit, with the gear switch in the up position, Walter began to work the hand pump to build up hydraulic pressure to raise the gear. It would not be easy work. The first retraction test would be made by hand. In the engine nacelles, where the gear would retract the wheel down, locks were disengaged. At six hundred pounds pressure, the gear moved —- ever so slightly, but it moved. Carl and Tony closely monitored each gear on the outside. Two arms got tired and Walter began to realize that to pump up the gear by hand was a young man's job.

A third arm started working the pump handle. At eight hundred pounds and, with some tire kicking to help move the retraction process along, the gear, complaining all the way, was retracting. At about twelve hundred pounds pressure, the gear was up and tucked away; and, with some minor adjustments, the gear well doors closed. 06 was flying along at seven feet or so above the ground. Well, not exactly; but she looked like she was flying.

The gear came down much more easily than it had gone up. With new batteries and the hydraulic pump on line, the new battery cables carried their energy to the switch near the up gear lever. With a snap of a finger, the toggle switch went from off to on, gear up position and with a shudder the gear apparatus moaned, creaked, and, ever so slowly, retracted on its own. Gear down and, with a swoosh, it rotated down. One more time and, with very little complaining, the gear was up and locked in about eight seconds. From all indications, nothing was bent, warped, or out of line. Again, the gear came down and, after a good look-see, no leaks. Let's try it again. Smoothly and firmly, the gear retracted instantly. No moans or groans this time.

Barbie III and Company

The bomb bay doors fell open and quickly flicked shut. The movement was so fast that, if a man were between the doors as they slammed shut, they would cut him in half at the rib cage. The tires were inspected. They were so-so but should last a soft landing or two. There would be some fast taxing tests and, if they held up, they would be okay. 06 was lowered and was once again resting on her tires. Another important item was checked off. New spark plugs were gapped and installed. Oil coolers were removed, flushed, and pressure checked.

On Saturday evening of the second week, it was time to start one engine. With anticipation, sweating hands, thumping hearts, a hard swallow, fire extinguishers in place, and cameras poised, the startup began. Batteries on, fuel pump on, a couple shots of prime, eyes, unblinkingly, watch. Switches on, energize the starter, cross your fingers. Count six propeller blades as they pass the cockpit, bite your lip, more prime, mags on, the engine coughs, shakes, belches a cloud of smoke. The starboard engine spins, shudders, catches again, gasps, backfires, and catches again, spins. Beg it to start and the -29 explodes to life, belching heavy clouds of blue smoke from the exhaust. 06 at last says hello to her owners.

To the uninformed, it idled like a raggedy old corncob. It was not smooth sounding or running. It was laboring and shaking. To the informed, it ran just like a twin-rowed, fourteen cylinder radial -29 was supposed to run. As the engine warmed up and reached operating temperature, the rolling blue clouds of smoke turned to white and diminished. Oil pressure up, oil temperature in the green, and cylinder head temperature in the green: the engine's performance was encouraging. Cowl flaps open to let the hot air out and cool the engine, cowl flaps closed to hold the warm air in as the engine warms up. Run the engine a little faster so it does not load up. All the engine gauges send their message that all is okay. At a faster than idle rpm, the -29 runs smoother. It does not like to run slow. It was not designed to run slow.

After many years, the starboard engine was experiencing life. Hopefully it would like its hot, tortuous world of whirling metal, pounding pistons, and thousands of thrashing parts that all had to move and work together. Similar to a symphonic orchestra, one sour note could mean disaster.

Sixty-percent power now. Held fast by her brakes and wheel chocks, 06 drops her nose and appears to take a brief mild bow. The entire airframe wants to go, but she just shakes and wiggles. 06 is getting comfortable and everything is holding together. Time to shut her down and check all the connections. No full power run up at this time. They would work up to it. Once the engine cooled down, they would check the oil strainers. In their own way, all celebrated. While the engine cooled down, the metal pinged and clinked from expansion to contraction. They patted each other on the back and shook hands. It had been a good preliminary run up. Hours later the oil strainers, much to everyone's relief, showed none of the slivers of metal that would indicate the engine was having a problem.

To warbird lovers, the only thing better than the sound of one big radial is two big radials. Sunday comes and, valves adjusted, timing checked, the same routine is initiated. Fuel pump on and the port engine chokes to life and is on line. The port engine is inspected and there is more celebrating. This engine, however, has a heavy trace of black smoke from the exhaust. The fuel/air mixture is too rich. Some field adjustments are made to the carburetor. It would be nice to have it calibrated in a shop, but there is no shop.

Once again on line, there is no more black smoke. Everyone gets to give the start up a try. It is a handsome reward for all their efforts and cash. They at last feel the beating heart of 06 and it is awesome. She flirts with them, tantalizes them, and responds to the experienced touch of Carl and Tony. Closer and closer they come to a full power check. As the -29's are raised to eighty-five percent power they are as sweet as they can be. That is if you are into that type of thing.

The time has come. One hundred percent power on both engines at the same time. If the engines were going to falter or have second thoughts, they wanted it to happen on the ground. So far, Carl and Tony cannot believe their good luck. The oil level is checked, a few tweaks here and there, brakes locked and set, wheel chocks in place, fire guards in place; let's do it.

It is a humbling sound. Some three thousand, four hundred horsepower is unleashed but under control. The unmuffled deafening sound is overpowering. If you are close by, it beats on the human soul to the point the brain becomes fragmented. You are insignificant; nonexistent, compared to the raw ragged power of the R 2600's.

With throttles to their stops and the fuel mixture full rich, 06 begins to compress her nose wheel strut. Propellers cut a blurred twelve-foot six-inch arc through the air. Vegetation close behind the blur is ripped from the ground and blown away. Tall grasses behind 06 weave frantically and are bent to the ground by the hurricane force of the prop wash. No human foolish enough to walk behind the wing could stand in the violent rushing mass of exhaust and wind. She is down on her knees. Gear struts are compressed as she crouches and braces her self to hold the thundering engines in check. She wants to leap over her wheel chocks. Rudders and elevators tremble and shake with the full power settings. Full power is overwhelming. Communication by simple shouting is not possible.

For miles around, the thundering R 2600's send their message. "I have arrived, my death has been greatly exaggerated. I am alive and well, thank you."

Her rumbling engine sound rolls and flows over and across the Illinois countryside. It bombards everything and everyone in its path. People leave their TV sets and step outdoors and wonder at the strange sound. Children cover their ears and cars stop on the county highway. Spectators who came to see and listen are not disappointed by her brutal power. Throttles back to a fast idle for about a minute, then to idle cut off, switches off, fuel pump off. Everyone is smiling. Everything stayed together under the tortuous run up.

The silence is very still: the contrast is like black and white. The overwhelming sound of power still roars in your ears. Slowly, you become aware of your pounding heart and that the ground is no longer trembling under your feet. Carl and Tony emerge from the hatch in the belly and Walter pops his head out of the top cockpit escape hatch. Thumps up and the boyish grins tell everyone that the 06 is about ready to go. They have arrived.

The group has tasted the reward of their months of work and struggle. They revel in the payoff of their rock-solid determination to go forward. They have touched, seen, smelled, and listened to their warbird. They all looked forward to the day they would sit between the thundering engines and, with thin cables, levers, rods, and pulleys, control the twin-engine, twin-tailed medium bomber. They were going to experience what few men today can ever experience. Others will only envy and wish. They are no longer ordinary. They are a cut above the rank and file. They own an operating warbird from World War II.

Again, the hot engines send their magic sound as they cooled down. Streaks of oil that had blown from the engine nacelles and exhaust is everywhere on the nacelles, rear fuselage and tail. The oil stopped its rearward, twisting journey when the engines were shut down. The prop wash as it churned and beat the air caused a swirling movement of air that wrapped around the rear fuselage and tail of 06. The hot oil was carried by the turbulent air and now gathered in rivulets that stopped their twisting rearward journey, hesitated, gathered, accumulated, in horizontal drapes and began to arch downward in graceful curves.

Oil, oil was everywhere. Had an oil line separated? No, Tony explained. The big -29's are noted for throwing oil. They will burn and leak about a gallon each an hour. If the engine is worn, there will be a bigger loss of oil. Carl went on to explain that, when the -29's were manufactured a long time ago, the tolerances were made very loose to keep up with mass production and reduce the reject rate. They were loose, so they could take a beating and keep thrashing away. Now Weary Warriors had the answer to why the oil capacity was thirty-seven gallons each. The point that the R-2600 could thrash itself and keep running would soon be painfully and expensively demonstrated to them.

The oil would be drained while it was still hot, all sixty-some gallons of it. Strainers would be cleaned and everything and anything that came loose in the engines would have to be removed. Oil was the gift of life to the engines. Any piece of metal that broke loose could jam a moving part or plug an oil gallery and would be the gift of death. Clean and flush would be the schedule for the next few days.

Some picked up rags to clean their warbird; others grabbed tools. Some worked on the airframe and some on the engines, all under the watchful eye of Tony and Carl. All clamps and every connection that could have been loose or vibrated loose during the long full power engine checks would have to be checked. They were close to the big day. They watched the calendar just as closely as they watched their bank account; they were running out of time and money.

Preflight
October 1981

It is late Fall in northern Illinois. Although most of the trees have shed their leaves, those leaves that remain still have some spectacular color. It is about nine months since Claude put the sharp end of the pick into the frozen dirt. In the bright October sun, afternoons are warm and jackets worn in the cold mornings are soon shed in the afternoon warmth, only to be put back on as the afternoon sun works its way across the sky.

The first taxi test is anticipated as a good time by all. The Weary Warriors will enjoy themselves the next few days. They will prepare, pulling the props through, getting better at starting the engines, running them up, and shutting them down. Some will play pilot and others will watch those playing pilot. Once introduced, they become familiar with her and find that she is not that complicated. She is big and noisy, but straightforward and honest. The three hundred gallons of fuel put on board earlier is used up quickly. They will need more, much more.

She is on her way, moving under her own power. Over the uneven grass runway, she sways in vertical oscillations as she picks her way over the grass stubble and weeds. Slowly at first, then faster, she seems to be bowing to her owners as they applaud and encourage her on. Faster now, she takes on a serious attitude as she comes to life. There will be no more fooling around.

She turns around at the end of the grass runway and makes her way back. The brakes are good and the engines sound good. Each trip down Dick's runway is faster than the previous one. 06 works her way up to eighty miles an hour and wants to leap into the air. She is light and ready. As they taxi back, everyone is shaking hands and congratulating themselves.

But wait! 06 stops. She is low in the nose, her big props missing the grass by inches. The engines stop. Everyone runs to her.

A quick look and the first setback is apparent to all. Her nose wheel tire is in shreds, beyond repair. With hands on hips, hats slid to the back of heads and some unconscious head scratching, they ponder their very flat tire. They have no replacement and the two ferry pilots are on their way.

If two groups are better than one then three groups should be better than two. Who knows who? Who has a tire? Weary Warriors have very few contacts.

Every tire supply in the Chicago area is called. The tire size does not exist. Tony and Carl think they have one in one of their desert storage sheds but are not sure. Some of the museum gang belong to the Experimental Aircraft Association up in Oshkosh, Wisconsin where there is a B-25 on display. They make the call. The EAA will lend them their tire but they have to come and get it. A couple of the museum guys hop in a light plane and they are on their way. 06 will have a nose wheel tire in a matter of a few hours.

Weight and balance is very important in an aircraft and 06 is weighed and goes through a rather complicated mathematical process to find her center of gravity. A ferry permit will not be issued unless this documentation, along with mechanical certification is complete. Subtracting the weight of the many gallons of oil, she weighs in at just over 18,000 pounds with a few gallons of gas sloshing around in her four usable tanks. She is very light compared to her combat-ready sisters who flew in World War II. With out her armament, bombs, and all the equipment needed for a combat ready B-25 she weighs almost half as much as her grossed out 36,000 pound combat sisters. Her lightweight is good: with full fuel aboard, 06 will get off the grass quickly and easily.

With the borrowed nose wheel tire installed and a few more taxi runs, 06 is ready for her inspection by the FAA, whose inspectors show up on time. They are, understandably, not too familiar with B-25's. They check Carl and Tony's credentials closely and are impressed. They will have to take their word as experts. An airframe inspection is made. After an engine run-up, gear retractions and a close look at the paper work, the FAA team is satisfied and issues the ferry permit. They will take a look at the pilot's credentials when they arrive at the airport. A ferry permit is actually a Special Airworthiness Certificate within the sub category of Special Flight Certificate. It must be carried aboard during the flight and is only good for a few days. The term "ferry permit" appears to have been coined in World War II because it was easier to say and write.

There are three restrictions on the permit. Takeoff will be to the south, away from any congested area, with the first turn to the left; and there will be only three on board; two pilots and Tony, the mechanic-observer. Weary Warriors and the museum members are disappointed. Some want to be on board 06. They have a flying warbird and cannot crew her on this momentous occasion.

Lou Fulgaro

First Try

As the FAA was issuing the ferry permit, the men who would be doing the piloting were arriving in the Chicagoland area. Brothers Mike and Dick Wright [no relation to Wilbur and Orville] were considered by most to be two of the best B-25 pilots in the world. Mike would be pilot in command and Dick, his copilot.

The Illinois bunch shudders at the tab as the four main inboard tanks are topped off. Six hundred and seventy gallons of aviation fuel makes for one tremendous gas bill. It would not take a bean counter very long at a dollar eighty-four cents (1981 prices) a gallon to add up the fuel cost. With a liability insurance policy costing six hundred dollars, the owners are ready but, financially, broke.

On Thursday afternoon, 06 gets a critical inspection by the Wright brothers. It will be their butts on the line and everything has to be to their satisfaction. Their conclusion after a good look is that they have flown worse. Saturday October 17th, the target date, is now just a few days off.

The Wright brothers plan their flight and start with the grass runway and the takeoff. They walk the runway, looking for any holes or soft spots. None are found. They calculate where 06 should be airborne and, if not, if there is enough runway to stop. They calculate that braking will be diminished considerably with slippery grass. What if the wind is not blowing in the correct direction for a takeoff? A quartering head wind is workable and they could live with a ninety-degree crosswind. A tail wind would be a real problem, seeing that they could only take off in one direction.

Mike and Dick examine air charts and plan their flight. Airfields are highlighted just in case. They will go low and slow and not work the old engines hard. One good thing about the Midwest is that it offers miles and miles of rolling flat farmland. It beats flying a questionable old relic over mountains or water.

Friday morning brings bad news. The weather will change. A warm front is coming through from the south and it is a big one. It will start to rain Saturday and continue to rain for two days with high winds. The only comforting news is that the wind will be from the south and ideal for the takeoff. The rain could make flying marginal but, worse, the grass runway could turn to mud or be just soft enough were a takeoff could be attempted and end in failure. There is a lot of comparing notes. The decision is made. They will go today, the 16th.

Carl and Tony are apprehensive. There are a few things they wanted to re-check. Moving the takeoff time presses them for time. Mike decides to go in the late afternoon. That will give them enough time to reach their destination with some daylight remaining. What Carl and Tony have to do will have to be done between now and takeoff time.

That Friday, everyone chips in and works. Cowlings and inspection covers are buttoned up. There are no more excuses. The time has come.

The early takeoff throws a lot of wanna-bes for a loop. The runway is still lined with some well-wishers; Chicagoland TV is on hand as are the major newspapers. How they got the news, no one knows. Carl and Tony load up on some spares that may just be needed; hydraulic fluid, duct tape, wire, and tools. Mike slides into the left seat and muses to himself that the seat belts are still G.I. Dick seats himself alongside him and Tony is behind them.

The fireguard stands by. They go through the preflight checklist, then the flight deck checklist. On the exterior walk around, the right nacelle and then the right wing are checked, then the fuselage and tail, interior waist, left wing and left nacelle.

Back in the cockpit, the Wright brothers buckle up. Fuel and oil are checked off. The hatches are secure.

Wheel chocks in place, hydraulic pressure at least 600 psi for the parking brakes. Fire guard posted. Props are clear. Master ignition switch on, right fuel boost on normal then emergency, engage and mesh right starter and hold for six blades. Right ignition switch to both, prime as required. 06 again faithfully explodes to life. After start, mixture control to full rich, adjust throttle to 1200 rpm. Oil pressure to 40 psi within 30 seconds. Suction about 4 psi. Hydraulic 800 to 1100 psi, brake pressure 1000 to 1200 psi. Right fuel boost off; check fuel pressure 7 to 9 psi. Same procedure port engine. Avionics master switch on, inverter on, generators on.

Flaps to takeoff position, wheel chocks removed, brakes off, and, without ceremony, Mike gets 06 moving and on her way. There is no grandstanding: he is all business. Ignore the crowd. Now is not the time to make a mistake. Put 06's nose into the wind and very carefully do the engine run-ups. Check idle rpm to 650. Advance throttles to 1700 rpm. Exercise prop controls. Full forward high rpm then to full aft, low rpm, should have a 400 to 500 rpm drop. Prop feathering check, 250 rpm drop. Generators are checked during the feathering check.

Check left and right mags, 90rpm maximum drop. Carburetor heat check for manifold pressure/ rpm drop. Run up engines to 2200 rpm and check manifold pressure to barometric pressure. Flight controls free, carburetor heat cold, throttle friction locks adjusted.

The procedure and run-ups are flawless. Everything says go. Even the wind is cooperating. Mike lines up 06 down the center of the grass runway and looks at his brother. Mike's brother Dick, as co-pilot, will monitor the instruments and assist. One more look at the instrument panel and all engine and flight gauges and they still say, "go."

With a final look at the big, raggedy sounding -29's, idling patiently, waiting with their props churning inches away from their heads, Dick nods in the affirmative. Mike looks at Tony, who nods an okay. Without a blink of an eye, Mike smoothly pushes the throttles forward and the ever-so-patient -29's respond without hesitation. With a roaring crescendo, they are on their way.

With an initial power setting of 34 inches manifold pressure and 2400 rpm, the waving, applauding people along both sides of the runway soon become a blur. 06, as light as she is and under the skillful hands of her crew, effortlessly launches herself into the air. 06 is in her element. She tastes the sweetness of flight for the first time in over ten years. Landing gear up, wing flaps up, lever to neutral, 06 climbs out of Lambert's field. The fuel boost pumps are off at one thousand feet above the Illinois countryside, reducing to normal climb power of 30 inches and 2200 rpm and 06 kicks up her heels at an indicated textbook climb of 160 MPH, faster than any of her chase planes can go.

Following the ferry plan restriction, Mike levels off and the air speed now sits at 200 MPH. Mike cautiously banks 06 into a gentle turn to the left and she responds like a lady. Once again, climbing at 160 MPH, Mike puts a good three thousand feet between 06 and the Illinois countryside. Leveling off, a bank to the right, 06 faithfully turns and heads back to the farm. With 30 inches on the gauge, Mike backs off to 2000 rpm, which is considered the best power setting at a medium altitude of three to eight thousand feet for the -29's.

With 06's broad sweeping turns, the one chase plane, carrying Carl, that took off before 06 is able to cut the turns short and stay reasonably close. Carl's eyes never leave 06 and he reports that nothing is leaking and nothing has fallen off. The gear is neatly tucked away. She looks trim and fit.

On the ground, the other chase planes are hurriedly getting their acts together. Mike will wait for them as this is picture-taking time —- the takeoff and climb-out had to be photographed. Mike lowers the nose just a bit and, as he crosses over Lambert's field, the air speed indicator is at 250 MPH at cruise settings. Impressive for her age. The deep rumble of the -29's and her twin tail design thrill all. It is time to baby the engines and slow 06 down and, at 24 inches and 1850 rpm, the air speed begins to bleed off as 06 loiters above her well-wishers and waits patiently. Below, all heads are turned upward, watching 06. Many hope Mike will give them a fast, low-level pass, but they will never know.

Suddenly, hands pointing and gasping sounds of "Oh No!" spread over the crowd. Smoke. Heavy, white, billowing smoke trails 06 from the starboard engine. Carl's voice on the radio from the chase plane advises Mike and his crew.

All three in 06 had been watching the chase planes on the ground getting ready to take off. The smoking engine now has their full attention. Tony scrambles and crawls through the small space above the bomb bay and is in the waist. He sits behind the trailing edge of the wings and the engines. The smoke is coming from the exhaust; an engine failure has occurred in their best engine. There is less than twenty hours on the engine since it was installed over ten years ago.

Crawling back to the cockpit, he advises Mike that, from all indications, a piston or piston ring has failed and oil is getting into the combustion chamber. The smoke is coming out the exhaust pipe and it is white. If it were black, it would mean fire. It is not a fuel or oil fire. Gauges for the starboard engine are all in the green and the -29 runs on, taking no mind that it may be running on thirteen cylinders instead of fourteen. The port engine, with over four hundred hours on it, was the one expected to have problems with if there were to be a problem, but it is running fine. They have an engine failure on the starboard side: the ailing Wright Cyclone is living up to its reputation. At least one cylinder is just going along for the ride.

She is a fickle lady. Something inside had broken. It is serious, but not serious enough to shut down the engine. Mike decides to leave it online. He may need it for the landing that is a few minutes away. Lambert is below them, but the expected rain means the grass runway may soon turn to mud. Clow Airport, a light plane airport a few miles away, lies over the nose of 06 with its one paved runway. It is minutes away and the expected rain will not hinder their next attempt at flight. Clow is where they will go.

The reduction in power had slowed 06 down, which worked well with their situation: as Mike reset the power settings to 2200 rpm, they had only about twenty inches of manifold pressure. 06 slows to a good pattern speed of 145 MPH indicated with wing flaps at 1/4 down and the gear down and locked. Their planning paid off much sooner than expected.

There is no control tower at Clow and the runway is narrow. If Mike put 06 down dead center, the wing tips might just overhang the pavement. Small, light aircraft were in the airport traffic pattern and all three aboard hoped they would spot the circus-red and white B-25, trailing miles of white smoke, flying a big round curve to line up with the runway. If the insurance agent had been on hand to watch the big event, he would have fainted away by now.

06 was headed away from Lambert and descending. Was she going down? The concerned owners all had cardiac arrest at the same time, considering what had happened and was happening. One brief radio message on the air-to-air channel cleared some of the mystery.

"We are going to Clow."

There was a mad scramble for car keys and cars. Some went by air, some by county road. Everyone deserted the farm and headed for about-to-be-famous Clow International Airport.

On the ground at Clow, the usual airport buffs gawked in disbelief. First, the throaty heavy rumble of the big 29's got their attention. Then came the "what is it?" question. They moved around looking in the direction of the sound. By some magic signal, they all drifted toward the runway where hangers and sheds would not block their view of whatever it was. Their eyes riveted onto the B-25 as it came into view, making a long shallow turning approach to Clow field in a power-on descent, belching white smoke. Aboard, there was calm, but some concern, mixture was to full rich, fuel boost pumps on normal, some carburetor heat, and wing flaps full down on final approach to the narrow runway at 130 MPH indicated.

The starboard engine was not aware that it was ailing.

All engine gauges in the green. Now was the time for the "they just keep on running till they totally thrash themselves" reputation to kick in.

Clow was witnessing a first. It was unbelievable, and Chicago TV and newspaper reporters a few miles away were in the wrong place at the wrong time. They were close but, with this development, they were not close enough: Mike and his crew were not about to wait.

At Clow Airport, people on the ground looked on in awe. The roaring monster coughed up white dense smoke as it bore down on them. The air traffic pattern at Clow became one of light aircraft scattering like dry snow in a wind. Not one pilot missed the circus-red B-25 with its trailing white smoke. No one who was at Clow that day would ever forget what he saw.

Mike's approach speed of 120 MPH over the airport boundary was faster than most of the light aircraft at Clow could go. Just off the runway, Mike slowed to 110 MPH; they had it made.

The air speed bled off and 06 touched down. With some gentle braking to keep 06 on the centerline, they coasted down the runway to the far end turn-off taxiway. 06 came to a stop and was silent. Once there, 06's crew began the post-flight checklist. It was just another interesting day for her crew.

There were many that day that said the cockpit of 06 was the safest place to be. The county roads between Lambert Field and Clow Airport with the speeding cars and light trucks full of owners, reporters, and well-wishers were the most dangerous places to be.

The Illinois bunch now had new and unexpected problems. Their worst nightmares and fears had been realized; one limping B-25 sitting at a foreign airport, four expensive pros on the payroll, the fearful anticipation of just how serious the engine failure was, and —- the big nut —- show me the money.

Clow International Airport

It is a very big name for a small but very nice airport. No international flights ever come or go, but the owner, Boyd Clow, says he was planning for the future when he named it. He is clearly a man of vision.

I have known Boyd Clow since 1971. He was a farmer who took a portion of his farm and created an airport. A good pilot, he is a master engine and airframe mechanic and a man with a heart and soul of gold.

During a five-year period from late 1971 when I owned a classic 1946 Fairchild F24 R46, Boyd was the man who gave generously of his time and expertise to keep it in the air. I flew out of a small, private, restricted field a short distance from Clow and was a frequent visitor. At that time, he had two runways and, later, would have just one, running north and south, which he paved. My R46 was powered with a heavy, inverted World War II Ranger six-cylinder engine that Boyd affectionately referred to as a "boat anchor".

He was a generous man and would, always with a helping hand, let me use his shop and tools when my aircraft needed work. On those lazy days, I would often motor over to Clow we would sit around and talk about the faded red B-25 sitting a few miles away at Lambert Field. We would talk about buying and restoring her and Boyd would say it would be a long and expensive project. He was not sure he wanted to get involved and the conversation would drift to another subject.

Let's get back to October 1981. At this point, the Illinois bunch was just about broke. This added to the overall gloom of that time and overshadowed the first flight euphoria. 06 was towed to a paved ramp in front of a small complex of hangers. At this time, Boyd may have had seventy-five aircraft based at his field. Boyd Clow as always was a generous and understanding host. Years later, he would tell me that 06's new owners were not very nice. They were actually rude. I would explain to him that they were not really that way; that they had very little money and a broken B-25; and that there was a lot of pressure and anxiety. He would come back with the statement that it was no excuse for bad manners.

With the engine cowling off again, the familiar routine was now accomplished with ease. From all indications, the number one cylinder was the one that had gone astray. This was determined the old fashion way by placing your hand on each cylinder after a engine run. The loafing (bad) cylinder will feel cooler than the cylinders that are working hard for a living. It appeared that a piston ring failed, broke, and chewed up the piston. The piston then failed at the piston skirt area and tore up the cylinder. It would all have to be replaced, including the valves and cylinder head.

The museum's B-25 would provide a complete cylinder assembly and they went by air to get one and a spare just in case. The crew at Clow would remove the failed cylinder; hopefully clean all the metal debris from inside the engine and the entire oil system. No metal could remain as it could cause another failure. With a plan of action they were comfortable and the pressure would lessen. All were tired and cold. They retired to the restaurant on the field, which was typical for an airport this size. Nothing fancy, just some good home-style cooking.

The owners were assured that, in two days, 06 would once again be on her way. Luckily, there was no serious damage. They had landed at a hard-surfaced airport and the rain would not affect their ability to get 06 off the ground. It was a smart move on Mike's part not to return to Lambert's field.

Suggestions flew around the table. All would have to stay a few days longer. A lot more oil would be needed. The entire oil system would have to be purged. They would have to repeat what they did before, but slip in a cylinder change in between. They did, however, have a small advantage: they were getting good at what had to be done.

06 was the news story of the day for greater Chicagoland. Her short flight made the headlines and was the top news story on TV. But the Chicago media were busy dropkicking themselves as they had missed the climax of the big event. They were not about to let that happen again. They would have to run with what they had for this day but would not let 06 out of their sight for the next few days.

I was not aware of what was happening. I missed all the hoopla and to this day cannot understand how that could have happened. After five years of ownership, I sold my R46 and tucked the money away. While 06 was doing her thing, I was looking for a reasonably priced warbird. My activity in the air had ended, my medical expired, and my pilot's license wasted away in my wallet. My trips to Clow were few and far between as I retired from one career and became totally absorbed in another.

The unanticipated expenses buzzed around in everyone's head. Hotel expense, food, labor, and material eroded what few funds Weary Warriors had left. The Weary Warriors part of the group decided to recruit another partner for their half of 06. They needed another four thousand dollars. This would turn out to be my four thousand dollars and, within a month or so, I would be a partner in the warbird group.

Back to Clow. The Wright brothers and Aero Traders boosted the sagging moral of 06's owners. They reminded the owners that a B-25 is a machine; and that machines tire, wear out and break but that it can be repaired. It can out live them and go on for generations to come. Okay, that helps.

The next morning, there was light rain and wind from the south. It was not too cold, but cold enough to wish you were somewhere else. There was no hanger large enough to house 06, so a tarp was thrown over the starboard engine and wing. The prop blades were used as tent pole supports. Being under the wing, out of the light rain, was a big help to those not under the tarp.

Spirits were better today, in spite of the rain. Some tackled the number one cylinder of 06 as, hundreds of miles away a cylinder was being prepared to take the number one cylinder's place. Busy hands with cold fingers toiled away. Every cylinder and manifold bolt was rusted and resisted removal with a vengeance. There would be many scraped knuckles today and profanity flowed freely. Finally, after some strong coaxing and a lot of leverage, the number one cylinder surrendered and was removed.

The -29 was cleaned of metal debris from the broken piston and rings. They did their best but they could never be sure they got it all. This was an emergency field repair; a quick patch job that hopefully would last a few hours. The engine would have to be overhauled or replaced after the ferry flight. Another reputation the big Wrights had was that, if they were to fail, they would do so during the first fifty hours of operation, the first twenty hours being the most critical. After that, they would run on forever or until they burned so much oil that range was limited by oil consumption rather than fuel consumption.

The museum crew arrived just as 06 was ready for the replacement. Eager hands pitched in and by Saturday evening they were almost finished. They would, from all indications, finish up Sunday. The timing was perfect. If they finished Sunday morning with the repair, they could test Sunday afternoon. If everything went well, they could fly out on Monday, October 19th.

The people kept coming. Millions of Chicagoans had seen or read about 06 on Friday [except me] and came to Clow to watch. Most had never heard of Clow and few knew anything about the tired old B-25; they were just fascinated by the event. Some came to wish them well: some came to photograph the crash and burn. There were a lot of cameras but no one reached into his (or her) pockets to help out.

It was time to give the starboard engine a try. They had, over the last three weeks, run both engines some ten hours each and they would not have that privilege this time around.

The start up routine began with pulling the prop through to get the oil out of the lower cylinders. The oil would ooze out the exhaust valves as the engine was cycled through its strokes by hand. It was a tiring but necessary ritual every time the engine was to be started: if not removed, the pooled oil could and would cause a hydraulic lock that could build pressure to the extent that a cylinder might destroy itself. The starboard engine coughed to life with the usual smoke, spun, and fell silent.

Trying again, Walter, on fireguard, spots it first: raw gasoline is running out of the engine compartment and onto the pavement. The prop is turning, the engine explodes to life, and the hot exhaust ignites the raw gasoline. The engine backfires, coughs again and spins to a silent stop. Walter, manning the fire extinguisher, fearlessly attacks the growing gasoline fire as hundreds of onlookers watch in a frozen trance. Walter wins just as the fire extinguisher goes dry. The white-faced, shaking novice owners are speechless as their eyes follow the billowing plume of drifting black smoke. This is another first for them.

"It is nothing", are the words of wisdom and they are, once again, comforted. "It is just some raw fuel overflowing from the blower. The big Wrights are noted for that little trick every now and then. That is why you will always have a fireguard standing by for startups. Preferably a brave one."

The starter is allowed to cool down and if you like to smoke now is the time to do it. The engine will rest for about ten minutes before they give it another try. Just to be sure, the fuel lines are checked: they are tight and secure.

With a new extinguisher on hand, the start-up begins again. The engine decides to get with it, belches to life and can't understand what all the to-do is about. She pulls strong at all power settings, the mag check is good and the prop cycles from high pitch to low pitch and back without hesitation. The engine gauges are all where they belong. The oil screens are checked and cleaned, revealing no real chunks of metal.

The group wonders whether to give her a try and take her around the patch. After some deliberation, it is decided that a short flight would prove nothing and would expose the crew to unnecessary risk. Let's not forget those marginal old main gear tires with who knows how many landings may be left in them. Everyone hopes they can get at least one more landing out of them.

With the rain still falling, they cover the cockpit with a tarp. 06 leaks water into her cockpit at an alarming rate. Mike does not like the idea of rain being driven into the cockpit at cruise speed. She will leak like a sieve. B-25's are noted for their ability to leak and after flying through rain, many crews emerged in to the sunlight, soaking wet. Since nothing in the B-25 interior is tight, 06 seems worse than most: and water can play havoc with the electrical systems. The rain is supposed to pass by Monday. They decide to run a power check in the late afternoon and, if all goes well, button her up and go Monday.

On the next day the rain has stopped. After some lunch and last minute tweaking, it is time to go. There are patches of blue in the sky, a good sign. The wind is still from the south, down the runway and in the right direction. It is clearing and seems to be getting colder. They will go at 3:30 PM. There always seems to be something to do.

Like magic, the people come. The grapevine must really work.

The few hours between lunch and takeoff time are put to good use. Everything will be checked and then checked again. At 3:30, they will be able to say that they have done everything they had to do. There will be nothing left but to go. They will give 06 another try at flight.

At Clow Airport the engines are warming up in preparation for her second attempt at flight. I included this photo as it shows the newly installed high profile air intakes. Photo Walter Wild.

Looking somewhat tattered, 43-4106 soldiers on after her starboard engine failed. With the starboard propeller frozen in place she precariously continues flying on one tired engine. Photo Barry Locher, State Journal Register.

One More Time

The cold dampness remained. If it got much colder, the engines could be hard to start. All that remained was to climb up the forward hatch, secure it and go. 06 was about to leave her gracious host, Boyd Clow. There had been no charge and, as always he allowed the Weary Warriors to use his tools, equipment, and shop. Feelings had mellowed somewhat and he hoped that, someday, the B-25 would come back.

The conversation piece that had gathered hundreds of people to Clow over the last three days was about to depart. Many regretted having to go to work because no one wanted to miss the takeoff. Boyd was smiling; he'd never had so much restaurant business. Mike put the fire to the -29's and they rattled to life. Again, without any pomp or circumstance, Mike worked his way to the runway with the crowd following along on both sides. Lined up with the white runway centerline, the Wright Cyclones again waited patiently.

The runway beckons, pointing the way. Throttling up, the reassuring rumbling roar is there. Nose wheel nailed to the white center line, 06 begins her takeoff. With the wide main landing gear, they had room —- but not much. It would be disastrous to let 06 drift to either side of the narrow runway. If a tire drifted onto the rain-soaked grass alongside the runway and sank in at this speed, they would rip off the gear.

Then she is airborne, humming like a sewing machine and as sweet as sugar. Gear up; get everything together; bank to the left, then to the right; bring her back over Clow at a good altitude and say goodbye to their host.

The chase planes are now ahead of her, strung out like a short string of pearls, all in a line. Quarter down flaps: slow her down to her minimum maneuvering speed of 145 MPH to stay in the air and slowly close on the line of light aircraft ahead of her. Her slowest speed possible to maintain altitude is much faster than the fastest speed of the chase planes ahead of her —- she is that powerful.

06 closes easily and slowly drifts by the string of light planes, posing for her owners. They admire her unique lines and twin tail design. She is indeed a living ghost from the past. As she floats past

them she is majestic: they are thrilled to view "their" B-25 in her element of flight.

At this moment, all the months of effort, worry, and expense all seem worthwhile. It is a dream come true and each owner has his own personal dream of his future with this machine of war.

Slipping past her escort, Mike orders the flaps full up and sets up for a 200 MPH cruise. At this speed, the engines are loafing, running easily; and 06 effortlessly pulls ahead of her laboring escort. She will leave them far behind in a matter of a few minutes. At long last they are on their way.

Mike uses the rule that less time spent in the air reduces the chance of an incident: the less time in the air, the smaller the risk. The load on the engines, however, must modify this rule. Mike could easily set up the power for a 250 MPH cruise, but the engines must work much harder to obtain that cruise and the risk rises with the power rise. He is comfortable and 06 feels solid at this power setting so he decides to keep her there. He wonders if, sometime in the future, a pilot will ever put her in a shallow dive and touch her maximum allowed speed of 340 MPH indicated. But for now, she rumbles along, burning very expensive gas at a rate of about 120 gallons an hour. Mike hopes the owners will appreciate the savings in fuel at this low power setting.

The crew in the cockpit relaxes just a little. They all have come a long way to make this flight. The less they adjust or move the power settings, the less likely it is that things will go wrong. The drab, flat countryside slips under them and the miles are clicked off at a good rate. The headwind that helped them at takeoff is now slowing them down.

The B-25 was not built for comfort. There is no heat and the cold wind is not only rushing past the cockpit, but through the cockpit as well. They are cold and they can see their breath. They snuggle deeper into their jackets. All three are happy that it is not raining. They would now be freezing if it were.

Early detection of anything going wrong is important; it could save the ferry flight. It would give them precious minutes to sort things out. Dick, sitting in the co-pilot's seat, constantly scans the engine gauges. His finger rests on the oil pressure gauge for the starboard engine. It has fallen off of its normal, optimal indication of 80 to 85psi; and the cylinder head temperature is rising. Dick taps the oil pressure gauge with his finger then gives it a good rap with his hand. Nothing. Minutes pass. All eyes are glued to the oil gauge. It is now indicating 60psi, the minimum setting running at slow cruise. The port engine oil gauge says a happy 85psi. Cylinder head temperature creeps upward, toward 190°C. Open the cowl flaps, try and cool off the cylinders. It helps cool the ailing Wright Cyclone.

Is it a faulty gauge? Could be; but they don't think so. Tony is back in the waist again and a good, hard look reveals nothing. The oil pressure slowly falls off. They suspect that a piece of debris from the previous piston failure might be blocking an oil passage. Now at 25psi, they are at the minimum pressure for idling the big Wrights. It is decision time. Mike elects to throttle back to idle and keep the faltering engine online as the power and prop settings are changed for the starboard engine.

The port engine wants to drag them around in a big circle. Directional control clicks in and first rudder and then rudder trim are applied to keep 06 going straight ahead. Power application is no longer balanced and the port engine must give them more power as they square themselves away at this critical time. The port prop is advanced to 2400 rpm to take a better bite of air. The throttle is set to 34 inches of manifold pressure or "boost" as some refer to it. The last thing Mike wants to do was work the older port engine this hard — will it hold on? Again, more rudder trim is applied to compensate for more power on the port side.

Much of what Mike and his crew were doing was automatic, their eyes all fixed on the air speed indicator. While maintaining directional control in a twin-engine aircraft is the number one thing to do during an engine failure, number two is to maintain flying speed. There is no sense to keep going straight if you're going to stall out and fall out of the sky.

Retrimming again gets things squared away. The starboard engine at idle, the port engine working hard, they are flying straight and level. Indicated air speed is much too fast for one engine and Mike aims for the magic number of 145 MPH. The port engine is working easier and they all breathe a sigh of relief. She is pulling strong and not missing a beat.

The oil pressure once again begins to fall off on the starboard engine. While they still have some speed over the minimum flying speed of 145 MPH, Mike decides to shut down the now dying starboard engine. Close the throttle, retard the prop, feather the prop, mixture control to idle cut off, fuel shut off, mag switch off, cowl flaps closed to reduce drag, and oil radiator shutter closed. Re-adjust power settings on the port engine and trim again.

06 settles at 145 MPH indicated, a comfortable air speed with one engine out. With engines idling, a B-25, with a light load of about 27,000 lbs. and gear and flaps up, will stall out at about 110 MPH indicated —- about the same speed at which she will lift off from the runway during takeoff. Approaching stall speed, some five to ten MPH above 110 MPH, the pilot will experience some slight buffeting before the stall comes. There is a tendency, if the control column is held back at the stall, for the left wing to drop gently causing the B-25 to fall off to the left.

With the gear and flaps down, the scenario changes somewhat; the starboard wing is the one to drop.

Most importantly, with the flaps down, there is no buffeting of the controls to forewarn the pilots. If they have a smooth touch, they will notice a slight lightness in the elevators to tell them they have run out of speed but there is little other warning of the pending stall. At the stall, the right wing drops steeply and the B-25 will fall off to the right. This tendency is accentuated if the control column is held back. Thus, when they approach for a landing with one big round engine, the feathered prop and nacelle just hanging out there, plus the gear and flaps down, excessive drag is something to be concerned about. Only the dumbest of pilots would minimize the importance of the pending landing.

That is why the 145 MPH indicated speed is considered the minimum flying and maneuvering speed. Some pilots will go as low as 135 MPH if they are very light, like 06 is today. But be careful: she can reach back and bite! Either indicated speed gives only a small margin for error.

Tony cannot believe they've lost the same engine twice in three days. She runs and runs on the ground but can't get the hang of it up in the air. Another look at both engines from the waist tells them that they are okay. The port engine is rumbling along unaware that her sister on the other side decided to take a nap. With the headwind and one engine turning, their true air speed, or ground speed (true speed over the ground) as some refer to it, drops to a pitiful 115 MPH. She is still indicating 145 MPH meaning there is a 30 MPH headwind.

Mike, wisely, gently climbs to put more space between the Illinois prairie and 06's belly. 06's life now rests on one tired engine and the skill of her three-man crew, now earning their money the hard way.

Altitude is always a pilot's friend. On the other hand, the higher you go the stronger the headwind. This, plus the climb attitude, slows you a few more miles per hour. If you have plenty of fuel, height is the smart move.

Somewhere behind 06, strung out for miles, light aircraft were straining to close on her, the fastest up front, the slowest bringing up the rear.

The owners are once again apprehensive. Weary Warriors just want her to get there and then they want to take a long vacation and forget about this ordeal. Their nerves are frayed and their pockets empty. They are worn out mentally and physically and their wives are about ready to leave them. While they have a strong attachment to their B-25, this is just about the last straw. The museum bunch can have her.

The fastest of the light aircraft catch up and gives 06 a once-over. They take one photo of 06 with her starboard engine shut down and her prop feathered. They then give her some room. Time slips by and then, ahead, the concrete runways of their destination are faintly visible as thin gray slashes in the brown autumn vegetation on the horizon. They are almost there.

The tower is advised of their situation and 06 is given permission for a straight-in approach. Some twenty miles out, the landing gear is dropped and locks down. The cockpit check for landing is completed early. This will give the crew time to concentrate on the approach and the landing.

Fifteen miles out, the hydraulic pressure drops off the scale. Something has let loose and as much as thirteen gallons of very expensive hydraulic fluid is vaporizing over the countryside. Tony begins to pour the spare three gallons into the hydraulic fluid reservoir. This process is agonizingly slow. Five miles out, at 145 MPH indicated, flaps are lowered to one quarter down.

With the nose lowered, power is reduced as the downhill approach makes up for the engine thrust needed to maintain 145 MPH. Rudder trim is again adjusted, as there is now less tendency to yaw with the gradual reduction of power. More down flap; steeper descent, less power, but always power on. Mike will fly it on to the ground with power and, once over the runway threshold, will let the indicated air speed touch 130 MPH, then 110 MPH. 06 is flared out with a slight, nose-high attitude.

A good crew makes the landing appear easy, like nothing has happened. Her main gear touches the wide concrete runway at about 100 MPH indicated. To slow her down, Mike keeps the nose wheel off the cement as long as he can. The nose wheel touches when it can no longer be held off. 06 coasts to a taxiway and Mike swings her off to clear the runway. The port engine continues to perform flawlessly as it coughs to a stop under the experienced hands of her crew.

06 has arrived at her new home. She will have to be towed to the museum, making a rather undignified end to a much-publicized, historic flight. She is beat up, bloodied, but still standing. She is aloof, distant, and indifferent as she looks over her new home and those that have gathered to welcome her. No one seems to mind the dripping oil and hydraulic fluid.

Mike and his crew are relieved to be on the ground. The port engine was a real runner and he could have restarted the starboard engine and run it into oblivion if need be. He is now happy that they decided to pass over the many airfields that they could have put 06 into along the way. Anyway, what would the owners do with a broken B-25 on a strange field short of its intended destination? He had a handshake agreement with them to deliver 06 to the museum on this airfield and he did just that. It has been one hell of a four days.

The numbers are hard to come by and again, if you ask five people the same question you get five different answers. From January 1981 to October 1981, Weary Warriors and the museum purchased over twelve hundred gallons of aviation fuel (some estimated only eight hundred gallons), two hundred twenty gallons of heavy weight engine oil and fifty gallons of hydraulic fluid. To get 06 from Lambert's field to the museum (with a scenic side trip to Clow Airport) cost thirty-six thousand dollars, give or take a few, dollars. Everyone agreed on the cost. This figure, of course, does not include bandages for mashed and cut fingers, antacid for nervous stomachs, and medication for headaches.

Enter the Author

Months had passed since the ferry flight. I heard about the white and circus red B-25's adventures and was kicking myself for missing the big event. I could not believe all this took place and Boyd Clow had not given me a call. He knew I had admired this medium bomber for years.

When I called to complain, his only reply was "You should drop in more often."

He was right. Since I had sold the R46, my visits to Clow were few and far between. To really top it off, I could not believe I missed all the TV and newspaper coverage. But there was no use kicking a dead horse. I should have realized that all this was an omen that said, "Don't get involved".

Every weekend, I would purchase the Chicago Sunday paper and religiously turn to the classified ads, looking under "Airplanes." I would read every one of the sometimes two classified columns. I was playing with the idea of buying a warbird.

One Sunday, an ad hit me between the eyes. "Wanted: Partner in B-25 Project". There was a phone number. I called the number and met Walter. He talked and I listened. As Walter filled me in, it was obvious he was talking about Lambert's B-25.

From that phone call, we met for lunch. Walter and I hit it off nicely. In many ways, we were very much alike. I felt he was down to earth and honest. We could and would get along.

Months later, I sat in a four-place, low-wing single engine airplane with three strangers. We were on our way to see 06. It was very nice of Weary Warriors to invite me now that they had my four thousand dollars. I at last owned a small piece of one half of a warbird.

Mike Butler and I sat in the cramped back seat and Walter Wild was in the pilot's seat. As we droned along, it appeared, and I assumed, that the young man seated next to Walter was his pilot instructor. We may have been on Walter's dual cross-country, which was one step of many to getting his pilot's license.

As we fishtailed, bobbed, and weaved along, Walter's instructor was getting annoyed with him. As Walter ranted and raved about the museum's lack of any progress with 06's restoration, his verbal expressions were telegraphed through the airplane's controls. Mike, like me, was a pilot and we exchanged glances as we merrily rolled along, enjoying the roller coaster-like ride. Walter was mad but, from the few words that Mike and I had, Mike was more disappointed than mad. They had sat quietly for months with this eating at them: with my money in the bank and my fresh enthusiasm, they decided to move forward.

Our flight was just about over. The individual seated next to Walter handled the radio and Walter made a nice landing. My first view of the white and red B-25 was through the cabin windows as we approached her.

The B-25, the object of our dreams, sat forlornly on a cement ramp this June day in 1982. There were some wires or cables dangling from her bottom side, which, to me, proclaimed neglect. All the years that I had admired her, I had never seen her sitting on a hard surface ramp. She looked very commercial. There were several museum members waiting for us but I would gather, after a few minutes, that none could make any decisions or answer any question on behalf of the museum. Very clever —- there would be no commitments on behalf of the museum.

While I poked around inside 06, I caught fragments of the conversation between the representatives of the two groups. I could tell that the honeymoon was over. Walter was doing most of the talking.

From Weary Warriors point of view, the museum was not living up to the contract agreement. Point in fact; 06 was not in a hanger and she was not going in any hanger because there was no hanger. There was a large utility building that the museum had leased, but 06 was twice the size of that building. Very little, if any, work had been done. I got the impression that the museum's mechanics were products of the jet age and knew very little of 06's systems and her engines except for what they had learned while preparing for the ferry flight at Lambert's field. The museum group had simply lied or misrepresented themselves, not a good way to start a relationship.

The museum had also played up their rare B-25H in magazine articles and newsletters with never a mention of the fact that Weary Warriors owned half of her. Feelings were hurt. It was also obvious that the museum was building up its membership by using the B-25 as a catalyst for membership drives, which would be the normal thing to do. They would receive the new member's dues and, in turn, take most of the money and put it to use for more advertising in more expensive journals, thus hoping to catch a very wealthy member who would sponsor a good portion of the expense of restoring the B-25. There was, perhaps, a little too much ego and not enough fact in their ads and articles. While the membership grew, no wealthy persons came forward.

As I listened to the conversation, it became obvious that Walter was no negotiator. Walter was older than I and Mike was considerably younger. Both were machinists. Talking in this environment was not their thing. They were also, to some extent, being stymied by the fact that the museum's reps could do nothing, even if they wanted to do. This was frustrating and it showed. All the work and expense that had gone into 06 for the ferry flight was sitting out in the open; neglected and exposed to the elements. All the systems that so many had worked so hard and long on would soon deteriorate, if they had not already done so. The B-25 had sat out, exposed to the elements the entire winter while Weary Warriors thought she was tucked safely away in a hanger.

As I sat in the cockpit of the World War II medium bomber, the reality of owning a small piece of her was overwhelming. I felt my four thousand dollars was well spent and that I would and could spend more, if necessary. I hoped that the two groups could work out their differences. They both wanted the same thing and should be able to work together.

The tone of the conversation outside the cockpit was going from bad to worse. It was time for me to say something to end the bickering. Nothing was being accomplished. It was time to bring the conversation to an end and end it with an impact. What the hell, I had just as much money in it as Walter and Mike and the guys from the museum probably had no more than their dues, which was about twenty-five bucks.

There is a big advantage to coming into a heated discussion late. Now, I had been a cop for about twenty-six years and, if need be, I could be one real mean bastard and come on strong. The guys from the museum would be a piece of cake compared to many of the low-life I had to deal with.

Climbing down the hatch, I put my most surly, unfriendly foot forward and I addressed them. I figured they would blindly cave into anyone who had the image of authority.

"While you can make no decisions, you can sure carry a message. You tell your conniving leader to get this B-25 in a hanger or your organization is going to be sued. We don't care if we have to come down here with a chain saw and saw off her wings and haul her back home on a truck. No hanger, no B-25. Just think what that will do for your fancy image."

Walter's mouth dropped open, Mike's eyes were like saucers and the guys from the museum huddled and leaned against each other for support. I spun on my heels and walked away. Walter and Mike did the same. We did not say goodbye. The point had been made with appropriate impact.

On the way home, there was silence in the airplane cabin. I sensed that Walter and Mike were apprehensive of me. They probably were wondering what kind of monster partner they had. I wondered if they were worried being cooped up with tyrant like me in a small cabin with no place to go.

I broke the ice and started a general conversation about how great things were going to be with the emphasis on the positive. We talked about our dreams. The cabin lightened up as we speculated about what was going to happen.

Mike said, "What do you think Lou?"

"If they can get the money, we go forward and keep our end of the deal," I said. "If they don't get the money to go forward, we take the B-25 back and we go forward without them. We can find more partners to invest. After all; you are already a not-for-profit corporation."

"But they can't get anybody to invest, what makes you think we can"?

"Mike," I said, "do you think I would have given you all that money if I did not have a share in her? That's the difference between the two groups. We each own her. With the museum, the museum owns her. Anybody that could afford to donate the big bucks they are looking for could afford to buy and own their own B-25."

Walter jumped in, "That makes sense, damn it! Where were you when we needed you?"

Mike continued, "The museum is tax-exempt and donations get a tax break. Do we have the same advantage?"

"No, Mike; all we get is the protection of a non-profit corporation. When we purchase something we do not have to pay Illinois sales tax. You can apply for a refund, I think."

A few months later, at our annual meeting required by Illinois law, I was elected president of Weary Warriors (no one else wanted to do it) and Walter was elected vice president. I don't remember who were secretary and treasurer. Mike and Claude each held one of the positions. We filed our papers with the state for the year and I introduced our small group to a simple form of management as we set our goals and objectives.

We move forward. First order of business is the status of 06.

I rented a plane, made a long one-day trip and found our B-25 exactly the way we had left her in late spring.

I report back to our group. We are disappointed with the project. Nothing is happening.

I memorize our contract with the museum and open up a dialog with the museum's president whom I had never met. To give our potential lawsuit a good set of legs (just in case), I start laying the groundwork. I get off several polite letters putting forth our concerns and log every phone call. We are invited to join the museum as members and we all do just that.

Time goes by and I smell a rat. While I know many criminal attorneys, I suggest we find a civil attorney who specializes in aircraft. Walter and Mike are given the task. The museum then suggests that one Weary Warrior become a board member for a better understanding and a better working relationship. Sounds good. More time slides by and I am selected to represent us on the museum board. I will have to be elected at the museum's annual meeting. My name is on the ballot. More time marches on.

Weary Warriors go to the annual meeting en masse. We are treated coldly and the handwriting is on the wall. Not only are the museum board and its officers cold, they are evasive. They already know the outcome of the election before the formal announcement is made. I do not get elected to the board. We should have had a stipulation in the agreement with the museum that Weary Warriors always would have a member on the board. Too little, too late. It's just as well: I would not enjoy suing myself.

The B-25 still sits. The phone call was encouraging, but changed in a hurry. The museum wants to go forward and had located two zero-time engines, in their storage cans and sealed. They were from an airline that had gone under. The price: thirty thousand. The museum would like us to purchase them per the agreement that we purchase the parts.

We advise the museum that we do not consider engines as parts. There is one good engine, we tell them: overhaul the bad one. We will buy the parts for the overhaul. You pay for the labor as per our agreement. If you don't have the money, put the mechanics, skilled help, and all those volunteers that you bragged about to work. The museum says they cannot do that. No explanation is offered.

Weary Warriors asks if the museum had treated and preserved the engines on 06.

Yes they had; they poured oil down each spark plug hole and put the spark plugs back in.

That is a good start but is not the way to do it for long term storage while the engines are still hung on the airframe. You need to start the engine and pour oil down the carburetor until the engine suffocates itself and stops running. All lower cylinder areas are then covered with oil and then oil is dumped down the spark plug holes to coat the upper portions of the cylinders.

We also asked if they had been pulling the props through every twenty days or so to keep internal engine parts freed up. They hadn't turned an engine for months.

Super. That is just great.

We touch base with our attorney. He suggests we try and work it out.

For some reason, Walter vents his frustration on 06's paint. If they do not know what to do or how to do it the least they can do is get the paint off 06 and get her down to bare aluminum and treat it with an anti-corrosive product. It sounds good. This is our last shot. If they say no, we sue.

To our surprise the museum says yes. We would later find out that membership was falling off. Members were not renewing and to keep the interest up the museum latched on to Walter's idea. It was just the shot in the arm they needed. It was a quick fix for a museum that was faltering.

Weary Warriors had pictures in their minds of buying several drums of paint stripper, brushes, gloves, eye protection, and renting a steam machine. On a warm sunny weekend, dozens of museum members turn out to work on the project. At long last, the camaraderie is present. Men do the work and their wives grill the hot dogs. Weary Warriors guess estimate that all the material will cost them about seven to eight hundred dollars.

Right?

Wrong. The museum takes the B-25 to a commercial paint shop on the airport and has the shop do the stripping at a cost of three thousand two hundred sixty one dollars and fifty cents. Our cost for material is two thousand, five hundred sixty-one dollars and fifty cents. Labor cost to the museum is seven hundred dollars.

I say, "Okay, we will take care of it," but I am thinking, "Whoa! Hold it! Wait just a minute. Are you guys' nuts? Give us just a little credit for having some brains."

I now had retired from law enforcement and was enjoying the work of a licensed private detective. I am licensed to work in four states.

On a slow day, I motor down, once again, to the museum. Circling the airfield, I see 06, glistening in the afternoon sun. She is no longer white and red. The tower directs me to the paint shop where I engage a very talkative employee in conversation. The boss is not there. He is awed that he is talking to a real private detective and cooperates fully. This guy is one in a million. He recalls that it took them days to get that damn oil and paint off. I get copies of the work order, materials, time sheets, and the invoice. I thank him, slip him twenty bucks for a cup of coffee and he readily agrees I was never there.

"Wow —- just like on TV," he comments. I smile and leave.

The tower gives me some complicated directions to taxi to 06 and I finally get there. I check out the strip job and it looks good. Using our key, I open the forward compartment hatch in the belly and I climb up into the cockpit. I am still mesmerized by the awesome depth of this civilized warbird. Seated in the beat-up pilot's seat, I go over the paperwork from the paint shop. We have been had. We were being held up without a gun. It appeared the material and labor costs were switched around. Clever. Very clever. If we'd paid the fraudulent amount, we could probably nail the museum for fraud. Maybe the paint shop also; or at least the board member that called me and sent the invoice. But, chances are, he was duped too.

I decided to recommend to my partners that we pay the material portion only of the bill. We would simply not pay the bill as presented. I had had enough. I would now join Walter and recommend we go to court and get our B-25 back.

I daydreamed just a little in the cockpit of 06 and was brought back to reality by someone slapping a hand on the side of the fuselage. It was the airport police, who ordered me out of the aircraft. Being a good boy, I complied. As I exited, he was fingering his handcuff case —- not a good sign. We went through the routine and once I showed —- and demonstrated —- the key to the hatch, he mellowed up. The retired copper bit put him at ease. He was not aware that the museum owned only half of the B-25. I got the impression he was a member. We said our good-byes and I headed for home.

I called a meeting, filled everyone in and gave the paint shop a call, advising them we were sending a check for seven hundred dollars which included the price of fifteen gallons of etch to preserve the aluminum. He was to collect the remainder of the invoice from the museum. We heard nothing more of the incident.

We were smoldering. It was the last straw. How the museum board could condone such behavior was beyond us. It did not occur to us that maybe the board did not know what was going on. But we would not forget the election and the rude reception we got at the annual museum meeting.

I liked the attorney that Walter and Mike found. He was alert to our concerns and he was mature. He drew up the documents and we gave him all the support documentation he would need, along with our personal logs of who, why, what, where, when, and how. He felt we had a good case. There were glaring breaches of the contract. We filed the lawsuit. There was no settlement money-wise so we would have to foot the costs, which he estimated would be at least five thousand dollars. He would need a retainer. We swallowed hard but we wanted the B-25 back. At that time, a so-so B-25 was going for at least one hundred twenty-five thousand dollars and some as high as a quarter of a million dollars.

Exit the Museum

By April 1983, eighteen months had gone by since the exciting ferry flight. 06's restoration program was just about stagnant. She sat in the same place and in the same condition as I had observed her during the paint shop visit. Our suit had been filed on April sixth. I tried to get it filed on April Fool's day, [just my sweet nature], but our attorney could not get the paperwork together that fast. Needless to say, the museum, for some unknown reason, cannot understand our posturing.

"Can we get together and perhaps discuss a new agreement? This has to be just a simple misunderstanding. Why spend all the money for legal fees when that money could be put into the B-25?"

We go forward with our legal action. The museum and our attorney do not realize the tenacity that Walter and I possess at this time. We will not relent. We have made the decision and will stay with it to the end. If that end is bitter for someone, so be it. We have exhausted all compassion. Mike and Claude are on the sidelines, but are with us. Lambert is getting less and less involved.

Word begins to spread and rumors are rampant. Questions begin to be asked by museum members. The answers they get from their own board members are evasive half-truths. Another partnership is going down the drain and we are elated.

The museum "will fight us to the death" is the word we get back from our attorney. I ask the attorney to explain whose death.

Weary Warriors are taking a beating on the warbird grapevine. Word of what a miserable bunch we are spreads from coast to coast. We do not have the contacts the museum group has and our reputation is soiled to say the least.

Walter is furious. Mike and I calm him down. We will have our day. We have done nothing that we have to explain or defend, but we will have our day. We dig our heels in deeper.

All five of us do not renew our memberships in the museum. We are unaware that there are a lot of others doing the same.

Our attorney suggests we offer to buy back our half and sends the message to the museum's attorney. The museum ponders the offer and replies that it cannot "betray the members and sponsors" of the B-25. They cannot sell. They will not sell. Would we like to sell?

Weary Warriors offers to sell its half to the museum for thirty-one thousand dollars —- a fair offer in that day's market. The museum turns down the offer. They have no money.

That admission throws some museum members for a loop. They begin to ask some very pointed questions, such as, where is the money? Where did the money go? More and more museum members become suspicious. There should be thousands of dollars in the restoration fund from all the pizza sales and donations from air shows where they showed off the B-25 on static display. How about the sponsors and membership dues? Much of the money was earmarked for the restoration fund and could not be spent for anything else.

Where was the money? There are delays and more evasions to their questions. At long last, the museum board begins to smell a stink.

The board members have not been paying attention to the operation of their museum. Some resign. With the pending legal action, they do not want to get involved or be responsible and they get out while the getting is good.

Out of the blue, some honest board members conduct an internal audit. As a result of the audit, the instructions to their legal counsel is to negotiate and do it quickly. They cannot make the principal amount payment due to the bank although they have been making some interest payments. The bank that floated the loan is holding an empty bag since Weary Warriors would not let the bank put a lien on the B-25. The museum needs money. The museum board members who co-signed for the loan were not about to be left holding the bag either.

The bank contacts me. The banker seems to be one hell of a nice guy who had gone out on a limb for the museum. I suspect he is on the museum board. I suggest he put the pressure on the museum. He wants his money; we want the B-25.

Some museum members balk, especially those that had turned to and had been working on 06 to demonstrate they were indeed restoring the bomber (a good point for their side and a smart move for their case). They have some time for the note payment.

It is spring of 1984 and 06's outer wings have been removed. Pilots and co-pilot's seats are out as are the controls and some wiring.

The banker is on the phone. The museum will settle. They would like to come together without going to court to keep costs down. I advise him to give us about two weeks: we will discuss it and get back to him through our respective attorneys.

The phone call is positive.

We call a meeting to go over the pluses and minus. Claude advises he will not put any more money into the organization. He wishes us well but will more or less stay on the sidelines and keep an eye on his investment. Lambert takes a pass and hints he would like to sell out. Mike, Walt and I will have to foot the entire bill for everything.

We put our heads together. We are committed. We cannot fly the B-25 now and will have to dismantle her further and truck her out. Where have I heard those words before? Walt and Mike will look into that cost.

I call around to a few friends of the museum. The museum has been quietly trying to sell its half, but no one wants us as partners, thanks to the nasty reputation given us by their rumor spreading.

But we are having our day. I also hear that there are less than twenty members in the museum and the president — with his ego — has left town. Walter and I hope they tarred and feathered him on the way out.

We put our heads together and, through our legal counsel, offer eleven thousand cash. The figure is firm. We will not bicker or bargain. It will stand at that figure, period. It will cost us four thousand to dismantle 06 and will take two semi flatbeds to truck her to a hanger we are looking at in Rockford, Illinois. With a lot of pressure from the bank, the museum accepts the offer.

We get another not-so-nice surprise. Our legal fees come to seven thousand dollars. I dig into my R46 money and then some.

There are three very understanding wives. Mike, Walter, and I split the total cost of $22,000 three ways. We each come up with $7,334. Walter, Mike, and I each have $11,334 invested and four of us own a B-25.

Four? I thought there were five?

Mike and I buy out Lambert, who remains a friend and visits us from time to time. Mike and I each now have thirteen thousand plus invested. I am one of the happiest guys around. I own 31.9 % of one of the rarest warbirds in the world.

As part of the settlement, we will not be able to physically participate in the disassembly of 06. We are not permitted to enter the museum's leased property to keep an eye on our B-25. I calm Walter down and our attorney assures us we will get all of the B-25 back. Let them have the parting shot. If we show up there will probably be a brawl as tempers are raw as are feelings. We've won; they've lost.

I figure the only ones who won are the two attorneys.

Weary Warriors now have a broken B-25 and we are broke ourselves. With all the expense and frustration over the past few years, there is an unexplained warmth of final victory and actual possession. The museum was correct, though, about the waste of money and years of energy. All of that could have been put into the rebuild of 06. We wonder what the museum's total bill was. We would never ask or find out.

The three of us look over the jumbled mass, once a proud medium bomber, of large and small piles of aluminum, dangling wires, bent tubing, and cabling lying on our hanger floor. It will be a long time before 06 takes to the air.

It is hard to believe. It is pathetic, but it does not deter us or dampen our spirits. We will be patient and wait. She is all ours. We can reach out and touch and embrace her anytime we want —- there are no rules against hugging. We will come up with a plan of action, but for the time being, we will bask in the aura of our precious B-25.

We wonder if she knows what the four of us went through to get her. Does she realize that, for the first time in over twelve years, she will not be rained on? The sun will not scorch her. No insects or birds will soil her. The cold winds will not touch her. Does she know we will pamper her and take care of her? She will be loved, not neglected. Will she trust us? Will she be a lady and be stand-offish and hard to get next to or will she be a woman and show her appreciation as only a woman can? We will soon find out.

We have an old, beat up, neglected hanger. It has two gas furnaces so rusty we will never turn them on. The roof leaks a little and there is no running water, which means no bathroom. We do have electricity. There is an attached office that we will not use for the first few years. The rent is a reasonable $210 a month. The office is an extra forty dollars if the time ever comes. The same thing, closer to our homes, is fifteen hundred a month. We will drive the seventy to one hundred miles, three to four hours round trip, to work eight hours or more every Saturday. We are that committed.

When Walter latched on to the hanger for us it appeared the landlord may have estimated the dimensions just a little too generously. When we get around to actually measuring the hanger, we find that 06, with her wing tips on, will not fit. With her eight-gun nose in place, she is too long. Well, we will worry about the fit when the time comes. Now, today, the piles of a B-25 fit and we have committed ourselves to the first bold step of her build up. Someday she will once again feel the pulse of motion. She will quiver with life and we will recapture the days of her glory. She will respond to our effort.

We will cautiously explore this mysterious lady. We will take her boldly by the hand so we may glimpse what she has kept a secret for decades.

The hanger doors are enormous, old, bent, heavy, and do not roll easily as they stack next to each other. We will spend considerable time on the doors, trying to get them to roll in their tracks without binding. It takes pure muscle power to operate the doors and it will always take two of us to push the doors open and pull the doors close.

It is hard to explain the deep inner satisfaction. The human soul finds satisfaction in strange ways. As we struggle to close each unfamiliar section of the hanger doors late that night, we are content. At long last, she is in a hanger. It has taken so long! She is now all ours; we owe nobody anything.

That night, on the long drive home, my mind wanders. There is a saying about people who own wooden boats, especially very large ones. It goes like this: a wooden boat is a hole in the water surrounded by wood into which one pours money. It occurs to me that owning a warbird, especially a big one, is like owning a hole in the sky surrounded by aluminum into which one pours money.

Lou Fulgaro

Counting Beans

Summer of 1984 brings sunshine and warmth. Walt, Mike and I assess 06 to form a plan of action. There was a plan of action of 1981 and we know how that ended up. Our plan for '84, which is elusive at this time, hopefully will not end the same way. But it is now a time to dream and we do just that.

We take a long look in to the future. Because we are daydreaming, the future looks good. We decide a few things that are more gingerbread than basics. Walter wants to call her Weary Warrior and she will have a reclining, semi-nude female painted below her cockpit. She [06] will be painted olive drab with a gray bottom. My eventual assignment will be to try to find a cannon-nose, as she is an H model.

I ask Walt and Mike if she had the correct low profile air intakes before they installed the new type carburetors in 81. She now has the box air intakes that look, to me, like stovepipes sticking up out of the engine nacelles. These stovepipes are so ugly the Canadians refused to mount them and came up with a modification to use the low profile intakes with the modern carburetors. They are not sure.

I bring up the collector ring exhaust system, which is not correct for an H model. The system is a civilian modification to quiet the -29's from the original, very noisy, individual exhaust stacks for each cylinder that gave the B-25 her reputation as a supreme noisemaker.

Claude thinks we are nuts but we decide to go ahead and try and make her original. They ask me to put together a model of what 06 will look like and I agree. We throw in a top turret for good measure.

To pay the hanger rent and utility bill each month, the three of us split the tab. Claude comes up with a few ideas to get people interested and to make money. They are all legal but I convince Weary Warriors that is not the way to go.

It is time for us to come to an understanding. First, and most importantly; if they want me to lead, I will lead, but not by committee. To keep things on track —- and with the best interest of Weary Warriors at heart —- if they want me to lead, I can only do so if I am the decision-maker once we have our goals set. I explain to them that, with four years in the military and twenty-six years in law enforcement, I do not believe in management by participation. I will listen to their input but the decisions are mine to make. There will be no voting. I will run Weary Warriors, period. If they don't like what I do, they can elect someone else to lead them. They agree.

The first thing I do is put Walter in charge of all mechanical operations. His word is law when it comes to mechanics. Walter will hold this position well into the twenty-first century and I will hold mine to 1992 when I retire and 06 goes from her rebuild phase into her flight phase.

Claude asked, "Lou what is your plan to raise money?"

"My plan is to have no plan. I do not intend to go out and find people to ask to invest in a B-25; nor do we need their piddling yearly dues. There will be no newsletter mentality. I intend to have them find us and ask if they can join Weary Warriors."

Silence.

We will need very little money for the next few years. Working together on Saturdays, it will take us that long to clean 06 up and start putting her together. We are going to be doing a lot of grunt work, as Walter calls it. Walter agrees it should not take to much money to start and predicts it will take $60,000 and three years plus the engines.

Walter's numbers are reasonable and lift our spirits even higher. Back to our now-agreed-to plan to do nothing. I convince them that warbird lovers will soon hear about us and, to while away a slow Saturday afternoon after their house and yard chores are done, they will come for a look see. To pilots and airplane dreamers, Saturdays are airport days. Our hanger doors will always be open. We will welcome all who take the time to come, to touch and to see with their own eyes. We will rely on word of mouth. We all like the idea because we have to do nothing.

The second item I insist on is that we will never go into debt. If we do not have the money to spend we will not buy, no matter how tempting the deal.

We have to have something to present to the visitors especially those who are interested and have money. It should be a well-typed handout that any of us can hand to a visitor containing one page with 06's heritage and how precious and rare she is and one page with a schedule of ownership. It should be in plain simple language, to the point and understandable; something they can take home and read over and over. Let them sell themselves. It plainly has to say, "If you want to play you have to pay".

Okay.

We give it a lot of thought as the three of us sit outside our hanger and admire our B-25. Our backs are against the hanger wall and we are warming ourselves in the sun this cool Saturday morning. As always, it turns into a brainstorming session. We are comfortable turning nuts and bolts and don't like to address administration-type problems but we have to have a foundation to build on.

From all these impromptu sessions, we come up with an agreement. We would like to limit the partnership to about fifteen members. We will review our partnership program at every annual meeting. Pilots who want to drive 06 from either seat will buy in at $10,000. Non-pilots who want to ride bomb bay forward [Upper turret, navigator compartment, jump seats on the flight deck] will have to come up with $4,000. Bomb bay aft members would buy in at $2,000 or, if they have a certified skill like a mechanic, $1,000. Those who just want to hang around and work on her and be part of the ground crew and, on occasion, go for a ride can do so for $1,000. To help pay utilities and odds and ends, pilots will pay fifty dollars a month, bomb bay forward, twenty-five and bomb bay aft and ground crew, twenty.

If you fall behind in your monthly assessments, you don't crew her until you are paid in full. Insurance premiums and hangar rent will be equally assessed to all members and, again; if you don't pay you don't play.

To encourage participation in the work on 06, a formula is devised. After you put up your front money [We do not take down payments and do not have a payment plan. We are not a bank], you will receive three shares worth one dollar each for every hour you work. And work you will do —- time spent around the water cooler and scratching your butt does not count. Walter will certify your hours. Goof-offs and party animals are in for a surprise in the years to follow. A lot of people get real mad at me but Walter and I are steadfast. The whole plan is to reward those that are conscientious and live up to their commitment. You don't have to turn a nut if you do not want to. Just come, sit and shoot the breeze if that is your liking, but don't expect to be paid.

Years later, in the summer of 1989, our plan to have no plan works out nicely. We would have a total of fourteen members in our one-of-a-kind squadron and a staggering $325,000 invested. 06 is about two years from flying and looks good. Many will have doubled and tripled their individual buy-in amounts. Walter, Mike, and I have each invested over $30,000 dollars.

As 06 begins to look nicer and nicer, we raise the buy-in amounts. Pilot shares go to $20,000 and are now at $30,000. The other slots go up also. Bomb bay forward is $16,000. Many who came and poked around and kept their money in the bank and their hands in their pockets now like what they see and drop a check in the mail for ten grand. We return the checks. Those that took a chance up front when 06 lay in a pile on our cement hanger floor are smiling. More people are mad at me. Who cares?

As we get partners, Mike's, Walter's and my percent of ownership drops. But that is okay. All fourteen of us feel that we own her and any apprehension that 06 is not ours is nonexistent. Much like a child, a parent does not question which of them owns the child: Weary Warriors have that kind of camaraderie. The harder and longer we work, the stronger the bond. We stick to our rules: there is no variance. Walter is still running the mechanics and is Vice President and I still sit at the top. Walter and I agree that to keeping everyone on the same page takes considerable effort.

Okay, back to summer of 1984 (just had to get all that paper BS out of the way so you the reader could understand us). The Aero Plane Factory, owned by Tim McCarter, a warbird rebuilder, is just a block away from us with his complex of hangers.

Ben, of Ben-Lar Transport of Rockford Illinois, has done a good workman-like job of disassembling 06 and transporting her. She had been taken apart and transported very carefully. Nothing was sawn, chiseled, or broken apart. 06 was neatly cradled, padded, and had no dents or twisting of any of her airframe structure.

Our precious B-25 was cautiously pushed, pulled, and carried into our hanger with loving care. The center section dominated the hanger and was placed in the central area were it would be the fixation of our focus. Resting on heavy timbers, it sat about two feet off the floor.

The center section is the heart of 06; every component radiates to, through and out of this section. It is the most critical piece of 06 and it is a big piece. Stripped and dry it weighs 1850 pounds. It is some 26 feet six inches wide and looked to me about nine feet long. About two feet off the cement, the top of the center section towered nine feet above us.

The cockpit/navigator section along with the eight gun solid nose was unbolted from the front of the center section and was off to the side in it's own cradle. The fuselage or by the book, "tail cone" was unbolted from the center section near the trailing edge of the wings and rested behind the center section. The two 23 foot outer wings, just outboard from the engine nacelles, had been removed by the museum and were stacked along one wall with the two vertical and the one twenty three foot long horizontal stabilizer.

The engines, firewall-forward, had been unbolted and rested on their engine mounts on the opposite side of the hanger from the wings and tail. The front of the huge engines faced the ceiling of the hanger. Close by, the removed props, flaps, oil tanks, oil coolers, and control services took up precious available floor space. The two heavy landing gears were partially retracted inside the engine nacelles that form part of the center section. The nose gear was propped in a corner.

Scattered all over the hanger were unbelievable stacks of aluminum sheet metal that included the bomb bay doors, gear doors, engine cowlings, control surfaces, two carburetors and their intakes; and inspection and access plates by the hundreds. To add to the general confusion, box upon box, crates on top of crates, and wooden barrels and drums by the dozen held pumps, wires, tubing, and nuts, bolts, washers by the thousands. Most components that had been bolted to 06 had been removed during her disassembly and, untagged, had been placed in unmarked containers. Many were not in containers —- they just lain on the floor in pools of oil and hydraulic fluid. It was a messy array of hundreds of odds and ends whose existence, to a novice, had no rhyme or reason.

Using our North American manuals, we attempted a detailed inventory and part identification, but soon gave up. It would take too long and the identification sequence was just about impossible. We did find that critical and hard-to-find parts were missing and, if they could be purchased, would be expensive. They were on 06 the last time we looked at her but, from all indications, had been pilfered. In our own minds, we knew who the thieves were. So much for our attorney assuring us that 06 would be returned complete.

The most obvious things that were missing were the two pilots control wheels [yokes] from the cockpit. In one of their places was a large, grinning photograph of the defunct museum's self-styled leader. Pinned to the instrument panel was a museum tee shirt.

Walter, as expected, was the first to react. Literally ripping the tee shirt out of the cockpit, he headed for the biggest pool of hydraulic fluid, saying, "I know what this is good for."

As he bent over the pool of hydraulic fluid, I yelled, "Hold it Walter. I have a better idea!"

Walter stopped and handed me the tee shirt. I pinned the tee shirt to some old nails in the hanger wall along with the photograph.

"This is just so the three of us will never forget our folly and we will never want to become like them."

The two items stayed on our hanger wall for years as a constant reminder. At times when we were really low, for whatever reason, we would glance at the photo and tee shirt and our energy would surge.

Several years later, I would purchase our two control wheels from a "source" (I was advised they had laid in someone's family room as souvenirs); but we had to replace most of the missing equipment ourselves. Our tow bar was gone and we would raise so much hell through our attorney that we would get it back. The tailskid was impossible to replace, so Walter made a Fiberglas mold off a museum static display and, from that, made a replacement (we eventually found whose B-25 our tail skid ended up on but did not get it back). The generator voltage regulators were also missing at a cost of $1,500 each. In 1988, we would have to purchase two regulators. Walter, Mike and I cursed the museum. If there were any regrets about the price we paid for their half of 06, there were none now.

We offered several museum members, who had been our friends through all this, invitations to join us but none could come up with the money. One day in 1987 while we were at lunch, we were advised by some of Tim's help that we had some visitors who looked familiar. Tim's men thought that they were from the museum. They kept an eye on them for us.

Weeks pass and the weather is just perfect. Major parts are identified, tagged and neatly stored. Before being put away, openings are taped up and sealed. Parts that would rust are treated with a rust inhibitor. Wire ends are wrapped, coiled, and tagged, as are the hundreds of feet of cables. Aluminum sheet metal is identified and neatly stacked with mating pieces. The hanger, at long last, is neat.

Narrow aisles weave and wind their way through a maze of neatly stacked boxes, crates, barrels, drums, airplane parts, and stacks of sheet metal. Everything is off the floor and on timbers, pallets or hanging from a wall. 06 patiently waits for her facelift.

We buy our first tool. It is a broom.

Our first material purchase is a lot of oil absorbent material.

Lou Fulgaro

This is a before photo of what our cockpit looked like when we got 06 back after the legal action. It was a real mess. If you look closely you can see the photo that greeted us. There are no control wheels.

We Begin Again

Resting comfortably on her heavy timbers, 06's center section was formidable. I knew the front from the back and the top from the bottom. After that, things became a little vague. While I was mechanically inclined, had worked on many engines, and turned a lot of bolts during my lifetime, I was simply overwhelmed. I had heard many times that the B-25 was one of the most straightforward and simple aircraft of World War II but this was hard to believe. It was not simple-looking to me whatsoever. I would ask Walter amateurish questions and he would give me answers that made sense. Walter knew a lot more than I did and, when it came to the mechanics, It reinforced my feelings that Walter would lead and I would follow.

The center section rested at the perfect height to be worked on. Mike, Walter and I walked around the center section, eyeballing it from every direction and every angle. We got down on our knees to take a peak at her bottom. Walter, the most knowledgeable, led Mike and I around and pointed out odds and ends.

Inside the center section, dirt, dust and a few years of neglect are very apparent. It was tattered-looking and beat up but nothing was torn. The peeling zinc chromate was complimented by the peeling paint. Whatever you touched or leaned against, you came away with the dirtiest black you ever saw. A crazy, tangled array of soiled wiring and limp cables hung everywhere. With the bent tubing, dangling hoses that dripped fluid, and all the pulleys, brackets and fittings, we had a confusing clutter and mess that went in every direction. The decision to restore was an easy one. We had no choice.

The three of us mounted our assault on the formidable center section. From home, we began to assemble the equipment and materials to support our project. Mike and Walter brought good tools and Mike brought the biggest rolling chest toolbox you ever saw, packed with tools. Walter showed up with electric drills, some so big I'd never seen anything like them. There were drop cords and lamps and some machine shop tools to cut threads on a bolt that fascinated me. Mike, being the playboy of our little group, brought a charcoal grill complete with charcoal and lighter fluid. We were so intense at our work that we would never fire up the grill. My contribution was rather mundane compare to my two partner's contributions. A very big hammer, a bigger crowbar, a few beat-up lawn chairs, two ladders, another broom, a large garbage can, and an old, tube-type radio that would play for the next ten tears. We purchased a good padlock for the hanger door and everyone got a key. A first aid kit was tucked away and a good size fire extinguisher mounted on the wall. Look out 06! Here we come.

Month after month, we would trek to our hanger every Saturday without fail. Year after year, the three of us show up rain or shine, warm or cold. We would neglect our Saturday home chores and the grass would not get mowed as often as it should. In winter, on those cold Saturday mornings when most sane humans would stay warm under the covers and resist getting out of bed, our feet would hit the cold floor by 6:00 AM and we would be on our way while the rest of our families slept in. Once again, I would not renew my pilot's medical and put any spare money I had in to 06. Walter got his license and did the same.

We always had to buy something, but if we could not pay for it we did not buy it. Weary Warriors always maintained this posture and it kept us out of trouble. There were times when we had ten cents in our checking account and times we had forty thousand dollars.

We were close to something that was a common bond. It brought us together and we formed, over the years, a camaraderie founded on dedication and contribution. We worked together, got dirty together, and, at times, bled together. Three strangers co-existed under an umbrella of commitment that would have tried the most successful marriage. We had something we wanted all our adult lives. We would love her only as a man can love a machine and we would curse her. At times Mike would say, "It's like trying to make love to a sixty-five year-old virgin —- it's not going to be easy."

Our B-25 resisted our amateurish efforts, our clumsy ways, and our inexperience. We wanted to be gentle and loving and she was downright ornery and stubborn. We worked on her as if she were a fragile lady. In realty, she was as strong as a steel locomotive. We wooed her with flowers and chocolate when in realty she wanted to be gathered up and carried off. We soon learned to match her spirited personality. She was giving into brute force. We were learning how to match her wily ways.

Occasionally she would resist, just showing her independence and, at other times, baffling us with her mysterious ways. Always with soft-soled shoes, we would walk over her ever carefully as not to mark or scar her. We would always try to treat her like a lady. I was the romantic when it came to our B-25 and Walter was the more practical one.

Walter and Mike, being machinists, put their skills to work. They even made special tools. Walter just about memorized the North American manuals. I always marveled at his ability to look at a bolt and know the size and thread. Mike and Walter never grabbed the wrong size wrench. They would give me a task, give some advice, and walk away. Compared to them, I felt I was not carrying my load at times when it came to the mechanics, but I was learning fast. As we grew in members, I slowly became the administrator of our small but growing group. I found the parts, paid the bills, went to hearings, conducted meetings, met with persons that were interested in joining us, prepared budgets and took care of our legal corporate matters. But on Saturdays, I was just another mechanic and the one that swept the hanger floor.

The first three years we dismantled, scrubbed and cleaned. The next three years we assembled, scrubbed, and cleaned. As our membership grew past ten, it was just about a full time job to keep everyone on the same page and going in the same direction at the same time. There were multiple personalities interacting and a lot of money involved.

We constantly took photos. Over the years, I would take over a thousand photos. It would pay off when 06 was being put back together.

We were going to remove everything from the center section. Anything that could be removed would be taken off. We would strip her bare, absolutely naked; she would be an empty shell. No B-25 would go through a rebuild like 06 was going to go through. We would find the true meaning of the phrase, "ground up restoration." We were determined that she would outlive all of us. What was nice was that we had thousands of visitors over the years that could verify our rebuild —- and we had those precious photos.

The main spars of the inboard wings between the center section of the fuselage and engine nacelles were critical. The two front spars carried all the plumbing, wiring, and cabling from the center section to the engines. If the pilots of her ferry flight could have seen the forty-year-old mess between the front spar and wing leading edges, I don't think they would have flown her.

The leading edges of the wings were hard to remove, but they were nothing compared to the main landing gear. Being the smallest, I was the only one that could get up in the nacelle, which was coated with dirty black oil and slippery hydraulic fluid. I would get down on the floor and crawl on my back under the nacelles that held the partially retracted landing gear. Then I would snake my torso through and around all the gear mechanisms, actuating levers, and hydraulic hoses, in the middle of which were the two huge, heavy gears with their massive struts. Each bare strut weighed 622 pounds.

The nacelle was big but, with the gear partially tucked up, it was cramped. If 06 ever slipped off her timbers, I would be nicely sliced and diced before being crushed. I was terrified that this could happen and, at times, I got claustrophobic and would almost panic. Because of the stretching and cramped twisting, cramps came often. Once I removed a few actuating arms, Mike could fit and would take my place. We needed big wrenches for the big bolts and soon understood why the gear was the strongest part of the B-25. We removed hydraulic and oil lines and came out soaked in the dirty black fluid. We would get so dirty that we would never get our work clothes clean.

My strength just caved in. I was simply not strong enough to do what had to be done —- not in the positions I had to work. I changed my position, got a longer wrench for more leverage and I still could not muster the strength. Mike gave it a try and with the same result. Walter still could not fit in. The three of us fell back and regrouped. There had to be a better way. We sat, frustrated, as 06 thumbed her nose at us.

Our answer came to us in a World War II jeep in the person of Tim from the Aero-Plane Factory who visited us every Saturday. He admired our tenacity but thought we were nuts to take on such a big project. He was a true friend and never charged us for all the advice he gave us over the years.

"El Presidente, why are you so glum?" he asked.

I explained.

"Well, why don't you jack her up and just drop the gear?"

Mike and I looked at each other at this simple revelation.

Tim gave us some "do's and don'ts" and was gone.

Walter scratched his head and said, "Lets try it. If the Egyptians could build pyramids, we should be able to lift the center section."

We had no aircraft jacks, but we did not need any. We got more timbers from around the airport and Mike and Walter showed up the following Saturday with more timbers, some fifty-gallon steel drums and the neatest little red hydraulic jack you ever saw, strong enough to lift the center section with ease. The problem was that there was only one jack.

"Don't worry Lou; we have a plan and it will take only one jack."

We located the center sections jacking points and position the jack. As president of this small but determined trio, I have the privilege of working the jack handle.

We position the jack and, with a series of "Hold it's" and "Wait a seconds!" comments, I worked the jack handle. In a few minutes, one side of the center section was six inches higher than the other side, solely supported by the jack. The other side rests on the timbers. We position a timber under the elevated side, place a soft scrap of carpet to act as a cushion and lower the jack about an inch and the center section now rests on a new timber. Moving the jack to the lower side, we repeat the process; the center section is now level.

We position a few timbers, some more rugs and continue to lift the one side another six inches. Add more timbers, gently lower the center section about an inch and then move to the other side to repeat the process. We keep repeating the process and the center section walks straight up with nary a wiggle.

Soon our hanger no longer looks like a lumberyard and the center section towers above us. The cribbing was now in place and rested on four steel drums. I marvel how we could lift the center section that now weighed over five thousand pounds, with the gear, wheels and four wing tanks with all the plumbing still attached. Tim shows up, gives us his approval, and suggests how to lock the timber cribbing in place and leaves. We can now drop the gear still retracted in the nacelles. It has taken five hours to complete our mammoth task and has given us new confidence in our ability. We can now walk under 06 standing straight up.

Walter looked and then all three of us looked for the large rubber mallet. We spent a lot of time looking for tools. We would always forget where we dropped them. Some tools would disappear for months before we found them again.

Walter was now able to squirm his way in to the elevated nacelle, then instructs Mike and I to slow down the swinging landing gear as it drops. We don't want the momentum of the dropping gear to dislodge the center section from its precarious position on the top of the timbers. Walter now takes the very dangerous position up in the nacelle. One slip and Walter could be maimed when the gear drops. Mike and I try and talk him out it but Walter persists: it's his turn to take a calculated risk in the cramped nacelle.

Walter begins to tap on the gear-locking mechanism. Mike and I brace ourselves. With a clunk and a swoosh of tight fitting hydraulic parts, the gear breaks free and the eight foot six inch long mass of steel drops and swings abruptly. As it swings forward, its six hundred-plus pound weight sends Mike and I flying. Walter is smiling as Mike and I pick ourselves up off the floor. We repeat the process on the other side and again pick ourselves up off the floor. The center section still stands. We congratulate ourselves. It has been a long day.

The following Saturday, we arrive, give our best to open the hanger doors and, much to our relief, find that the center section still rests on top of the drums and cribbing.

The first order of business is to remove the tires and rims from the axles. This was done to remove weight once we dropped the gear. We had re-installed the tires to act as cushions just in case when we lowered the gear. The wheels are big; they stand thirty some inches high and are about nineteen inches wide. Most of the morning is spent with that task, which includes disconnecting the hydraulic lines to the brakes. By lunchtime, the tires are off the rims and rolled into a corner. I look at the large axles and am amazed at their size.

Tim arrives as usual to check up on us and advises that, in his opinion, the three of us will not be able to handle the weight of the gear. After lunch, we will pull the gear and Tim will send a few of his men over to help out.

At lunch, the three of us discuss the best way to remove the huge pin holding the gear and lower it. We know it is heavy and that we cannot allow it to drop and hit the cement floor. We decide to design a makeshift sling to lower the gear to the floor. On the way back to the hanger, we stop at a hardware store and buy some heavy rope.

Walter makes the sling and asks our opinion. We all agree it should work. Walter will be up in the nacelle and will knock out the pin. Mike and I will hold the free end of the rope that is looped over a cross member and lower the gear to the floor as gently as we can. Tim arrives with two volunteers who have two cot-type mattresses with them. There will now be four of us on the free end of the rope. The mattresses are placed under the gear, just in case.

The gear has to be held in position until the pin is completely removed. If not, when one side of the pin is knocked free of its bearing, it will twist and bind the pin in the other bearing. We block up the axle with boards. Tim is on the end of the long crowbar to leverage the heavy strut upwards, taking the pressure off the pin caused by the weight of the gear strut. We all have to work together. The four of us on the rope brace ourselves, Tim leans on the crowbar and Walter hammers out the pin with relative ease. Tim instructs Walter to come out of the nacelle.

Tim wraps a belt around the bottom of the gear and Walter knocks out the boards holding the gear up. As we lower the gear, Tim and Walter pull the bottom of the gear forward. The rope is strained and stretching. It's making strange sounds from all the weight. The gear settles on the mattress with a gentle kiss.

We are all elated but where do we put the gear? Tim suggests we will have to have the gear lock lugs checked for cracks and might as well store the gear on some timbers at the hanger door.

Six of us struggle to carry the six hundred-plus pound gear to the hanger door area. Strength-wise we are all working at our limits. I am, once again, amazed. I now know the true meaning of dead weight.

Mike asks, "How in the hell can this thing fly with all this weight?"

Walter replies, "Horse power."

The only thing wrong with this picture is that we have one more gear to go. The other gear does not come down as easily. Tim tells us that it is the same as the first and that we are just worn out. At long last the gear is off and secure.

"Okay, El Presidente. See you next Saturday."

Twenty thousand pounds of dismantled B-25 lie in piles of aluminum and steel that no longer resembled an airplane. The important center section rests on cribbing and steel drums. Note the landing gear. Rear view.

A mass of mechanical mechanisms. This is what the author squeezed into before the center section was raised.

In the early years our guardian angel Tim McCarter came to visit us every Saturday via one of his World War II Jeeps. Here he ponders the removal of the heavy landing gear strut that weighed 650 pounds.

Lou Fulgaro

The Fuel Cells

Mike and Walter join me. We Sit back and relax. It is the end of the day. If I smoked, it would be the appropriate time to light a cigarette. My shoulders and arms actually ache from all the exertion today.

Walter says, "What's the matter kid?"

I reply, "I think my arms are going to fall off."

Walter pats me on the back. "We got it done, your arms will grow back —- don't worry."

The sun was warm on my face as fall sent its subtle message. The cold winter would soon be here. We dreamed, once again about the good times to come. We were still determined to persevere. Our thoughts drifted back to the museum. After the lengthy legal battle, we were battered and beat up but we had emerged victorious.

Mike comments, "It all seems to be uphill."

I came back with, "You can't slide up hill, we have to work for our dream. No one is going to hand it to us."

Mike comments how ugly the eight-gun nose looked attached to the cockpit. "It looks like a droop snoot."

We all laugh and agree.

I talk about Dirty Dora. "It had a like eight-gun nose and was pretty. We may want to consider calling her Dirty Dora." We are not too keen on the idea, but we would think about it.

"We could get a glass nose and we could carry another person."

That sounded good but, like the eight-gun nose, there were a lot of B-25's around that carried either nose.

"I think we should have a cannon-nose." I am thinking out loud. "I think we should be unique. Why be a run-of-the mill B-25? Just think, we have an historic "H" model and if we can locate a cannon-nose we would have the only airworthy cannon-nosed "H" model B-25 in the world."

Mike wondered, "Were are we going to find a cannon-nose? They don't exist."

Walter said, "If we are going to restore her to her original configuration, it should be a cannon-nose. One of those museum guys mentioned offhand they thought they had a lead on a cannon-nose."

Mike speculated, " I don't remember that, but we would be different and would probably get invited to a lot of air shows because of the cannon-nose."

Walter looks at me, "Well kid, it's your job. You're the private detective. If it's out there somewhere, find it. Let's get it and be done with it."

We all agree to pitch in three thousand each —- anymore we will have to talk about it.

"Are we sure that is the way we want to go?" I ask. "I don't want to waste my time on a wild goose chase."

Mike answered for Walter, "The model we have put a cannon-nose on it. The more I think about it the more I like it."

We were going to have a cannon-nosed B-25. It was settled.

The next Saturday, we spent all morning finishing up the stripping of the center section. All of its plumbing, wiring, cabling was off and pumps, brackets, and pulleys soon followed. It was easy work compared to the landing gear. Mike and I were actually joking around as the last piece that could be removed was set aside. The center section was stripped clean. Mike and I advised Walter, who was stripping the cockpit, that we were done. What was our next project?

We all took a break and, afterward, Walter said, "Lets get back to work and finish up the center section. I will help with this project."

I asked, "What's left?"

We walked under the center section and Walter pointed upward and said "Those. There are four of them. Two on each side."

Above us, covering the entire bottom of the wing between the center section and the engine nacelle, were two huge plates. We would call them stress plates. They were so important that, if an engine was hung without them, the engine's weight of twenty four hundred pounds would twist the wing. With the four hundred-fifty pound prop at the front added to this weight the wing would bend and have to be replaced.

The plates were held by closely-spaced, large Philips bolts with rounded heads that had to be about one half inch across. There were about a hundred of them on each side.

The stress plates formed the bottom of the main fuel cell bays. There were four main fuel bays, two on each side. More importantly, between the fuel cells were the center main wing spars plus the fore and aft spars. Everything hung off these spars and without them there was no B-25. The wing spars would have to be inspected; and if they were corroded, 06 would be reduced to a parts airplane. If the spars were good, we had a B-25 that could fly.

Now I find out. Visions of the museum's B-25 danced through my mind. This is what caused their B-25 to be worthless.

My left hand reached for my wallet: it was still there. How would I explain something like this to my wife?

We looked at the hundreds of huge Phillips bolts holding the stress plates and wondered. They had been up there for at least twenty years. It would be a tough job and we would be working over our heads.

Walter grabbed our biggest Phillips head screwdriver and put the point to the bolt head and twisted. The screwdriver slid out of the unique cross point bolt head like it was buttered. We got my favorite tool, the big hammer, and once again Walter put the screwdriver to the bolt head and gave the handle end of the screw driver a couple of good blows. Laying the hammer down, two hands on the screwdriver handle, push hard and twist, and —- nothing. Try another bolt: nothing. The third bolt squeaked and came out. The same with the fourth bolt. Two out of four is not good. We fall back and regroup.

"I suppose they did not use common socket bolt heads because they wanted the bolts exposed to the slip stream to be as streamlined as possible," I guessed.

Walter said, "Sounds good kid."

I continued my thought. "A socket wrench with a long handle would do the trick. If we could turn the center section over, that would make working easy."

"No we can't do that," said Walter.

"How about putting it on one end? That would make it easier."

"No. We can't do that either."

Mike and I worked hard for three Saturdays and twenty percent of the bolts were still up there. Those that remained were well-rounded from our efforts. As the Saturdays turned colder, our hanger echoed with hammers hitting big screwdrivers. I purchased a mechanical tool that had a heavy weight attached to it. As the weight slammed down, it gave the screwdriver a slight twist. Mike and I were down to ten percent and frustrated as hell. Our B-25 was being completely uncooperative. We still had not removed one stress plate. Mike and I checked in with Walter, who was still working in the navigator/cockpit section.

We had to laugh. He was covered with red hydraulic fluid. Walter referred to it as "bomber blood".

"Use a chisel," was Walter's advice.

With a chisel firmly embedded in the head of the bolt, Mike struck the handle of the chisel with a hammer in the direction that the bolt would unscrew. A few more bolts came out, but we also knocked off many heads. Things were looking dismal.

As a last resort, we would drill out the remaining bolts and bolt shanks. We kept four loose bolts in place on the four stress plates and, on the fourth Saturday, we were ready to "drop" our first plate.

The plates were heavy gauge aluminum that appeared to be about five feet long and four feet wide. They were a sizable piece of 06.

After the plates came off, we saw the fuel cells looming above us. They were big and appeared to be made of a black neoprene-like material. The two front fuel cells held 184 gallons each. That's close to 2245 pounds of fuel plus the weight of the two cells which was substantial. Each cell appeared to be about three feet deep. The rear fuel cells carried 151 gallons each.

I had to ask the question. "What's holding them up?"

"Fuel cell hangers and the pipe connections." Walter pointed them out in the manual. Bolts came in from the top of the wing and mated to nuts embedded in a heavy strip of rubber at the top of the cell. Looked simple enough.

The fuel connections were another story. The tanks were interconnected and had to be uncoupled from the inside of the cells. The bottom of each cell had a good-sized inspection plate. We removed them and I could get the top half of my head and one arm through the opening. It was a tight fit. With an extension light in the cell, I could see all the connections. We would have to weld wrenches together to reach all the bolts.

I was the only one that could fit through the opening. I got the short end of the stick again. It was so tight that, once I was able to place the socket on the bolt head, I could only turn it half a turn and then would have to start over again.

Mike worked on the top of the wing and had his problems, too. It would take three Saturdays to disconnect the lines. To unscrew a two-inch long bolt would take half an hour. I came to the conclusion that North American must have used midgets to work in the fuel cells.

In the middle of this, we got our first new member, a friend of mine named Milt Gaden. He had spent many hours with me working on my Fairchild and was now a private pilot. He came on board as an aft of bomb bay member and wanted to go for just one ride. He would show up every Saturday for years and do whatever was asked of him. He came on board just in time to wrestle with the fuel cells.

Gaden was a computer programmer by trade and a detail person by nature. Walter put him to work at our neat little pump-operated degreasing tank, cleaning and scrubbing every part that came off of 06.

The hangers were disconnected, the internal connections were removed and the fuel cells just hung there. In theory, they should have fallen out. No such luck. 06 firmly embraced her fuel cells and was not about to let loose. She was thumbing her nose at us again. We were cold and our patience was wearing thin. We were missing something. We pried with boards and the cells would collapse where we pried but they would not come out.

"El Presidente, having another bad day?"

I explained the new problem to Tim who looked things over and he suggested we try heating the cell so it would be more pliable.

"They are too stiff, too rigid from the cold temperature," he says. "Give it at least two hours of heat," and he is off in his jeep.

We start on the six auxiliary fuel cells in the wings. Next Saturday we will have heat and will take on the main fuel cells. Heat applied by any safe method should do the trick.

The following Saturday, Mike and Walter showed up with a portable propane heater. It had ceramic tiles that actually glowed with heat but I could not see any flame. We placed it under one front fuel cell and decided to leave it alone for two hours. Two of us worked on the auxiliary fuel cells and two in the navigator/cockpit section. It is amazing how much can be accomplished by four persons when the work goes well.

Walter announced it was time. This time we had a few pry boards with smooth rounded ends to lever the cell with. Checking again to make sure everything was disconnected, we pushed the heater off to the side and eyeballed the fuel cell. It was somewhat pliable and was sagging in the middle which was a good sign but it still just hung there. We slipped the two boards between the cell and wing spar and began to apply pressure, gently at first, just to get a feel of things. To our surprise, the cell moved!

Encouraged, we pried a little harder and the cell moved more. We tried a different angle, then a different side and the cell was dropping. It was on its way out but needed more coaxing. There was no place to get a handhold, as all the sides were smooth.

We coaxed, pushed, pulled, and wiggled it and it began to slip out. Eager hands braced the about five-foot cell and we gently lowered it to the hanger floor. It felt like it had to weigh at least three hundred pounds. By the time we got to the fourth fuel cell, we were experts at removing B-25 fuel tanks.

They all looked good. In fact, they looked very good! We were relieved to find out they were not original. Searching our aircraft logs and the dates stenciled on the tanks, we were very happy to find that they had been installed some fourteen years ago, much better than our original estimate of twenty years.

The six auxiliary tanks were a different story. All six were totally collapsed and had been disconnected and just left in the wings. We were intrigued by the stenciling stamped on each tank. "1943- BULLET PROOF-SELF SEALING". I took the best looking cell and cut out the stenciling and kept it as a memento. To keep the weight and costs down, we would not replace the six auxiliary cells. The 670 gallons carried in the main four cells would give us a good cruising range with a reserve. At 200 MPH, the fuel burn would be about 120 gallons an hour, which would translate to 1,100 miles or 5:58 hours flying time. Anyway, as we got older, our bladders would not last much longer.

The real good news was that the main wing spars were like new. The mechanics that put in the new tanks, treated the main spar with an anticorrosive primer and a good grade of paint. In the few places where the paint and primer was peeling, the bright aluminum just glistened. We had a good one. She would outlive all of us.

Our spirits soared at our positive find. Tim gave his okay on the tanks and suggested we coat them with glycerin inside and out. Once that was done, we would wrap them in plastic and seal them. Mike and I would scout drug stores trying to find glycerin in a bottle bigger than a few ounces. One pharmacist ordered up about a gallon for us. Tim looked at the spars and held back his opinion until they were stripped. This brought us to the next step.

Our hanger did not have any water let alone any drains. We would not be able to strip paint without water. If we did have water, the hanger was so cold the water would turn to ice. We negotiated with Tim to do the stripping. Again, the three of us would foot the bill.

I got my second look at the aircraft logs we had. Many early logs were missing from her younger years. This was not too important as the hours accumulated are carried forward to the latest log. A lot of her history was a mystery with the missing early logs. She had a total of 1,946 airframe hours. While she was long in the tooth, she was young in airframe hours. We decided to have a historian to research her past. Walter got the job.

One of four very large fuel cells. It was heavy, slippery and had no handholds. The round opening is where the fuel cell filler fitting attaches through the wing.

This photo shows the piece of cut out fuel cell that I saved because of the bullet-proof wording. As of this day when I bring it out it gets the warbird talk going. It is amazing what was so common half a century ago is so prized today.

Top: A solid eight-gun nose B-25. Behind the prop blade is a low profile air intake. Bottom: A glass nose B-25 with the stovepipe air intakes that I do not like. Wild is standing just under the prop hub. Photos Pat Habel.

Mike Butler and Milt Gaden at work on the fuselage. Both of them worked every Saturday for years.

Thinking Positive

Word of our rare bird was spreading in the warbird community. Over the many weeks of many summers, we had hundreds of visitors. They came by plane and by car.

That they found our obscure hanger was an accomplishment in itself. If they arrived by plane, they asked the tower where the guys with the B-25 were. If they came by car, any waitress near an airport restaurant would say "Oh, that crazy bunch of guys!" and point the way. When they found our hole in the wall hanger, they gaped. They also talked, pointed, looked, gave advice and suggestions (some good); and, most importantly, they dropped names and phone numbers of contacts. If I had been around in 1981 at Lambert's field, I would have said that history was repeating itself.

In 1981, though, there was an airplane — now there were just neatly stacked piles of airplane parts. To many, it was beyond comprehension. The project was just overwhelming. Many of our visitors belonged to groups that had, as a club project, restored light antique aircraft. Many had spent years with these projects but their projects were small in comparison to ours.

Some of our visitors have been around a long time and appeared knowledgeable. Most of them guessed that it would take seven to ten years and a quarter of a million dollars to finish. Walter would counter with three to four years and sixty thousand dollars. I hoped Walter was right. Way in the back of my mind, expensive thoughts kept popping up. They gave me the nagging feeling that I should get used to the idea that somewhere in the lower six figures was more realistic.

One of those visitors was a young man by the name of Frank Serrano. He was a student aircraft mechanic and he started to show up more often: one day we just sort of adopted him and gave him a small piece of 06. Frank was an energetic worker and he worked hard and long. At some point, Frank had mentioned that his father was an airplane mechanic who had worked, years ago, on P-47's. Frank's father would visit us from time to time and give his son —and us — some good advice. Walter and Frank would work closely together for years. We where attracting some talented good workers but no big money.

The awesome landing gear would now have to be addressed. Tim suggested we get the gear magnafluxed to check for cracks that were invisible to the naked eye. We should also have the tire rims dye checked for cracks. Two different methods to make sure the parts were airworthy. The certified gear and rims could then be refurbished and once the center section was cleaned up we could hang the gear. Mount new tires on the rims and install them also. The idea was to bring these key elements together at about the same time.

Walt, Mike and I talked. [Milt and Frank left all the planning and the related expense to the three of us, as did Claude.] To attract some big money [pilots position] we should get 06 to start looking like an airplane as soon as possible. That was to become our top priority at this time. We should get 06 off of her pile of timbers and standing on her own. With no further use for the timbers we would have some much-needed working room.

Hoisting the heavy gear into Mike's van for a trip to the FAA inspection station was a task. Again, the weight —- the awesome, unrelenting weight. Many willing hands pitched in during times like this when we were going to have a special. Word would spread and every Saturday they would show up. Many times we did not know their names. They were just there when we needed them. Many of them thought we needed our heads examined, but they loved warbirds and when their Saturday home chores were done they headed for our hanger many bringing their own chairs. As we had predicted the warbird lovers were finding us. We did not have to find them. Some who were regulars got to know our story and would show a new visitor around pointing out the high lights of our rare B-25. Like two pitchmen, Mike and I would size them up. Mike would get acquainted and, if they looked promising, pass them on to me.

We needed some big bucks. With just the three of us paying the tab, we would fall far short, dollar-wise. The three of us set a ceiling, more or less, of no more than thirty thousand each. If my wife had ever found out, she would have had a stroke. That was a lot of money in mid-1980. Little did we realize how far short we would really be.

Walter crossed his fingers, Mike did his beads and I said a prayer. There had to be pilots out there that had some money and, like us, could not afford to purchase a warbird for more than the cost of a trainer. The next best thing would be to get into a limited partnership. We would be patient. They would come when the weather warmed up and 06 started to look like an airplane.

The report from the FAA inspection station was devastating. The down locks on both of our main landing gear had cracks. Our landing gear was not airworthy. It was junk but the nose gear was good. I filled out the forms for a structural defect and sent them off to the FAA as required by Federal Law. We paid the inspector his two hundred dollars and took our broken gear back home. The main gear joined other odds and ends on the scrap metal pile that was growing. 06 had done it to us again.

Meanwhile, we had come on a real find: two new tires sat in our hanger. They had been expensive: seven hundred-fifty dollars a piece. We had looked for months to find tires that had the original diamond threads just like in World War II. We did not want to mount modern thread tires (that were also expensive, but not like these). When the dye checking was done and the word came back from the inspection station, we were relieved to find out the tire rims were okay. We would clean them up, paint them the original silver and mount the tires.

I kept worrying that someone would steal our tires. Many people saw them and every now and then some real characters would show up. We chained them to a steel hanger support column.

Lou Fulgaro

Live and Learn

Walter kept showing up with a warbird nut by the name of Jerry Fencel. Fencel, I think, was the origin of the term scrounger. I gathered he was in his early seventies. He knew a lot of ordinary folk in the warbird circle.

He had a motto: "Never pay asking price for anything. Trade for it, borrow it, do everything you can to avoid paying for it." I was sure he had money buried in his back yard in an old fashioned tin can.

I never found out exactly what Fencel did in the Air Force. I did know he could find parts; and over the next few years, he was a great assistance to me, bringing in a few pilots and their checks. But I had one hell of a time getting him to let loose of any money. After a few years, I had to write him a letter saying if he wanted to play, he would have to pay. I liked Jerry but rules were rules.

The rims had been cleaned and painted and were gleaming like new. Fencel had latched on to two truck inner tubes for the tires and we decided to mount the tires. I watched Walter struggling to get a new tire on its wheel. We all pitched in to help. Lubricating the tire with soap did not help. Next we tried the big crowbar, assisted by the big hammer. The tire would not go on. We had been advised that the tires would be difficult to mount but this was way past "difficult".

Mark Clark dropped by and watched our losing battle with the tire and wheel. Mark was a knowledgeable warbird person as he brought, sold, rebuild, and consigned warbirds for sale. He was located across the field from us.

"Lou, are you ready to sell?"

"Never," I muttered, frustrated.

Mark kicked the tire and said, "It's too small".

Well that's simple enough. But if the tire was the correct size so the wheel was obviously too big.

Mark said goodbye with the comment, "It does not look like a B-25 wheel."

Armed with rulers, calipers, a camera and some strange measuring devices I never saw before, a few of us headed off to a static-display B-25 nearby in Wisconsin. The base commander was very helpful and I watched Walter eyeing up the tailskid.

"Lou, think he would trade a fiber glass one for the real one?"

"I don't think he has the authority to do that Walter," I said. "These things are on an inventory that is monitored by some vague branch of the military."

From our observation, we reached the conclusion that our wheels were not B-25 wheels. We also found out the bottom half of our main gear struts were not B-25. The top half was and that was the end that was cracked. Just our luck; the right half was the bad half. The brakes were also not B-25 standard. We needed answers. We'd had just about all the surprises we could handle.

Some of her mysterious past was about to become known. Of all things, Walter located the crew chief for 06 when she was with the Bendix Corporation. He would eventually visit us and tell us that, when Bendix got her, they scrapped the cannon-nose and installed the eight-gun nose. Our B-25 was used as a test bed all her years with Bendix and she worked hard to earn her keep. The long nose was installed to test the nose gear for a hot new fighter in the development stage, the McDonnell F-101 jet fighter. Bendix did not mount the long eight-gun nose to streamline her but to house a second nose gear. Yes, 06 flew with two fully retractable nose gears. Either gear could be extended or retracted independently of each other. This solved the mystery of all extra hydraulic lines in the nose and navigator section.

She also had a crosswind main landing gear installed. An auxiliary power generator was installed in the tail gunner's position, as the engine generators could not supply enough power to run all of the test-measuring instruments. A small wheel extended from the bomb bay to measure side load forces. At speeds up to 110 MPH she would roll/drive over two-by-four boards bolted into a taxiway in an attempt to break down the F-101 gear. It was a rather straight-forward method considering they did not have computer imaging at that time. This information certainly explained the cracks in our down-locks.

We also learned that the B-25 brakes were inadequate for this type of braking after running the boards. The pilots soon found themselves out of pavement: they were at take off speed anyway, so they just took off. They would circle around and begin the process all over again. This was time consuming and the technicians had a deadline. New modern brakes would mean two modern wheels to house the new brakes.

We begin to see the light. With the long idle speeds, one of 06's generators had to go, which explained one generator with more capacity than the other. It was still not enough. The big hole in the tail gunner's plate glass face shield was for the mounted portable gasoline generator's exhaust. The big rough patch in the bomb bay doors was for the fourth wheel that measured side forces.

Well, we wanted answers and we got answers. It added to the mystique of 06. It would also add to the expense of her restoration. We junked the idea to make her up like when she flew with Bendix. I can remember the day when our wheels and brakes joined the landing gear on the wooden pallets that our junk pile was housed on. Come 1988, they would be in the same spot where we dropped them. We gave Mark Clark the old tires and wheels because they would fit a B-26.

For just a few days we are down in the dumps. As usual, though, time takes care of disappointment. We will replace what was broken or not original. We stay the same path. Weary Warriors will not compromise our B-25 and our goal to own the only original, flying cannon-nose H model in the world. It keeps us focused and together.

The time has come. In about two weeks Tim will have room for the center section. He will chemically strip the interior, the leading edge of the wings, fuel cell bays, and the nacelles where the gear retracts. We include a few other odds and ends.

Walter puts all his skill to work, aided by Mike and Frank, to design and build a cradle to transfer the center section to Tim's shop. Gaden, Fencel, and I wait for the design to become a reality.

We all gather all the wood we can. We buy nuts, bolts, and washers. Some of the bolts are over nine inches long. They are ordinary stove bolts and not too expensive. We find more carpeting to pad her delicate bottom.

Under Walter's direction, we all turn to and start building the rolling contraption that will carry our precious center section. Again, we remind our selves the center section is the heart of 06 and we will not take any short cuts. It's a tricky job, transferring the now lightened, nineteen hundred-pound center section from her stacked timbers to the spindly-looking cradle. The twenty six-foot beam looks twice as wide from the bottom looking up.

The transfer is successful but not without some real concern. All we would need to do is "drop" the center section to the cement hanger floor. Especially with some of us under it.

With cameras clicking, we cautiously and slowly roll the center section out of the hanger and aim it toward Tim's shop. Eager volunteer hands help with the big push about a block away. I, like all the Weary Warriors there that day, am profoundly relieved and thankful the short trip was with out incident and the center section is tucked away. Our hanger has a big void.

Once the doors are closed, we all notice Tim has heat. We had purchased two drums of paint stripper to do the job, hopefully with some left over to do the rest of 06. We would be wrong again.

I would say that, while sitting in my office at my work place, at least an hour a day was spent on the phone to find parts. While Walter got such things as cleaning solvent and paint stripper, I was putting together a list of contacts and talking to just about everyone in the USA and some in foreign countries that had or knew somebody that had B-25 stuff. I really met some characters and some real slick con persons where the words "a fool and his money are soon parted" were most applicable.

The same night of the center section move, I received a phone call. Was I the guy looking for a cannon nose? He had the bottom half of one, it was brand new, never been mounted on a B-25. It was in perfect shape and better than new. Still in the original crate, none other exist, and it is for sale. The price was a no-haggle $6500. Yes I was and consider it sold. What a day! I am keyed up over the day's success.

As my mind wanders and fights sleep, I wonder who the gentleman was that shows up at our hanger from time to time. He shyly stays on the fringes. He was interested but just sort of lays back, sizing us up. He was taking a good long look. Within two months, the stranger would join us.

A Real Experience

Winter 1984 has arrived in Northern Illinois with the winds blowing across the Rockford area farm fields. It is one of the coldest winters in recorded history. Our hanger leaks and is cold, damp and drafty, even with the doors closed. We at last admit to ourselves that our portable heating units are so puny that, once the temperature drops below twenty degrees, working conditions are miserable.

We devise working conditions to beat the cold. With hot air blowing in one end of the tail cone [rear fuselage] and blankets draped over the top, the inside of the fuselage is a toasty 40 degrees. We do the same with the navigator/cockpit section and soon both sections are stripped of all equipment. As we unbolt the eight-gun nose, we wonder if we can sell it to help defray the cost of the bottom section of the cannon-nose. It has been our experience that, if we want to sell something, it is junk, but when we need to buy, it is gold-plated. As Tim approaches, I wonder if we will be as good putting 06 back together as we are at taking her apart.

"El Presidente, I have some bad news for you. My crew and I will be gone a few months on a warbird expedition."

Work on the center section would come to a halt. He had advised us this may happen and now it was about to happen. The morale of Weary Warriors present sags. They don't take the news well.

Tim and I go for a cup of coffee. We talk and negotiate a price to rent his hanger and use his equipment on Saturdays. He agrees as long as I accept the responsibility of turning things off, locking the doors and paying the utility bills. No one will be permitted in the shop unless I am present. We shake hands and we retire to his hanger and shop where he shows me around, explains how to work the equipment we will use, and hands me the keys.

While he would be in Rockford a few days, he will not be at the airport and he suggests we plan on getting the other sections over to his place to strip the paint off of them. I never did find out where he was going. It was a secret.

A few hours later, I gather the Weary Warriors around me. I love to give them good news. Early this same morning I gave the news on the cannon-nose and their spirits soared. Tim's news dropped that spirit like a rock. I explain and the upbeat spirit returns as we discuss what has just happened and realize what it will mean.

What started out to be a good three to four months of no work for us because of the cold was now going to be our most productive period and get us ahead of schedule at very little expense on our part. We will take full advantage of this development. While Tim would finish the center section when he returned, we had a lot of basic labor to do in the meantime.

We cannot miss this opportunity. Walter and his personnel crew start to design rolling cradles for the rest of the B-25 sections. The cannon-nose will have to wait a few weeks.

The junked pallets were stacked high. More planks and dollies —- Walter and Mike seem to have a magical, endless source for this material. They both have many business contacts in Chicago and, from broken wooden pallets, we could save the good boards. We would put the big hammer and big pry bar to good use.

We work like we are possessed. Nails and spikes groan as we lever them out of the rough sawn, warped, dry wood. We work so hard physically that the cold did not touch us. We save big spikes and purchase more cheap bolts. It is Gaden's job to straighten out the bent spikes. He does such a precise job they are as straight as new.

Two Saturdays later, with more rug material for padding, 06's sections are sitting on their cradles. We are ready to roll her out.

Later that evening, our entire airframe (minus the nose, tail and wings) is sitting in Tim's shop. Our hanger looks empty. Walter, Mike, and I once again put our heads together.

Number one. I had been searching for the gear, wheels, and brakes. The gear could be purchased, yellowed tagged [airworthy], minus the levers hydraulics, pins, etc. We have all that. Wheels and brakes were readily available. Yellowed-tagged wheels were not too expensive but we would have to clean them up and paint them. New, certified brakes were expensive. Walter and Frank would concentrate on those accessories and rebuild the hydraulic actuating struts and all the parts that send the gear up and down and permit 06 to roll on her own tires. They could do all this while Mike, Gaden, and I did the stripping of paint. We would get all the gear accessories into Tim's shop and literally abandon our hanger for months.

Number two. Now that the air frame sections were in Tim's shop, I was worried about the cannon-nose and thought we should make a quick run down to Kansas City, Missouri where it was located, take a look, see if it was okay, buy it and bring it back. I wanted it in our possession. Mike agrees. We will make a kamikaze run during the week using Mike's van: drive down to KC, turn around and come back — a total of 1100 miles with no sleep. We want to see the nose before we buy it. We know the cost and will split it three ways. We hate to reach for our wallets but we have no choice. I set up a date agreeable to all including the seller. We have three weeks before the trip. Yes, the bottom half of the nose will fit in to Mike's van.

The two thirty-gallon drums of paint stripper had been ordered and received. We purchase a variety of brushes. Tim supplied the boots, wet suit, gloves, and the hood with a see-through, plastic face. He also had the steam machine that produced no steam, was pump-driven and produced the coldest water under a lot of pressure. At the end of the hose was a six-foot nozzle and, if you did not hold it tight, it would buck like a wild horse.

Tim had given us instructions on how to strip paint on a grand scale. The important information was that the stripper could eat up aluminum and we would have do it right the first time and wash the chemical away quickly.

Walter and Frank did the mechanical work, as Mike and I did not possess the "technical skills" they did. Gaden bounced around. Fencel had disappeared when it got too cold — we had not advised him we had a heated hanger, as he was not a member. Walter had recruited him and if Walter did not want to tell him it was between Walter and him.

Mike and I ended up in the fuselage and encountered a real experience. I, like most adults, have stripped a chair or two in my lifetime, but the interior of 06 was going to be a real challenge.

Apply the pink colored, noxious stripper over your head with a large brush and watch it run down the sleeve of the rubber suite. Use a smaller brush for the smaller areas and a tiny brush for the hard to get areas like the inside corners. Step out and wait about twenty minutes. When the stripper starts to bubble, but before it dries [it has to have time to work], you hit it with the high-pressure water. Knock off the peeling paint, primer, or whatever with the long nozzle, keeping yourself away from the flying stripper and water. The nozzle should have been twice as long.

Water was everywhere. Mike and I took turns but we could not escape the bouncing water. The more we rinsed, the wetter we got. The more we rinsed, the more slippery our footing became. The more we rinsed, the deeper the water got in the bottom of the fuselage. It collected everywhere and ran out more slowly than we were putting it in.

Repeat the process over and over again.

Trip over a stringer, bounce your head off a bulkhead, knock over the bucket of paint stripper, trip over the hose, get tangled in the hose, and try to maneuver the six-foot nozzle in the small confines of the fuselage. Do all this while you were ninety percent blind from all the water, stripper, and peeled paint on your facemask. Keep the light cord out of the water you were standing in ankle deep and try and not get electrocuted.

Some paint would come off as good-sized sheets, revealing beautiful new looking aluminum. It actually glistened. Then there where areas were the paint stubbornly resisted our efforts to come off. The brushes became frazzled, Mike and I became frazzled and we broke light bulbs like we had stock in the bulb company. We inhaled the fumes, our eyes watered. We were so wet and dirty we could not tell what we were doing.

We shed the cumbersome slippery gloves first. We could not hold on to anything with them on. We took off the hood and the facemask, as the mask would steam up so we could not see and the hood was too hot. Then the wet suits went, as we got soaked anyway from sweat. Even the safety glasses got in the way but we kept them on.

As we worked our way from the front to the back, it seemed to get easier —- maybe we were just getting used to it. The space was also getting smaller as we progressed towards the tail. Halfway back, we entered and exited through the waist gunner's positions, as we did not want to get the already-cleaned portion dirty. As we got the hang of things, we would have two projects going at the same time. Only one could fit inside and one of us would stand outside of the waist gunner's position and direct the light while the other rinsed away. Frequently, the cold water would stray and spray a hot light bulb and another bulb would shatter.

When we started we were standing up and did not realize how good we had it. Soon we were hunched over, then stooped over, then kneeling and sitting, as the fuselage got smaller in height and width. Every now and then, we would spot Frank and Walt doing their "skilled" work and we would give them a good shot of cold water. With the pump running, they could not hear Mike and I laughing. We usually would get them twice a day. They eventually got wise and when we started with the water, they would move to a location where we could not get to them.

At first, we did not notice the little stings on our hands and faces. A few days later when I shaved in the morning and looked very closely, I could see the tiny burn marks.

The stripper was getting to us. Three Saturdays had gone by and we were about seventy percent finished and just about out of stripper. We order up one more thirty three-gallon drum. We could see a lot of clean aluminum. It looked great and we were pleased with our progress.

The call from Frank Howerton (the man with the cannon nose) was disturbing. He was going on a trip and could we put off our trip a few weeks? He assured us that everything was going to be okay and his cannon-nose had our name on it. He had a few other goodies for us. They would be a surprise. We tried not to be paranoid about the whole thing, but we were apprehensive. Weary Warriors wanted the cannon-nose and we wanted it bad.

Two more weeks meant two more Saturdays. We were just about done. The gleaming airframe made Milt, Mike, and me forget the hell we had gone through during the past weeks.

Tim arrives back for a few days to pay some of his bills. He gives our work a close look.

"Nice try, El Presidente, but not good enough." Tim was using a mirror on a handle to look at the bottom places underneath the fuselage members that we could have seen if we stood on our heads.

"It's your B-25, El Presidente. If you want a so-so job, it's okay, but I would think you would want to do it right."

Looking in the mirror there they were, mostly in the corners. Small patches of green paint, some no larger than a quarter-inch square.

Armed with small brass brushes, we attack the remnants of the OD interior. We use toothbrush-sized brushes and sponges this time.

We make ourselves comfortable and toiled away. When we are about to break for lunch, we power hose it down and let the water drain while we have lunch.

I was in the fuselage giving it a final flushing. Tim had instructed us to spend at least two hours flushing. In real estate, they say, location, location, location is important: with aluminum and paint stripper, flushing, flushing, flushing was important. I was enjoying myself with the familiar job of washing out the fuselage for the last time. Water had gotten into a bandage on my left leg between the knee and ankle where, the Saturday before, I had scraped my leg on a jagged piece of stripper-covered aluminum. I ended up with a four-inch scrape that would take nine months to heal. To this day, my skin does not feel right at that location and if I get an insect bite in that area, it takes months to heal.

Through the pebbling effect of water on my safety glasses, I again saw the mysterious man. He had found us In Tim's shop. He was very careful around the B-25. He was in his sixties, wore glasses, and kept to himself. He did not talk to anyone. Mike touched base with him and soon pointed me out to him and Mike took over the flushing.

I said hello to Glen Hanson. He was a personable Airline Captain, nearing retirement, who had flown B-25's in the South Pacific during World War II. He flew "G" model B-25's, which were as close as one could get to an "H" model. The "G" model had two machine guns in the nose compared to the "H" that had four machine guns in the nose. Our top turret was toward the front of the B-25 while the turret on the "G" was towards the rear and it had no tail turret. From that point on they were pretty much the same.

I spent about an hour with him, showed him around and filled him in. We were both into model railroading and I discovered that he had once owned a Fairchild F-24 W-46 as I had. His was equipped with a Warner radial engine while mine had the Ranger inline engine. We showed each other photos of our Fairchilds.

Glen was keen on the cannon-nose and I could see a gleam in his eye. He showed up a week later and we went for a cup of coffee. He had more questions and a few old magazines with him that featured the "H" model and he was positive one of them was ours. He gave me a duplicate of one of the magazines. I still have the magazine; it cost fifteen cents in 1944. Glen popped in a few times, we went for a few more cups of coffee and we had a new pilot member and ten thousand dollars.

Glen, like Walter, became one of our devoted workers. Living the closest, he spent a lot of time working on 06. His sheet metal work would become legendary. He was one of those persons who could do just about anything and do it well. Besides that, with his thousands of airline hours and his military flying, we had our first real B-25 pilot. Mike, Walter and I would be considered amateur pilots when compared to Glen. We also had a new teacher in Glen and for the remainder of that winter we would be cutting out dents in 06's skin, covering unwanted openings and getting rid of corrosion here and there. Glen was meticulous and taught all of us how to cut and make aluminum patches. We were soon riveting and bucking.

I thought at one time that we were going to re-skin the entire airplane. Those of us who were learning spent a lot of time on the top of 06 where no one could see our not-to-perfect patches. Those who were really good spent time on the sides and bottom where everyone would see the almost invisible patch. Milt and I patched a lot of holes on the top of the fuselage from bygone antennas. Glen watched and checked our every move.

As I filed the square corners of a patch to make them round, I listened to the sounds of electric drills and riveting. How the sounds had changed from the big hammer days! It was obvious we were using the big hammer and big pry bar less and less. We were indeed moving forward.

Lou Fulgaro

Top: Our precious center section is pushed into Tim McCarter's shop. Wild's rolling contraption worked. All the gang is there. Bottom: The cockpit section and its cradle are on its way being pushed by Tim McCarter's crew.

Top: The fuselage, (tail cone) and its rather skimpy cradle. We got tired of pushing and McCarter hooked up his jeep and pulled it to his hanger.
Bottom: Turned upside down, the outer wing is used as a light workbench.

Lou Fulgaro

The Cannon Nose

The time had come. Walt and I piled into Mike's van. We were on our way to Kansas City Missouri to meet Frank Howerton. Mike's van was not one of those plush vans many of us are used to today. It was a cargo van with two utilitarian seats. Mike —- or Walter —- had placed an easy chair with fine upholstery on the bed of the cargo section of the van. As President of Weary Warriors I got the plush chair (seat belts were not mandatory then). As we aimed the van south towards Kansas City some five hundred fifty miles away, we talked B-25 talk and about how lucky we were to find Glen or, more accurately, how lucky we were that Glen found us.

Howerton's directions were good and helped as we weaved our way through the 5:00pm rush hour traffic of Kansas City. The closer we got, the more excited we got. None of us had ever seen a cannon-nose and we wondered what the surprise was that he had talked about.

We were there. As we turned into Frank's driveway, we were greeted by the sight of Frank, seated in the doorway of the garage, buffing the bottom half of our mythical cannon-nose with an electric buffer. What a way to sell something!

Frank flashed a smile and all three of us liked him right away. Introductions were made as we admired the shine on the cannon-nose. While it was still light, we went out to the airport and examined Frank's B-25, the "Fairfax Ghost." I had not known he owned a B-25.

"Frank," I said, "you never mentioned your B-25."

"Lou," he answered, "you never asked."

We went back to his place and, as we talked, Frank asked me if we were still going to build up a real B-25 or settle for a "pussy cat" like everyone else had. We advised him it was going to be as original as we could make it.

We went down into Frank's basement, which was a very special place. The entire basement was full of B-25 parts. The walls were lined with shelves stocked with part after part. As Frank talked, he started handing us parts we would need for our rebuild. When we talked on the phone, I had mentioned the problems we had with the gear. Frank's surprise was what he was handing us; pumps, oleo struts and brackets for the bomb bay as well as everything from jump seats to cup holders and toilet paper holders.

All were new, GI-issue.

"Still going to get rid of that "pussy cat" exhaust system?"

"Yes Frank we do not want it."

"Good. Save all the parts. You can use them to trade for the system she was designed for. You should be able to trade for complete modification systems which will let you fly with the low-profile air intakes and individual exhaust stacks. But you need to make some modifications to the carb, cowling, engine mounts, and dishpans. Your exhaust system is in demand and you can get an even trade off. Here —- hold this box."

Frank started throwing exhaust stacks into the box. Some were steel and some were porcelain coated. He included more than enough with a few extras as some would burn off or vibrate and crack apart. There was an exhaust stack for each cylinder. He even included the hard-to-find "Y" exhaust stacks that routed the exhaust gas around the low-profile air intake. We had in our hands what made the B-25 the noisiest combat aircraft of World War II.

"Lou," he said, "these will get you started."

It would take me about two years but we did negotiate a trade for the old exhaust system. As I heard it, the Canadians had developed the modifications for our collector exhaust system as they could not stand the new box air intakes [stove pipes]. Our longtime friends at Aero Traders would give us a good trade, including the low-profile air intakes that I wanted so much. Oh happy day! I never met Tony and Carl but if I did I could have kissed them for that trade. Thanks again, Carl and Tony.

We took Frank out for a steak dinner and then he took us out to a small airfield. Stopping in front of a small hanger-like building, we opened the doors and beheld more B-25 parts! Under two of the dimmest light bulbs I ever saw, Frank pointed out a large, open wooden crate. We had to look hard to see what it was. Inside the crate was a huge steel frame contraption, gray in color.

Frank said, "Take this with you. If you don't use it, you can trade it off. It is rare, it is the only one that exists, and I have had it for years and will never use it. It's yours if you would like it. But you can't sell it. Hell, I could sell it. I want you guys to have it."

"Frank," I said, puzzled, "what the hell is it?"

"Did you guys just get off the boat?" laughed Frank. "It's a torpedo rack for a B-25. Fits up in the bomb bay. It's complete and ready to be installed."

A torpedo rack? You've got to be kidding! Before he could change his mind, we grunted and groaned to horse the five hundred pound rack in to Mike's van. The van sagged and groaned with all the weight.

"Here," said Frank, hauling out another treasure, "take this too. It needs work and some parts are missing, but take this thing with you. It's the gunner's pedestal for the top turret."

I was astounded. "Frank you got to be kidding."

"Nope. Take it before I change my mind and get the hell out of here. I got things to do. You guys keep in touch."

The pedestal had to weigh about two hundred pounds and was about four feet tall. We said our good-byes and headed back to Rockford. I could not believe our good fortune. Frank single-handedly had made up for all the people that had and would rip us off.

With the parlor chair in the cargo area we were cramped for space. There, alongside us, was half of our cannon-nose. It was hard to believe but there it was, at long last. Walter was not the sort of person to smile and laugh a lot but on the return trip he was a different Walter.

Frank Howerton would become a good friend and over the years we talked often and he gave us good advice. We figured the bottom half of the nose cost us nothing when you counted in all the bonus parts.

Now another challenge awaited me: to find the upper half of the nose. Mike and Walter were on a high and would give me a year to find one. If not, they would build one up. With Glen's sheet metal ability, it could happen. As we changed seats and took turns driving, each of us in turn sat in the parlor chair; Walter slouched down and rested his feet on the nose, Mike hung over the side of the chair and leaned on it and I kept a hand on it. We all had to touch it to make sure we were not dreaming. We were going to have a flying, cannon-nosed B-25 after all.

We all had our daydreams that night as the overloaded van made its way back north. I dreamed of a cannon-nose B-25 with nicely cowled -29's, all those exhaust stacks and the beautiful low profile air intakes — all, of course in flat GI OD brown/green — we would take 06 back to the way she was. Walter and I would always keep this as our goal. Others would not but through this late evening I dreamed on. With our roaring exhaust stacks, everyone would know when we were coming and they sure as hell would know when we'd arrived. When we left they would know we had been there.

Yes, the heart can find satisfaction with a machine. In our own modest way, we would recapture the years of glory of our B-25. All those that would stand and admire her would envy us; the crazy bunch of guys who called themselves the Weary Warriors.

Frank Howerton and his glass nose B-25J named "Fairfax Ghost" a highly polished bare aluminum version that he sold in 1996. This is the B-25 that would eventually knock Barbie out of the first place bomber award (by two points) at the Sun and Fun show in 2000. Howerton collection.

A rare smile and a beaming Wild prepares to unload the bottom half of the cannon nose. Note the shine on the aluminum, courtesy of Frank Howerton, and the size of the hole for the cannon.

The corrosion treated bottom half of the cannon-nose has just been bolted on. The cockpit section, with its interior stripped bare and canopy missing, rests in its cradle and has not been attached to the center section. Note the streamlined muzzle blast vent just behind the cannon opening and the rug padding on the cradle. We were very careful with our prize and did not want to dent or scratch her in any way.

Buyer Beware

Sometimes it becomes obvious the old adage of "buyer beware" is most appropriate. When I consider how we spent some of our money over that ten-year period, I shudder. I thought that warbird people would have a common bond that would build an honest camaraderie, but like any other area of life there were the con artists and the crooks. Shopping for a part was not like going to a supermarket to pick up your groceries. You had to rely on instinct and maybe you could get a recommendation. You were thousands of miles away from the fifty year-old items you wanted. It could be new, but it had been sitting somewhere for a very long time. How the person on the other end of the phone call could drop names, say "trust me —- like new, yellow tagged, still in the original box, original issue, you can't go wrong", and all those things a buyer likes to hear and then send us rusted, corroded junk amazed me. We'd send the money, wait for the check to clear, pay to have the object of our long search crated, pay unheard of freight charges and then, when it was delivered —- surprise! You get so paranoid you hate to open up boxes.

We order a life raft door for the fuselage and get wing tips: order a fuel pump and get a hydraulic pump. Part numbers, proper nomenclature diagram numbers, page numbers, and manual sections for reference meant nothing. You run to the bank to stop the check. Too late —- it already cleared. You start all over again. More long distance phone expense, crating time, and freight expense.

Turn around time was measured in months —- if they would take the part back. Phone messages left on recorders went unanswered. Call at different times, maybe you could catch them. You know the seller is listening to you but he will not pick up. We learned to beware of sellers that never picked up; they were hiding behind their phone answering machines.

It was common for a person selling the part not to have the part but to know someone that did. You send him the five hundred dollars, he cashes your check; he goes and buys the part from his source for three hundred dollars and sends it to you. A good example of this was the bottom half of our cannon-nose.

One party called me and said he had a new lower half of a cannon-nose. It is in mint condition, price $9,500. I hesitate, would like to think about it, want to look a little further. A few weeks later, Howerton calls me —- you know about that phone call.

I begin to wonder. Everyone is telling me no cannon-noses exist and all of a sudden there are two new lower halves of a cannon-nose on the market. When we picked up the nose from Frank, it was obvious that both he and my first caller were selling the same nose. The first party, as the result of our phone conversations, was so sure we would go with the cannon-nose that he had promised Howerton a thousand dollars to hold the nose for him. He was going to make a three thousand-dollar profit on the sale! He never sent Howerton the thousand dollars.

A few years later, the first party calls me. They would like to come to Illinois and make a fiberglass mold of our nose. They think there would be a market for them. Weary Warriors can make a few easy bucks. We give them a polite no. 06 was going to be very valuable some day and the one of a kind real nose was part of what would make her so valuable. They got real mad at me. But what's new? I think we should have been the ones that got mad.

Let me give you another example of buyer beware. This one cost us some big bucks.

This expensive example would be our engines. We had a deal going in 1986 that seemed like it was right out of heaven. We had some money and Weary Warriors decided that two zero-timed engines would be nice. We had, if you recall, one broken engine and one mid-time engine that was running perfectly in 1981 at the time of the ferry flight. Again, the voice on the other end of the long distance phone call was reassuring. He had, he said, two military overhauled R-2600's, still in their sealed engine cans, missing only starters, generators, and mags. He had dozens and the sale was to settle the estate of his partner. His partner's wife wanted out and he was selling the engines at give-away prices. There are no buyers; interest on loans is close to fifteen percent. She needs the money. After all, how many buyers are out there for a -29? He wanted $7,500, which included delivery, payment on delivery, for the two of them.

I am hesitant. Weary Warriors are not sure. We have the money but we are suspicious. We have been burned before. The voice on the phone invites us down to take a look. He tells us to take our pick and he will open the cans. In our presence, he will rotate and bore scope each engine.

The seller throws in two extras. Both engines will have overhauled carburetors. We already have two and can sell or trade two. Good carburetors are going for five hundred dollars apiece. The seller has a warehouse of other parts all being sold at good prices.

We are getting greedy. We want the engines. Glen and Walter will go and take a look at the engines to make sure. It will be a twelve hundred-mile round trip. Arrangements are made to meet the seller and they are on their way.

On time, at the right place, Walter and Glen patiently wait. The seller does not show up. After many phone calls, they make contact. They have lost a day and still do not know where the warehouse is. At last they meet and the seller apologizes. His wife took suddenly ill and he had to rush her to the hospital. He looks tired as he shows the frazzled Weary Warriors to his warehouse.

In front of Walter and Glen, in a can with the top removed, is a gleaming Wright Cyclone -29. The seller cannot stay. He has to get back to the hospital. He lets Weary Warriors have the run of the place. He tells them to stack anything they find alongside the engine. He will talk price with Lou later and deliver the parts with the engines. He tells them to lock up when they leave and is gone.

They examine the engine. From the outside, the seals look good and appear to be like new. In a field behind the warehouse are more sealed cans. The lot numbers, dates, and codes are the same. Walter and Glen spend the good part of the day looking around. They are anxious to get home. They lock the door behind them and head for home.

I didn't buy the hospital story. I was more suspicious than ever when I heard what had happened. They had looked at one engine, which was probably a "bait" engine. My guess was that none of the engines had been rotated or bore scoped.

I made several calls to a B-25 researcher by the name of Bob Hany in New Jersey. He knew just about every B-25 in existence and most of the people in the B-25 world but he was out of town and not expected back for a few weeks. I tried more contacts to get a read on the seller. I inquired around and got the name of a fellow that owned a TBF, a Navy single-engine, torpedo bomber that carried the same engine as the B-25.

I made the call to Florida and talk to the man that owns the TBF. Yes, he purchased two engines. Took one out of the can, oiled it up, and hung it on his TBF. It runs just fine. I report, Walter and Glen report and we decide to go ahead.

I send the seller fifteen hundred dollars up front. He tells us that the engines will be delivered in a few weeks; the balance will be due when the truck rolls up —- cash or cashier's check only.

What else can a person do? Did I do everything I should have? The rest of Weary Warriors are satisfied. Relax, already. I still wished I could find Hany.

On the appointed Saturday morning, the seller arrives on time with two enormous engine cans on a trailer. They look at least six feet wide and eight feet tall. The seller has just completed a day and a half trip and he is anxious to turn around and head back.

Walter pats me on the back. "See, kid, what were you worried about?"

The man is a walking B-25 manual. He knows page numbers in the manuals that pertain to certain subjects, right off the top of his head. He looks 06 over and makes a lot of good suggestions. Walter, Frank, and Glen soak up the info like dry sponges.

Me? I buy him lunch.

We borrow Tim's forklift. Tim wants nothing to do with the heavy steel engine cans. Unloading the cans will be our responsibility. The forklift is small compared to the enormous cans. Walter will do the honors. If the engine had weighed one more pound, the forklift would have collapsed.

It takes us hours to unload the cans. The seller is getting anxious to get home.

The cans are off the trailer but they are so big we cannot turn them on end to break them open. We notice that the seals are broken and the top half of the cans are tacked to the bottom half by four heavy bolts. The cans, I am advised by the seller, were opened to inspect and bore scope the -29s as promised.

The day is ending. We are physically and mentally exhausted from the ordeal of unloading the engine cans and trying to turn them on end. We were not properly prepared.

I give the man his cashier's check and he waves goodbye. We've just spent $6,500.

No matter how hard we try, once we get the cans on end the forklift is not tall enough to lift the top half of the can over the top of the engine bolted inside the can. As we rolled the hanger doors closed that night, we still had not seen our engines.

That night, Hany gets back to me. He knows of the seller and his engines. All the engines he has had indeed been sealed by the Air Force years ago, just as the seller had stated. The bad news was that all the engines had been earmarked to be overhauled. Every engine in that lot was broken and they were sold at auction years ago by the government for two hundred and fifty bucks each. Rumor was that some of the cans were filled with rocks.

That did it.

First thing Monday morning, I am on the phone to Tim. I just about beg him to open our engine cans and take a look. I advise him he will have to build a low ramp so his forklift will be high enough to get the top of the can over the engine prop shaft. I ask him to please let me know what he finds.

Tim calls back. "El Presidente, the good news is there are no rocks. The bad news is that it looks like you have one engine that looks new but it has two bent valve stem guides and one engine looks so old and rusty it may just be run out."

I can't believe this is happening. My phone messages go unanswered. The seller has disappeared. We now have three bad engines and maybe one good engine. Tim suggests that we tear down the three bad engines and try to put together one good one from parts off the three. If we are lucky, we might just get away with some cylinder changes. Frank and Fencel start to take apart the engines.

Six months later we are not lucky.

Let me tell you one more story about the landing gear as it demonstrates to what extremes a person can go to rebuild an old warbird. A warbird parter told us he could get new landing gear, wheels, and brakes in Bolivia for a price, at Port of Entry, of $4,500 a pair. He was recovering several B-25s in Bolivia and the Bolivian government had piles of crates of parts for the B-25. All he had to do was get to the right government official and hand him an envelope of U.S. currency and the parts were ours. He had found the right official and the deal had been made.

Now, when our government gave the Bolivian government the B-25's, they sent along shiploads of parts. As most of the Bolivian government's Air Force flew out of some real rough fields, this shipment included dozens of landing gears. The Bolivians never had to replace any gear, though, as the landing gears were so strong. They had all of them left. Sound familiar?

What did the Bolivian Air Force do in the years following World War II? They beat up a lot of guerrillas and bandits from the air. Currently, they were using the B-25s to fly sides of beef over the steaming jungle. With the hot climates and poor roads, the meat products were moved around by air to avoid spoilage.

We order the complete gear. It will take about thirty days. No money up front is necessary —- a welcome change. In thirty days or so, we will be done repairing the skin of 06 and will be bolting the sections together.

We are still beating the cold weather.

Tim continues to let us work in his hanger on Saturdays. Tim is back and working on the center section. The thirty days goes to forty days, then fifty days and on to sixty days. I start asking questions of our supplier. The answers go like this: the riverboat sank; the cargo plane broke down landing at a remote strip; there is a mini revolution going on and we can't get to the warehouse. Or: the gear got lost; my partner who is handling that end of the deal went into a Bolivian whorehouse and never came out. Then: my partner has been hospitalized with the clap; the gear went to the wrong port of entry; I can't find my partner —- he may be in jail somewhere; we lost the gear. Finally: the gear is on the way —- just hang in there.

As winter wanes, we finally give up and buy the gear in the U.S. minus the brakes. We will have to skip the brakes for a while. We can get 06 on her gear without the brakes.

Walt and Glen change their mind and advise we really need the brakes to get the gear hooked up right. New brakes are $650 a set. We order up two as I watch our checking account drop under a thousand dollars. The brakes arrive: they are new and perfect.

Walter breaks the news. "Lou, we made a mistake. We actually need four brake assemblies. There are two per wheel."

Cute. We'd been had again. I phone the seller. I had said two and he sent two. He was waiting for my phone call. He had the other set ready to go and would send them as soon as he received our second $650.

We got the two freshly painted wheels. The problem was that the supplier had painted right over the mud and grime. We strip the wheels and get them checked. They are certified airworthy. The wheels are repainted and look good.

The seller from Bolivia calls. They've got the gear when can they ship it? We take a pass and thank him for his time and effort.

We are back in our hanger as winter gives way to spring. I look at the like new wheels and decide it would be nice to have our new diamond thread tires mounted. Fencel had gotten the correct tubes a few weeks earlier and the first set of tubes joined the growing junk pile.

Mark Clark, after watching our first attempt at mounting the tires, suggests we take the wheels and tires to a tire dealer in Rockford he deals with and Mark makes the call for us. They can take us in about an hour. Since our checking account is almost down to zero, I will pop to get the tires mounted and balanced. Frank and I throw the wheels, tires, and tubes into a borrowed pickup truck and head for the tire dealer.

As we leave, I glance in the rear view mirror and admire the lower half of the cannon nose that is now bolted to the cockpit. We had installed the refurbished nose gear complete with a new tire once the nose was attached. Everything is still on its cradle. Soon, though, she will be standing on her own. The nose gear weighed a piddly 194 pounds and was a lightweight compared to the main gear.

As we make our way to the tire dealer, I am pleased that we have the diamond threads and I am anxious to show them off, mounted on their wheels. They will make 06 really look military.

I had talked to a guy who for years, he said, had been trying to get a tire manufacture to locate their original molds for the main gear tires. His fascinating tale went like this: the diamond threads were not around any more —- all B-25s had modern rib thread tires —- not very 1944 military-looking. After months of searching, Goodyear had located the original tire molds in Brazil. They would make a batch of twenty tires for us —- no less, no more. Then they were going to destroy the molds. The price was $750 for each tire. He was trying to line up some guys and had to move fast. Were we interested?

Yes, we were indeed interested.

Weary Warriors had dealt with this man before and we trusted him. We sent him the money. In a few months, the tires arrived and they were beautiful. We rolled them out constantly to show our many visitors, who were noticeably impressed with our dedication to our restoration.

But back to mounting the wheels.

Frank and I wait in line at the Goodyear dealer. Frank will watch the mounting. Our turn comes and I back up the pickup truck for the unloading.

The shop foreman looks at our wheels and asks, "What the hell are those?" as he points to our wheels." I never saw tractor wheels that looked like that."

I explain they are wheels from a B-25 bomber circa 1943.

"Okay," he says, "we will mount and balance them; twenty-five dollars each."

Then he says, "If you would have purchased the tires here, we would have mounted them for you at no charge."

I hesitantly and very carefully answer. "I did not realize you had these tires here."

As the shop crew unloads the wheels and tires, my brain is clicking but it keeps on tripping as I sort out his statement. I hate to look stupid and, right now, I'm feeling very stupid.

The man goes on after taking care of another customer. "We always have a few of these in stock, especially in the spring —- and a few in the fall."

I am thinking, "We had these made special in Brazil. Am I hearing this guy right?" I do not know if I am turning red but I can feel the blood pressure in my face.

Still not trying to look dumb I ask him the going price for a tire. He walks to the counter, opens a book, flips a few pages and says, $375, including mounting." I feel the blood draining from my face.

This cannot be happening.

"Is that a special price?" I ask.

"No," he says, "That's the going price."

We had been had again.

I sat on the tailgate and mulled things over. How my outlook had changed in a matter of minutes! I am not from Missouri, but I like the show-me state attitude. I have to be sure.

"We may need two more tires," I say, "can you show me what you have?"

He points to an outside lean-to enclosure with a tin roof and chain link fence as siding. Frank and I walk over and take a look. There, in the piles of tires, are our diamond thread tires. The markings and numbers are the same. Someone made himself a lot of money. We had paid twice the retail price. I would check with the tire manufacturer in a few days and find out that the tractor tire is the old B-25 tire and is still made in the good old USA. The tire is readily available anywhere in the states. I am furious. Vengeance, though, will be mine in about a year.

The tires are loaded and they look good, which is little consolation for our being had. As we drive back to the hanger, Frank is grinning.

"What the hell are you grinning at, Frank?" I ask. "We got ripped off again."

"Lou," he answers, "it's the only way I can stop from crying."

We roll the tires and wheels off the pickup bed and everyone admires them, then we tell them the story. They are all stunned and go back to work. We do not look back; it hurts too much. I can tell by the silence that all of us there that day were hurt. It came too soon after the engine fiasco.

Walter and Glen announce that they will hang the gear the next Saturday. This lifts our spirits but I will miss the great event.

The following Saturday night, Walter gives me a call and brings me up to speed. The gear is hung, complete with brakes and wheels. She is still in the cradle but looks good.

Midweek, I take a few friends out to see our gleaming B-25. There she sits still in the cradle but she is on her own legs and the tires are resting on the ground. As I show my friends around, something strikes me as being wrong. I have spent many hours with this gear and it looks good, but it doesn't look right.

Then it hits me. The gear is mounted backwards.

There is a scissors-type component that connects the top strut to the bottom strut. In almost all gear applications, this scissors trails the gear. In its application on the B-25, however, it faces forward. I check the picture on a model kit of a B-25 and, sure enough, they had switched the gear or each gear was on the wrong side.

I leave a note attached to the starboard gear: "Mounted backwards, El Presidente."

Walter, Glen, and Frank showed up Friday, as they wanted to surprise everyone the next day with 06 standing on her own and the cradles dismantled. They see my note.

On Friday night, Walter was on the phone to me and he was laughing. Frank kept telling them they had the gear switched, but he and Glen would not listen to him. The gear is now on the correct way.

The next day, we all admire our B-25. There are no more cradles to bump into or trip over. Today is a grand day. Our pile of pieces and parts is starting to look like a B-25. Our gear sits with new bushings and wheel bearings. Every nut, bolt, and washer is new. All the arms, levers, and actuators look like new. It will be a shame to start the engines someday and get all those gleaming parts full of dirty oil.

"Lou, what's next?"

I eye up the tail section. The tails on B-25s are notorious for being corroded.

"We will attach the fuselage to the center section, hang the bomb bay doors and clean up the nacelles."

To be fair, there were many that sold quality parts as advertised and, with their goodwill and help, we moved forward. With regard to the others, however, I formed a "hit" list and vowed never to forget those persons.

Revenge is sweet, though. As the years passed and the word spread about our restoration, I would get calls from others restoring or repairing their dinged B-25. These calls came from around the world looking for advice, parts, or a solution to their problems. I would tell them whom to avoid. There are not that many people building up or repairing B-25's and buyers are rare to say the least. Over the past twenty years, the bad guys have lost some big money.

I still have that list.

Wild, the borrowed forklift and one big engine can.

Jerry Fencel tweaks a 2,800-pound Wright Cyclone R2600-29 engine that produced 1700 horsepower. Its size and especially its weight were beyond comprehension.

Lou Fulgaro

Bingo a Couple of Times

Many great things happened in 1985 and 1986. Most importantly, we do not run out of money. Magazines oriented towards warbirds are beginning to pick up on us when they run out of things to write about. We are mentioned towards the back pages but that is okay.

"Fly Past", a warbird magazine in England, prints an article about a cannon-nosed "H" sitting wrecked in the jungle on some island with a forgotten name. In the article, the author mentions that it is a shame that it appears that there will never again be a flying, cannon-nosed "H". One of Tim's employees reads the article and writes a letter to the publisher with a couple of photos of 06 and tells them about us. The letter starts an eight-year romance with this magazine and its North American expert, Dave Graham that follows 06's progress for years.

Somewhere, a great World War II air warrior reads about us and calls. His name is Victor Tatelman. I am mesmerized as I realize whom I am talking to Lt. Col. Victor Tatelman U.S.A.F., retired. He would like to come up from Florida and see our B-25. I bring him up to date on our progress and send him all our information. I am very honest about our slow restoration progress but he still wants to come.

He takes a commercial airliner to Chicago and I pick him up at O'Hare in the evening. He is all class. That night, we go out for dinner at one of the finest restaurants in the Chicago area. There are four of us at dinner and it is one of those rare pleasant dinners that one can remember forever. We like each other, hit it off well, and early the next morning we are on our way to Rockford. Tatelman is like a kid on the way to a candy store.

Tatelman has over four thousand hours under his belt and is approaching nine hundred hours in B-25s. He has an aeronautical engineering degree, has built a Pitts Special and an Acroduster II. He had just completed rebuilding a Bell 47 helicopter. What a find Tatelman would be if he would join us!

He pours over 06 with the knowledge, talent, and expertise of a man who has been there and done that. He asks questions I never heard before. He writes a check for ten thousand dollars and we have our second experienced real, live, B-25 driver. I am ecstatic that we would be attracting such talented persons. A year later, he comes out for a second visit. When he realizes Walter, Mike, and I each have thirty thousand invested in 06, he writes a check for twenty thousand dollars. I jokingly remark if he thinks he can buy us with just money he has a second surprise coming.

Tatelman has a well-equipped, hanger-sized shop at his home in Florida. I point at the fabric control services. Tatelman leaps at the chance to inspect and recover them. He flies his son up by commercial airliner, rents a truck and the rudders, ailerons, and elevators are loaded up and on their way to Florida. Months later, they have been rebuilt and recovered with the finest of fabric. There is no bill for materials or labor.

"Lou, what else can I do?" he asks.

"Vic, the rest of the tail awaits you." I express my concerns over the rumors I had heard for years that the tail feathers on B-25s were prone to corrosion, rust, and general deterioration as the manufacturer who supplied some of the tails to North American used an inferior, contaminated aluminum. He will have to open up the tail and take a look.

The same process takes place again; only this time a bigger truck arrives to accommodate the twenty-three foot-long horizontal stabilizer and the two vertical stabilizers.

I visit Tatelman at his home in 1988 and we take a good long hard look. Tatelman has done a quality level of work on the tail. He has worked at it for months, just about every day.

"You know Lou, the tail of a B-25 shakes like hell. It actually vibrates to the point we used to think the damn thing would fall off."

"You've got to be kidding," I say. "Did any fall off?"

"No, some were actually blown off, though. We took a real beating over there with all those low level attacks."

"Can we beef it up as long as you're cutting out some of the bad structural frame work?" I ask.

"I am already doing that."

As we continued our inspection, I ask Tatelman, "What do you remember the most during your combat days?"

"Its strange, Lou; I can remember that image like it was yesterday. The Japanese fighters —- they had some damn good pilots. I remember when they would make a run at us, the flashes of gunfire above the engine cowl and on the leading edges of their wings. And waiting, not knowing where the bullets would impact. It bothered the hell out of me."

"It was different over in Korea," I laughed.

Tatelman nodded, "The Chinese and North Koreans were lousy pilots."

"Vic, you were in Korea?"

"Yes, I flew F-86's."

"You know, Vic, the MIG-15's used to tear the hell out of the B-29 formations. It got so bad we had to go to nighttime bombing and pray they would not find us."

"Lou, the MIG was designed to intercept bombers, not take on an F-86. The slow firing canons could shred a bomber in a matter of seconds."

"I can assure you, Vic, the guys sitting in the antiquated B-29s appreciated you guys and your blow torches. While we appreciated you, we despised the architects of that air war that sent airmen into jet age combat with propeller-driven relics from the past while all those jet bombers sat, pampered in the states, waiting for an imaginary attack that never came."

I returned to Chicago and advised all that we would soon have our tail. It would be a good tail.

Pat Habel, a non-pilot, came to Tim's as he had heard that the actor Cliff Robertson's Spitfire had stopped at Rockford for some light maintenance work on its way to the EAA Fly-In at Oshkosh. He walked past our hanger, said hello to Frank, who was sweeping the floor, and admired our B-25.

Pat was a technician at a nuclear generating station and a confirmed warbird buff. He liked what he saw and we had another member who would join Walter, Glen, and the other whiz kids that were doing all the mechanical things from scratch. He spent years putting the cabling and hydraulics together. I, as did many others, admired his ability to take the most complicated schematic and make sense out of it. We had another winner. Pat, as we entered the year 2003, would be one of Weary Warriors leaders when it came to maintaining 06.

As long as we are talking pluses in this chapter (as compared to the negatives of a previous chapter), it is important to know that a lot of this took place before "www dot com" and such things as "surfing the net" existed. For every person that ripped us off, there were as many that did not. The next few paragraphs will demonstrate that there were a lot of persons out there just as honest and helpful as Frank Howerton.

As we worked on, most of the dirt, oil, grease, and all that stuff that makes you look like you work in a coal mine had disappeared. We could see clean, meticulous progress. Where at one time we dreaded to show up, as we knew what lie ahead of us, now we looked forward to Saturdays with our B-25. Every Saturday, we joyfully worked our way toward putting 06 back together.

Word had spread of my quest for the top half of our cannon-nose. The bottom half was hard to get our hands on but the top half, called the hood, was really elusive. There was not one B-25 parter that knew of one. We reached dead end after dead end. I was close to giving up. Walter and Mike were talking about having to build one up. It would take years to do.

The obviously young voice on the phone got my immediate attention as it said the magic words, "Mr. Fulgaro, are you the gentleman looking for the top half of a cannon-nose?"

The young man's name was Taigh Ramey and he was calling from Los Altos California. I was impressed; he did not call collect and he pronounced my name correctly. He thought he knew where there might be two of them. I was stunned. He had a friend who a few years ago had two of them in his body shop. When he worked there, they were going to throw them out but, instead, stacked them in a corner of the shop and used them as trashcans. He volunteered, if I were interested, to go down and take a look for me.

I got the impression that Taigh was about eighteen years old and very much into warbirds. I could not thank him enough for his time and consideration. The days passed and we all waited like expectant fathers. We needed the hood and were willing to pay for it. We talked price among ourselves and decided we would go the same as we did for the bottom half.

Thigh was back on the phone. Yes, the hoods were still there. One was badly corroded and had no hinges or latches. The other had some corrosion but had all the hinges and latches. With a little work it could be made airworthy. Was I interested?

I wanted to cry out, "YES! YES! I will cut my heart out for one! I will give you anything you want!" I sat down to prepare myself for the shock that would, undoubtedly, follow the utterance of the price.

"Are you there, Mr. Fulgaro?" He still calls me "Mr."

"Yes, Thigh, I am here. The second one sounds good. We would be interested in it."

In the most innocent of voices Thigh asks, "Is four hundred dollars too much? I think I can talk my friend down a little if that is too high."

My brain is whirling.

"Hello? Hello? Mr. Fulgaro, are you there? Can you hear me, Mr. Fulgaro?"

"Yes, Thigh, I hear you and that is good news." I have to be honest or at least make a feeble attempt at being honest. "Thigh it's worth more than four hundred dollars. There are not that many around."

What am I saying? Am I nuts? I am feeling guilty. "Thigh it's worth at least a thousand bucks." I still feel rotten.

"No. All we want is four hundred."

We have a deal. We take the better of the two. I decide that, even if it is rotten with corrosion, we can take measurements and make patterns and build one. Thigh will go and get it, build a crate, and ship it. Total price, six hundred and fifty dollars. I trust the young voice on the phone and send the check. I don't cross my fingers as I drop the check in the mail. I believe in this young man. I give Weary Warriors the good news. We will take a wait-and-see posture. Is it too good to be true?

All our freight was sent to Tim's as he was always there to receive it. He had a way of breaking news to me. It was the same with every phone call. It would go like this.

"El Presidente, you have a box. In the box are like-new brakes." Or: "You have a crate and there are two wheels with nicely painted dirt." Or; "You have two heavy crates with the main landing gear. They look good and are yellow-tagged."

If they were shipped freight collect and it was the beginning of the week, I would send Tim a check immediately. Toward the end of the week, I would see him first thing Saturday morning. He did not have to do this for us. I think he liked opening boxes and crates.

My phone rings at my office. My office personel go nuts trying to figure out who "El Presidente" is, but they eventually get the hang of it.

"El Presidente, you have a large crate. Inside is a beautiful hood for the cannon-nose. It appears complete and needs a little work."

Oh, happy day!

The nose and navigator/cockpit sections have been bolted to the center section. Glen will spend weeks working on the hood for the nose. He has to rebuild the hinges and latches. He finds himself a corner and lovingly goes to work. Tatelman calls to report that the tail is about ready.

"When are we going to attach the fuselage to the center section?"

"Soon, Vic, soon."

All the sections that have been separated are re-attached with new bolts. We never use an old bolt, nut, or washer. Glen spends some time working on the bow strip at the top of the windshield. Ours is corroded. I find another and, from the two, Glen will build one. Gaden is working on the nacelles. Frank is attaching the gear doors and all the apparatus that make them close when the gear is up and keeping an eye on Fencel, our hanger-arounder, who is taking a -29 apart.

Mike is in the cockpit, Walter is in the bomb bay and I am in the navigator compartment, all-preparing for paint. The shine of the new bolts holding the sections together is nice to see. At certain angles, you can see a blurred reflection. It will be a shame to paint them. As we enter this final phase of preparation before painting, we decide that we will do the main spars first and then the fuel cell bays. We will attach the fuel cells with all-new bolts and new inner connectors, plumbing, and seals.

We also decide it is time to buy an assortment of bolts, nuts washers and cotter keys. Not the special bolts, but the thousands we will need to hang brackets, pulleys, and tubing. We will also have to buy rubber inserts that fit into the hundreds of openings of our airframe structure that cables, aluminum tubing, and wiring must pass through. This has to be done to prevent chafing. Over the years, we will spend in excess of twenty thousand dollars on nuts and bolts. No cut rate or imitation bolts from foreign countries will ever go into our

B-25. I keep looking for the gold plating that this hardware must be coated with, it is so expensive.

To attach our wings in 1988, [not including the wing tips], will take three hundred and fourteen wing bolts. The cost is a staggering five hundred and sixty dollars just for the bolts. We have to add the nuts and washers.

To my surprise, I reach under the flooring of the navigator compartment and come up with a handful of dried debris. It is a combination of stripper, paint, and years of dirt. All that paint stripping process had washed all the debris into the nooks and crannies under the aluminum floorboards. For some reason, we did not think to remove the floorboards as we had in the fuselage. Walter and Glen advise that it has to come out, and then be cleaned before painting. Their words of wisdom are always followed and are final.

It's almost an impossible task. We fall back and regroup. This has put a burr in our paint schedule.

Walter will man the paint spray gun and will practice and learn with the fuel bays and under the flooring of the fuselage. These areas will be hidden from view. He will then show up mid-week to paint. When we show up to work on Saturday, the paint will be dry. We make our selection of interior OD paint. Through modern science, it is a perfect original match. The interior will be semi-gloss, whether we like it or not.

Walter advises that I will have to "walnut shell" the bottom of the navigator section. We are back in our hanger and have no water and cannot use stripper.

"Walter, what the hell is walnut shelling?" I ask.

"You're going to learn something new, kid. Walnut shelling is a process were crushed walnut shells are directed to an area to be cleaned, under air pressure, through a special nozzle."

Walter shows up with a few sacks of crushed walnut shells and the apparatus, which includes a hopper for the shells. Keep in mind that we cannot scrape the aluminum with anything that is made of steel, as it will mar the soft aluminum. This includes such things as steel wool. We put our new air compressor to work and I learn a new technique.

It works and works well, especially on all those hard to reach places like corners. You point the nozzle and pull the trigger: the blast of walnut shells comes out and, before your eyes, the paint disappears like magic in a shower of bouncing walnut shells. One of the problems is that you also get bounced by the stinging, sharp-cornered shells, making eye protection a must. Gloves and long sleeves help ward off the shells.

"Hey guys, this is terrific! Why didn't we do this in the first place?"

Everyone shrugs their shoulders and I hear a few "I dunnos."

I soon find out why Tim told us to use paint stripper. I watch in horror as a piece of aluminum disappears before my eyes. I turn the gun off after about five minutes of work. Everyone comes and takes a look. We are all interested in every phase of our restoration and are curious. Walter decides there is too much air pressure and lowers the delivered PSI at the nozzle. The soft aluminum again is eaten up like butter. The shells may work fine on steel but most of that cleanup work is already done. We stop.

So much for crushed walnut shells. I vacuum up the shell debris. The sacks of walnut shell join the growing junk pile

I make inquires. Carl of Aero Traders advises glass bead is the way to go. It is fiberglass and is much softer than the walnut shells. We buy a few sacks of glass bead. It works just great but it is slippery and I have trouble keeping my footing. It's like being on roller skates on ice. Everyone is so impressed we decide to do the cockpit as well. I direct the nozzle of the vacuum and suck up glass beads by the tens of thousands. The navigator compartment is spotless. I am very proud of my work and it was easy. Walter comes over with an air nozzle that is attached to our air compressor and directs the nozzle and lets the air fly. Glass bead is bouncing all over the place. I am dumbfounded and vacuum again. The same results. Over and over again the same results. Frank takes over. I guess he will have to show me the way. The results are the same.

I find a phone booth and give Carl Scholl a call. He is laughing —- and it is my dime.

"Lou, never use glass bead on the inside, you will never get it all out. We learned the hard way also. It is so slippery it will actually get between two pieces of aluminum that are riveted together."

When I return, Walt, Glen, and Frank are using rubber mallets and blocks of wood trying to jar out the elusive glass bead. I fill them in on the conversation with Carl.

When Weary Warriors was painting the interior, the glass beads were a nightmare. Even with low air pressure, we would still scare up glass beads. They all got painted OD brown/green.

Fifteen years later, the cockpit crew will watch a stray OD glass bead occasionally march across the cockpit floor, keeping time with the vibrating beat of the -29's. The old-timers smile.

Out of the thousand plus photographs I took during our restoration this ordinary shot is one of my favorites and shows the dominating size of 06. Wild and Serrano are relaxing which was rare. Note the outer wings stored against the wall of the hanger in the background.

August 1987. The forward half assembly is starting to look like an airplane. After years of searching we located the bottom half of the cannon nose in a barn in Kansas City, the top half in a body shop in California where it was used as a trash can. The two slot like openings in the fuselage side are for the internal stored ammunition to feed the two external side mounded machine guns. In front of the slots are the outline locations for the muzzle flash deflectors.

Anybody for Paint

As mentioned, the "anybody" was Walter. We had many discussions about paint. Our discussions focused on the interior only; from where to start to the shade of olive drab; to prime, then paint or whether use the new, very expensive epoxy-type paints that were primer and paint all in one. The exterior was years ahead of us.

Our first discussion was when to paint. We all sat down during lunch and I conducted an impromptu meeting where there were differences of opinion. Some wanted to paint the stripped down interior before we added anything like pumps, brackets, wiring and tubing. Others wanted to hang everything and then paint; their point being that attaching everything last would ding, scratch, scrape and mar the paint. The other side felt that, for a neat looking job, it had to be painted first. If there were a ding or a scratch it would be touched up. Walter advised that we would be hanging all new tubing and the new tubing would be natural aluminum color as was the original. It would contrast nicely against the OD paint, as would the exposed electric wiring that would be white.

It turns out that we will paint first then hang everything, and we would use the new epoxy paint that went for forty-plus dollars a gallon. There was some vague hocus-pocus mixture that Walter had to add to the paint to get this fabulous paint started and then paint very fast as it could not be used after about an hour. Whatever was left after this time would have to be thrown out.

Walter mixed up about quart of the paint during the week and painted a test patch in the bomb bay, cockpit, and did the entire one side of the main spare and fuel cell. Saturday came and Walter approached me and asked for my approval. I was flattered that he would ask. He had done the research and purchased the paint. The effect of the OD paint was perfect and we all agreed it was as close to the original interior as we could get. We could match the outside 1943 paint but the inside seemed to have a little more green in it and the Air Force archives were a little vague on the interior paint.

Walter approached me cautiously one Saturday and when he did this I stopped what I was doing and listened very carefully.

"There is no more paint" were his words.

I replied, "We have money in the bank. I will give you a blank check, just write in the amount when you pick up the paint."

Walter replied, "No, that's not what I mean. I mean there is no more paint like we have been using." His words sunk in. The paint was no longer available. There was another color that was very close but not the exact color. We all agreed to try the second color OD.

We had saved some interior paint chips years earlier and this is how we tried in part to match the original interior OD that had a lot of green in it. Walter was right, it was a different color. We all said "no" to the new paint. The paint shop recommended some paint pigment to bring the color closer to where we wanted it and the color was worse than the second stock paint. Walter tried a third stock paint and we ended up with four shades of OD. The test spots on the interior looked like hell. We had a four-color interior that was about ten percent painted.

Each paint application took a week. Walter would apply it mid-week, we'd look on a Saturday and say no and the next week Walter would give it another try and we would start the cycle all over again. Five weeks of this was just about all I could take. That was enough for me.

We had a second meeting on the paint. Let's try a new brand, a new paint shop. There would be no pigment mixing of our own brew and we would use a stock paint. We all agreed and a very frustrated Walter went on a paint-hunting expedition that took days. God bless Walter.

We had our fifth test spot and on the sixth week we all gathered and viewed the test patch. Some liked it; some did not. But it looked good. I held up one of our original paint chips, placed it against the test patch, and it damn near disappeared. I did it several times and all the "no" votes changed their minds. Some still did not like it but it was the color it was supposed to be and, at long last, it was settled.

I patted Walter on the back said, "Buy enough to do the full interior with some left over to touch up for ten years." I gave him a Weary Warriors Squadron blank check.

It was Pat Hable who came up with the safety-orientated suggestion. Walter was not to paint while alone. The new paints were deadly and there should always be a safety standby person. Walter would be painting in some very confined areas and that, in itself, was dangerous. We all respected Pat's input as he had spent years in the Navy and served on two nuclear powered subs. He had been a machinist's mate and his official title was Engineering Laboratory Technician. I never knew exactly what that meant but it had to do with controlling mixtures on a nuclear sub and, in those days, that was a very dangerous place to be. We went one step further and decided to paint on Saturdays only as we felt if Walter's backup did not show or was late Walter would put caution aside and paint anyway. We would all eat the paint so to speak and help out where ever we were needed.

  We placed a fan set at a low speed at one end of the fuselage that pushed fresh air in and one at the tail end that pulled air out. There was no doubt that Walter was doing the worst of all things that had to be done. No one volunteered to paint for him. With goggles, a paint mask, gloves, a hooded sweat jacket, and the oldest of throwaway clothing, he would prepare himself for the task that lie ahead. While he was getting prepared, some of us would mix the magical concoction and fill up the paint spray container. Then Walter would crawl in and start spraying the green sticky concoction called paint.

  One of us would help guide the air and paint hoses so they would not get tangled up or get hung up on anything. Two would man lights, as a rule working through the waist gunner's openings. One would aim an input fan to blow the sticky green over-spray away from Walter. The green drifting spray came billowing out of hatches as, inside the fuselage, Walter was immersed in a sea of green mist that would get thicker by the minute. We would all worry about him. He would only emerge when his goggles were so coated with paint that he could not see. While Walter gulped fresh, clean air we would take off and clean his goggles, and change the filters in his mask. With clean goggles and filters, he would plunge back into the fuselage. He would never complain. It was simply his turn to do a miserable task.

  For those unfamiliar with a B-25, there is a tunnel about eight feet long and twenty-four inches square that runs from the navigator's section, along the left side of the fuselage and under the pilot's seat to the glass nose, where the bombardier had his bombsight. It was the only way in or out. It was not the place to be if you did not like small spaces. It was designed for agile young men to crawl through, not old duffers like us. In the cannon nose version, this crawl-way is where the eight hundred and forty-pound cannon was bolted in. It was bad enough to strip this tunnel of its old paint, but painting it required the heart of a lion and the patience of a saint. All four sides had to be painted, and only the bottom was smooth. The remaining two sides and top had small bulkheads and stringers protruding to contend with. Enter the tunnel from the front, spray and let the paint dry. Then enter from the rear and spray the sides of the protruding structure members that could not be sprayed from the front. Let it dry again and check for missed areas and do it all over again.

We would soon realize that over the years that most of us that came to work would share the dirty jobs. We individually would realize that it was our turn, step forward and do it. Gaden spent a lot of years at the solvent cleaning tank. There were so many accessories, parts, and small odds and ends that had to be prepared to paint. Some got the OD treatment, some silver and some ended up black. It was all painted the way it was in 1943 whether we liked it or not.

It is amazing what a coat of paint can do. The freshly painted silver parts contrasted brilliantly against the new OD paint. I would watch our visitor's eyes get big and round as they viewed two or three years' progress. They no longer commented, "You will never get it done." The "wows" came more and more often. They would then bring their friends, armed with cameras. What was important, though, was that many of our visitors knew what kind of hard work lie beneath that like-new paint. There was no dirt, rust, old paint, corrosion, or poor workmanship hidden beneath a thick coat of paint.

Word spread throughout the warbird community. We had changed from "the guys who screwed the museum and thought they could build up a cannon-nose B-25" to "the guys who were building a cannon-nose B-25." We got more and more warbird visitors that flew in just to take a look. It gave us the opportunity to set the record straight as far as the museum was concerned. The warbird community was slowly embracing us and a lot of nice things were being said about us. We were earning their respect for what we were doing and how well we were doing it. The makeup of Weary Warriors Squadron was new and unique in the warbird community and the concept was working.

Some began to take projects home. Glen took on the cockpit instrument panel. He would make a new one. It would be exactly the way it was in 1943. Glen would not allow the radios to go into the instrument panel. This was going to be interesting, as some did not agree with this. I had located and purchased a gun sight that went in the cockpit of the "H" model to be mounted on the pilot's side. Gaden took on this project. Walt took home the pedestal for the turret and kept that project at home for years. Frank and Hable took on more mechanical work.

Fencel began to talk about the exterior paint scheme and armament. I would try and talk Fencel into going to his back yard and digging up one of those tin cans full of old dirty money. Fencel would eventually do that but we had to bring him in screaming and kicking all the way. Our buy-in rates where going to go up and he had thirty days to come in. If not, I had to sadly advise him he could no longer participate. No pay, no play. It was a hard thing to do, as he was very likable, but very stingy. He joined us bomb bay forward status. It was hard to believe anyone could hate to spend money as much as he did. In Fencel's defense, he did have warbird contacts and brought a lot of people to visit us, many of who reached for their checkbooks.

To end this chapter, it is most fitting to let you know that the original paint for the interior, that we worked for so long to match, was not discontinued. It was still available from a distributor in St. Louis. Walter's first paint retailer had a falling out of sorts and stopped carrying that brand of paint. The paint retailer could have referred us to someone else but we had another greedy person to deal with. He was well aware of the time and expense we were going through and could not have cared less. I gave him a call and let him know we were spending thousands with someone else. The greedy one that made a few hundred dollars off of us lost thousands over the years, not only from Weary Warriors, but many who liked the new concoction of paint we used. The honest paint retailer got all the referrals.

Lou Fulgaro

A New Shop Boss

A Few New Members

Walter approached me one day and said he thought he should step down as restoration boss. It was his opinion that Glen Hanson should take over as we phased out the take-it-apart years and entered into the put-it-back-together years. Glen was knowledgeable and not just a good worker but a hard worker.

I was apprehensive. Glen had a tendency to be a loner like me, only more so. He did not like decisions made by a committee. I never could get close to Glen, as he liked his space. Weary Warriors was not like the inside of an airline cockpit where he ruled supreme with no questions asked. We were all volunteers who laughed together and cried together. Glen was indifferent to all that nonsense.

The decision was made and Glen was now our Restoration Project Chief. Walter gave a sigh of relief and would assist him. Glen took over. Glen tried to mellow up a little as he worked at his new role. I appreciated his effort and it again demonstrated what a fine person he was. Glen had his role and I had my roles.

You noticed that was plural. Not only did I have to sell 06 from time to time I would also have to massage some hurt feelings. Glen would schedule work and we would go over his schedule together in a quiet corner of the hanger. I wanted to get 06 to look like an airplane and Glen wanted her to go back together in a logical fashion, which also made sense. We both would give a little to have both avenues work.

Being well aware of our cash flow —- or, at times, lack of it —- I would constantly try to get projects going through Glen that, at first glance, would impress interested persons. When the first impression wore off and they took a second look, I wanted them to see the detail work: they should, again, be impressed. We needed some big-ticket members and their buy-in money.

Glen did years of sheet metal work and he more or less set the pace. When I thought we should bolt the fuselage to the center section, he advised me that he had a lot of sheet metal work to do at the back of the bomb bay. The fuselage would get in the way so joining the fuselage was put off. It would have been nice to have the fuselage attached but Glen felt the top half of the cannon-nose would be more impressive. It would take him six months to work the top half of the nose.

Glen turned the bottom of one wing into a giant workbench. The hinges and the latches had to be rebuilt and there was some sheet metal work that had to be done. Once that was done, it took three more months to fit the hood. It worked like the hood on a car. When Glen was done, it worked as smoothly as the cover of a fine pocket watch. When closed, it matched perfectly with the bottom half and the close fit matched the coachwork on a Rolls Royce. It was incredible.

Glen spent more time at the hanger than anyone else. Being retired and living the closest was a big advantage. If something did not turn out to Glen's high standards including his own work the project would have to be redone.

There, always in front of us, were the monster fuel cells. They had waited in their wrapped plastic for years and still looked like new. Now that the fuel bays were painted and we had warm weather, it would be a good time to install the fuel cells.

Glen inspected them and decided we needed new filler openings and all the fittings including the drain sumps, which were beat up and rusty. The repair parts, however, were readily available.

While Glen took on the hood, some of us took on the fuel cells. Fencel worked the engines, Gaden the nacelles, Frank brackets and pulleys, and Mike the brakes.

It would be nice to hang our one good engine. To do that, the fuel cells and the stress plates had to be in place. The backing plates and collars of the fuel cells were complicated and hard to get to. Nothing, it seems, had changed.

Glen would run over and see what we were doing and try and find a better way. He would end up doing some of it himself. Then, he would then check on Mike, help Frank get the brackets sorted out, show Fencel how to remove a stubborn cylinder from a -29. He was like a mother hen watching over her chicks. We all appreciated his concerns but when he helped us, the sheet metal work stopped.

Throughout the process, Glen was as fussy as an old mother hen. Later when we had a mechanic he mounted an electric junction box with dozens of wires coming in and going out. The box was located in the navigator compartment. It was a quarter inch out of plumb, although you had to step back and study it to notice it was not right. Glen had several of us take it off and reinstall it plumb. It made no difference to us but it did to Glen.

Another time, some aluminum plumbing in the bomb bay had an eight-foot run that dropped about an inch. You guessed it. It had to be ripped out and reinstalled perfectly plumb.

The mechanic would eventually get the hang of it. This was good since someday our butts would be in 06 and a simple cotter key installed upside down could be disastrous.

I talked it over with Glen and Walter. It was time. We needed a certified engine and airframe mechanic, someone who knew what he was doing. Some of the work we were about to do had to be inspected and written off. Everyone agreed —- but more on this individual later.

Thanks in great part to Fencel, we started gathering pilot members and our bank account grew with the membership. During this three years period, we gathered some good pilot members. Ray Hillson, MD, a heart specialist, was one of them. He had a lot of twin beech time and had recently moved up to the Chicago area. We used to joke with him that we had our built-in flight surgeon.

Another fellow, Ralph Quatrine, had been a B-17 pilot and had many combat missions over Germany in World War II. His wife, Elaine, came on board bomb bay forward and we had our first and only woman member.

Jerry Macomber, a Rockford resident and confirmed warbird nut, came on board as a crew member at a most critical time: Macomber was a master painter retired from the Chrysler Corporation where he had prepped and painted their cars for the national auto shows. Of all things, he raced pigeons. He became a good, dedicated worker and eventually did a paint job on 06 that was second to none.

Jerry Schiera, a corporate pilot, also came on board. Dave Morris was an electronic wizard from the Motorola Corp and came on bomb bay forward. We put his talent to work. A fellow by the name of Jim Taylor was another electronic whiz kid and came on as a crewmember.

More would come in time but for now I was amazed at the intelligence, talent, and the diversification we had. There was no way we would not succeed. Whether an old timer or the new kid on the block, we were all determined to have the only cannon-nose flying B-25 in the world. We all owned a piece of her but it was getting harder and harder to keep everyone dancing to the same tune and singing on the same page.

Glen was having trouble with this development. I could see it in his eyes and hear it in the tone of his voice. He was short on patience and could not tolerate repeated mistakes. There would be some tough decisions to be made.

Jack Robinson scavenges a –29 for parts. The engine being built up is on the engine stand behind Robinson. Serrano, behind the engine is trying to free up the mechanism to tilt the engine on the stand. If you look carefully you can count five engines in the photograph, all them bad.

Again the Fuel Cells

A Mercenary Mechanic

As our membership grew, the percent of ownership that Walter, Mike, and I had shrunk at an alarming rate. What amazed the three of us was that we did not care. Our determination to show the museum, share the joy of ownership, reach our goal and show the world our cannon-nose B-25 was that strong. You did not have to be a multi-millionaire to own a warbird debt-free. We were demonstrating that the little guys, if well orchestrated, could pull something like this off.

What helped, though, was the way all our members treated the three of us. There was a certain respect and trust for the three of us and what we had gone through to be where we were. To the rest of Weary Warriors, we were the founders and Walter would always be revered as the person that got it started.

As we peeled off the plastic wrap off the fuel cell, we beheld the shiny, like-new slippery fuel cell. Those of us who were involved in taking them out years ago remembered well what we had gone through. Tim suggested that, in spite of it being summer, we still pre-heat the cell, encircle it with several straps and collapse it. We took his advice without question.

Six of us heaved the heavy slippery fuel cell over our heads and stepped up on to a makeshift wooden platform. We pushed, shoved, twisted, pried, and swore. We fell back, regrouped, talked about it, and gave it another try. We were to the point of giving up a second time when it popped in and just hung there all by itself. Our lovely lady was once again embracing a fuel cell. While we were on a roll, we decided to do all four fuel cells. It took us five hours to fit the cells up into their bays. It would take us three months to get them properly secured with new stainless steel hangers and another three months to install the new plumbing. None of which mattered much as we had come to measure time in years, not minutes.

While we waited for Walter to finish making the fuel cell hangers, Gaden and I were assigned by Hanson to finish up the nacelles. I sat in the sweet-smelling nacelle. The nacelle and the gear were spotless and the realization of how far we had come occurred to me while we were scrunched up in the nacelle. We had to install hundreds of new bolts and nuts to attach the nacelle to its framework and support brackets. We had worked all day in one nacelle and we were still clean. There was no more filth, no more rust, no more leaking fluid, and no more black oil! We were, at long last, on the downhill leg.

Bolt by bolt, the floppy nacelle became rigid and when we had all the bolts in place the nacelle was rock steady. We would complete the starboard nacelle the following Saturday. Walter advised he should have the new, machined hangers for the fuel cells finished by the Saturday after. They were unusual type bolts. They came through the top of the wing and screwed into a threaded metal recess embedded in a thick, raised layer of material at the top of the cell. The metal threaded recesses did not come through the top of the cell and, from inside the fuel cell, you could not know their location. The hangers helped secure the cell but also held the top of the cell taut and prevented it from sagging. If it sagged, it would rob the fuel cell of precious gallons of fuel.

Walter would work the top of the wing of the center section and I once again squeezed one arm and my head up into the cell. We would place a board under our famous red jack so we would have a stable platform for it. Before this, we had built a crude series of braces to hold up the sagging bottom of the cell. We pumped up the jack and, as it reached the top of the cell, inserted another board so the rising jack strut would not damage the top of the cell.

As I pump the jack handle, the top of the sagging cell begins to rise and, hopefully, the threaded metal recess will line up with the small hole in the wing where the hanger is to be inserted. Walter, on top of the wing portion of the center section, will watch the cell rise and, with a long blunt probe and a flashlight, feel for the recess and try and line up the holes.

It was a frustrating exercise. Not once did we get it right the first time. The slightest movement at the top of the cell would cause the jack to come tumbling down.

"Hold it Lou! We have to come to the rear a half of an inch."

I grab the rubber mallet and give it a feeble swing trying to move the cell. Nothing. Glen drops his sheet metal work, grabs a smooth, rounded wooden board, slips it between the front wing spar and the cell and tries to lever the cell to the rear.

"Hold it!" Walter yells.

With the force of the board the front of the cell, it begins to give. When it does, the bottom of the cell begins to fold and down comes the jack. The top of the cell sags and falls away from the wing.

"Jack it back up Lou, I can see the threads. We got to come up about six inches."

Glen freezes and tries to hold the position while I fumble with the jack and boards with my one free hand. The odor from the cell material at times is overwhelming. The dingy, forty-watt bulb in the pitch-black cell is inadequate but a larger bulb causes the cell to heat up and the odor really gets bad.

"Keep coming Lou."
"Hold it, Glen.
"Looking good."
"Hold it. Nobody move."

Glen and I freeze. I hear Walter dropping tools on the top of the wing.

"Got it lined up, hold it steady."

Walter inserts the threaded hanger and slowly and carefully turns it to catch a thread. No luck, the recess hole for the hanger is a hair cockeyed. Walter is muttering and swearing and Glen is trying to calm him down. My nose is itching and I think I am going to sneeze. Glen calls Frank and passes the board off to Frank and Glen is up the ladder. I hear his footsteps above me as they cross the wing. More tool noise and I just know Glen has taken over. Glen gives constant steady instructions. He always lets you know what is going on. I sneeze, nothing happens.

I hear a clunk from the top of the wing and a rolling sound. Something is rolling on the downward slant of the wing and I hear more profanity and someone scrambling above me. I hear whatever rolled as it hits the hanger floor.

Glen says, "Milt get that flashlight and get it up here!" The jack is once again beginning its journey and we have about five seconds. The glycerin, applied years ago, makes the inside slippery. It falls. We once again fall back and regroup. I offer a suggestion.

Let's change tactics. Once we get two lined up, the rest should just fall in line. Let's build a post-like affair with handles and insert it through the inspection plate opening. This would provide space for a board to cover more area; timbers and boards we have a lot of. Two of us will push up while someone levers the cell.

Glen and Walter work it up in about ten minutes. We give it a try and the top of the cell is up against the bottom of the wing. A little to the left and a little to the right and we have one, then two, then three hangers are installed. We become experts at installing fuel cell hangers. It takes three Saturdays to complete this task.

While Glen watches over us, no one is doing the sheet metal work. We now have to address the fuel cell vents, the crossover pipes, intake pipes, transfer pipes and the wing tank filler openings. This will take four more Saturdays but help is on the way.

I spoke with someone at the Combat Air Museum as I searched for our mythical mechanic. They knew about a round engine mechanic that, according to their sources, traveled to most of his jobs. Now, a good detective never ends a conversation without getting a name to further his cause. It is a basic rule. You have to create your own leads. You never say thank you and hang up without another person to go to. Someone had heard of a doctor who owned a B-26 and lived in Arizona. And Mark Clark just happened to know the doctor's name.

I was on the phone with a very busy nurse and yes, she worked for the doctor and he owned a B-26. I dropped some warbird community buzzwords and she stopped the office work for five minutes while she searched and gave me a first name and a phone number in Nevada. I called the number.

They have not seen the mechanic in years, but I get a last name this time and an engine overhaul facility in Oklahoma where they think he may have worked. From Oklahoma, I am on the phone to Texas and on the other end of the phone is my mark, Jack Robinson.

Robinson is an Air Force veteran who was in Korea when I was. He was an aircraft mechanic all his adult life and worked on many -29's. He liked warbirds but there was never a lot of work in one place, so he free-lanced. He worked north in the summer and south in the winter. He had all the tools and special equipment to work up an engine and he was also an airframe mechanic.

As we talked, I was surprised when he made the comment, "are you the guys up there with the cannon-nose?" Yes he could work up our engines but we would have to have a -29 engine stand to mount the engine while he worked on it. This we did not have.

He would be available in a few weeks. We talked money. We would have to pay him thirty-one cents a mile to drive up to Illinois and he would need three thousand a month for a six-day week. If everything went well it would take three to four weeks to work up the basic engine and another three or four weeks to mount the accessories and "hang" the engine. One more month for whatever. He could scavenge parts from our other engines, provided the parts were okay (this he did, frequently). If not, he could get parts at wholesale prices and would pass the savings on to us. But he told us to beware; engines that are built up this way will have problems the first twenty hours until the bugs are sorted out. He would need one month's pay in advance and work the first month with no pay. He would expect to be paid every Saturday afternoon thereafter without asking for his paycheck. When he arrived, he would expect his mileage check.

Weary Warriors conferred. At the rate we were going, it would take twenty years to finish 06 by ourselves. This would give us a good jump time-wise to say the least. Most important we needed a warbird mechanic to oversee our amateur efforts. We seesawed back and forth.

"Glen, you're the boss. Can we work with a certified mechanic and not get in his way or he get in our way?"

"Lou, we need someone like this. I hate to spend the money, but I think we should try it. If not, we will fire him, but we need a pro at this point. When I think of all the plumbing, cabling and wiring that has to be done, it's scary that we do all that by ourselves."

Walter agreed. Weary Warriors had about forty thousand in the bank, thanks in most part to Fencel. We could do it. I have a good feeling about Jack and he comes well recommended. We send him his up front check. I assign Fencel, our chief scrounger, to find an engine stand. He asks how much we want to pay and I tell him nothing.

Robinson had asked that we pick what we think would be our six worst but workable cylinders, pull them off the engine case and build a heavy crate to ship them to an overhaul shop for exchange. He will check them over first and send them, just have them ready to go.

Two Saturdays go by and on the third Saturday there is no Walter or Fencel. Fencel sort of comes and goes but it is unusual for Walter not to show up.

Walter and Fencel finally pull up two hours later in Claude's pickup truck and there, in the back is a beat-up looking engine stand. Fencel is so proud his buttons are popping off his shirt. Fencel had found a trade school that at one time taught students to work on the big radials. They no longer had a need for it. They had wanted to sell it but Fencel talked them into donating it to us. We were all impressed.

We had been successful in bartering our collector exhaust system with Aero Traders. We had all the parts including the precious low-profile air intakes. Our original broken engine had all the cylinders pulled by now.

In my desk drawer were two pieces of aluminum-type alloy from a piston skirt. During the ferry flight, there had been a piston failure. When the starboard engine lost oil pressure, these pieces and a few smaller ones plugged the oil sump. Thanks to the museum who, wanting to let their members hear the engines run, started both engines even though the one low-time engine had low oil pressure, they burned it up. A simple cylinder exchange and cleaning up the sump could have saved the engine. They could have repaired it for under five hundred dollars. What a bunch of idiots. An overhauled engine with no accessories now cost thirty thousand.

We now had six and a half engines. How did we get six? Fencel also conned the trade school out of two and a half -29 engines. Students had been taking the engines apart and putting them back together for years. The trade school gave us the engine stand, provided we take the engines off their hands —- obviously, they had no more use for them in this day and age. They looked worn but had never been run. We assumed we had one good mid-time engine and that was the port engine from the ferry flight. We felt that we could get one "slightly used" good one from the rest of them. We just wanted one. We all got ourselves used to the idea that we would have used-looking engines. We would not win any warbird trophies with our beat up-looking engines. But we could clean them up and, though not new-looking they were clean.

The telephone call to my home [collect] put me at ease. Jack was on his way and would be at our hanger Saturday morning.

Off to a Good But Bad Start

The next Saturday when I arrive at our hanger, Jack is already there and Walter and Fencel are showing him around. I give him his mileage check and checked his ratings. Jack picks up on the exhaust stacks and says he noticed that the low profile intakes had been modified to accommodate our new carburetors. If I recall correctly (we had switched from Strombergs to Hollys because the Holly was more efficient and reliable).

Jack says, "You guys must like noise. With those exhaust stacks, you're going to take a beating in this thing."

Walter laughed, "We are all half deaf from old age anyway."

Jack says it will take him a few days to get set up and squared away. First, he has to find a trailer park. We unload boxes and crates full of tools from his trailer and I give him a key to the hanger. We all like him and are comfortable with him.

The next Saturday, I arrive and Hable and Walter are pacing. There is no Jack. Walter advises he is in the county jail for drunk and disorderly and the only way he can get out is to come up with the bail money. Glen is furious but everybody else is laughing. This is a new turn of events for us.

Walter, Hable, and I pile into my car and we are off. Being a retired cop helps a little and we get Jack out. The three of us pool our money and, thanks to a kind judge, the bail is reduced to what we had. I think they were glad to get rid of Jack but our work Saturday is shot.

Jack can't stop apologizing for his actions but says he had to defend a girl's honor at a local bar. We laugh it off —- he would pay us back over the next few paydays.

As the months passed, Jack would demonstrate over and over his knowledge of big engines. He opened all the engines but one and could do in a day what it would take Fencel two months to do. He bore scoped them, checked the gears, bearings, valves, and pistons. He could glance at an item and tell you immediately if it was good, marginal, or a throw away. He made the decisions. He would use our like-new engine with the bent valve stems as the main parts engine. We had all thought he would choose to use the look-like-new engine but we did not question him.

For a while, there was no noticeable progress but the engine junk parts pile was growing at an alarming rate. Jack would literally toss a crankshaft, or a half of an engine case onto the pile. Fencel would peruse the junk pile every Saturday he showed up, pick out a part and ask Jack what was the matter with it. Jack would stop working and go over the part and show Fencel why it was no good. This started rubbing Walter the wrong way, as we were not paying Jack to educate Fencel.

Fencel was going nuts trying to figure out how to make use of the engine junk pile. He could not stand to throw anything away. There must be some way to get some use out of all those parts. Glen suggested we load them in a dump truck and drop them off in Fencel's basement when he was not looking.

Jack was confident he could make one good engine but he thought we would need at least three cylinders up front and we should get three more for spares. He was convinced we would use them up in the first few hours that the engines were on line. Fencel was flabbergasted. Not counting our assumed good engine, we had some seventy cylinders lying around. Jack explained that some of the cylinders we had were melted, some rusty, some pitted, some scratched, and some cracked. He could use only eleven of the seventy and then we would have to cross our fingers. We sent six cylinders to the overhaul shop for exchange. Fencel wanted to send the real bad ones but again Jack explained they would not accept, for example, cracked cylinders or pistons with holes in them.

Jack set out to rework the front gear assembly from all the combined engines. The front gear assembly was the most expensive part of a -29. Propeller shafts joined the junk pile like falling snow. Two were rusted, one was bent, one was pitted and one had rounded splines. Only one was good. This is how it went week after week. As the engine went back together we cleaned what we could and painted here and there. Slowly, an engine began to form on the engine stand. It was looking real good, almost like new.

The fuel cell parts arrived and Jack started installing them. He advised it had to be done right and we could not afford a leak. The B-25 was prone to burning. We all remembered, not too long ago, a burning B-25 crashed at Midway Airport as the pilots tried to land it. Both pilots were leaning out the cockpit windows trying to escape the smoke. They did not survive. Jack advised there was an FAA advisory issued from that accident to plug up the openings of the wing roots where they entered the center section. It was The FAA's opinion that opening the cockpit windows sucked the thick black smoke from the interior of the wing into the cockpit. He would take care of that when the time came. He also suggested we install a fire suppression system for each engine. They could be chemical or the new, expensive halon type, although the chemical type would eat up the engine if not washed off at once.

We once again discussed the auxiliary tanks. Would we use them or not? We had made the decision once, but more people were involved now and we had some real pilots. With the four main tanks, we could carry about six hundred and seventy gallons. Jack advised us to forget about the 29 inches of boost and 2000 rpm. That would suck up about 164 gallons of gas an hour. The engines were too old and we should baby them.

We should cruise at least at five thousand feet but less than ten thousand feet. With a lean mixture, we would set the cruise at 1850 rpm and 20 inches of boost in the summer and 24 inches in the winter. At this low rpm, we would have to make sure the generators had enough output. If not, we would need to crank up the rpms by ten until the generators did produce.

With the new carburetors, we should consume about a hundred gallons of fuel an hour in the summer and about one hundred twenty gallons in the winter with the additional boost. With the main tanks in the winter, we would have about five hours cruise time with one-hour reserve. In summer, in cruise mode, we would have about six hours with about three-quarters of an hour reserve. This however, would vary with carburetor settings and weight.

Jack held us spellbound. He had an audience thirsty for knowledge and he went on.

"At a climb speed of 160 MPH indicated, the engines will burn twenty-five gallons of gas to get you up to five thousand feet. If you climb to ten thousand feet, you will burn about sixty gallons at the same air speed. All this effects your consumption and that can again vary, depending on your weight. You're going to be light so the consumption should be better. The six auxiliary tanks hold about three hundred gallons. They are expensive, heavy, and a maintenance nightmare. All those connections increase your chances for leaks."

Jack recommended we not use them and put the money into engine fire extinguishers. This we would do.

Once the fuel cell system was put together, Jack sealed off all the openings and with air, pumped up some air pressure and the fuel cell system held. Glen was impressed.

Jack suggested he work on the good port engine, as he had to wait for some connecting rods and piston rings for the engine he was building up. He started with the generator and advised us that we needed new brushes. Did you know one little brush for an aircraft generator cost fifty-five dollars? For a car generator the brush cost three dollars.

Jack also advised (for those that were not around at Lambert's farm) that we had modern direct starters, meaning that when the starter turned, the prop would turn. We were not sure we liked that as, for the sake of nostalgia, we wanted to hear the whine before the engine kicked in. Jack told us that the momentum starters used centrifugal force and their flywheels were heavy: we should keep what we had. The starter and generator were overhauled, as was every other engine accessory. They all looked like new when they were attached to the portside engine.

Jack would spend three years of springs, summers, and falls with us. We liked him and needed him. Besides the 29's, Jack would give us constant advice for what ever we were doing. He did most of the cabling, wiring, and plumbing. Always soft-spoken, he was literally a walking, breathing library of information. We would have never been able to do it without him.

We Hang an Engine and We Learn

We would spend an entire Saturday afternoon just hanging one engine, not including all the preparation time by Robinson.

While securing the port side fuel cell stress plates, we ran out of bolts before they could be fully secured in place. The two fuel cells disappeared forever as far as I was concerned. I would always put them down as one of the most frustrating tasks we ever had to do.

Weary Warriors once again asked a very understanding Mark Clark for a favor and we borrowed his hand crank crane. It had the capacity to lift the two thousand, eight hundred-pound engine. The engine mount was a weird-looking system that the engine was bolted to and, in turn, the mount was bolted to four airframe attachment points. Two bar frames extended from inside the bottom of the nacelle. At the top, the mount mated to two more attachments on the front wing spar. Jack assured me it would hold but I had some difficulty comprehending how the spindly engine mount with four attachments could hold all that weight, hanging six feet outward from the wing spar. Add the weight of the prop plus the centrifugal force of the spinning prop and engine and, in my opinion, that should twist the engine right off the airframe.

First, Jack had made a three-point sling out of chain to hoist the engine; once we had it rotated so the prop shaft was horizontal to the floor the chain sling would be attached to the engine. The problem was that the engine now sat on the hanger floor bolted to its mount with the prop shaft pointed straight up. We would have to lift, tilt, and then rotate the engine to the horizontal position. We were not sure exactly how to do that. We did not have the proper harness to lift and tilt the engine but once again, Glen, Walter, Jack, Frank, and Hable but their heads together and, with some heavy rope, tied off the prop shaft.

We could not just sling the rope under the engine. This is how valve guides got bent and cylinders got cracked. None of those were designed to individually carry the weight of the engine. We were all very apprehensive. Glenn was outright worried. He checked and rechecked while Robinson patiently waited for him. We formed a plan and Jack assured us it would work. He had done this many times before. We would lift the engine about a foot. Once the engine was suspended, we would place some heavy wooden pallets under the engine so they formed a crude cradle. Then we would have to tilt the engine by lifting on the ends of the engine mount. Once we had it tilted so it was horizontal, we would lower it to the wooden pallets until the boards started to crack, then carry some of the weight by the rope and some by the pallets. Jack cautioned us to watch our feet and hands as the -29 would be very unforgiving if it came to rest on our toes or fingers.

With fingers crossed, we cranked the engine up off the floor and placed three wooden pallets underneath the engine forming a cradle-like affair. We heaved on the opposite end of the loaded engine mount and it barely moved.

Jack said, "Come on guys. Let's put some muscle into this. You have to do it. There is no other way."

We put our backs into it and, with some ingenious leverage, we tilted it a few degrees.

"Hold it that's all we will need." Jack lowered the engine while we held the mount. The problem was that, as he lowered the engine, our end of the mount went with it.

"You have got to hold that end up. Once we have it past top dead center and it will pivot."

Someone suggested we place a brace on our end of the mount and let the brace hold up our end.

"Can't do that. The mount may get kinked or bend. You have to hold it; the more it pivots the lighter your end will get. All together now, give it everything you got."

There were some real straining Weary Warriors that day in spring of 1987. Mark Clark, who was watching, could watch no more and left, wishing us luck. I thought I was going to bust a gut when the cracking, splintering, crunching sound of dry wood collapsing echoed in my ears and Jack said the magic word, "Relax."

The engine rested comfortably at a slight angle. We were all awed by the sound of the collapsing wooden pallets and it reminded us of how frail we really were. It really hit home when I realized the engine alone weighed more than my entire four place Fairchild, in fact a good eight hundred pounds more. We all stood back while Jack hooked up his chain sling. Walter asked about the wing twisting with the stress plates not secured and Jack advised he would take care of that.

With the chain sling in place, the weight was transferred to the chain and the rope removed. Cranked up about two feet off the mangled pallets, the -29 hung parallel to the floor. We started our precarious ten-minute journey from one side of the hanger, outside and around the nose of 06 and then back into the other side of the hanger. If the massive weight and bulk of the engine started to swing from momentum (which it constantly did) we had one hell of a time slowing it down to stop the swinging motion. We were useless, like paper confetti.

We lined up on the port nacelle and jockeyed the crane to get it lined up as close as we could. The crane's hard rubber wheels would hang up on a thin washer lying on the floor and the crane would stop dead in its tracks. The massive -29 would want to keep on going and start to tilt the crane. Slow and easy please.

The -29 was cranked up to about the right height and its mass towered above us. It hung by a thin cable attached to the chain sling and we were intimidated by its size and potential if it fell. With Glen and Frank up on the wing and Jack and I on the ground, the idea was to guide the mounts to the attachment points. Walter and Pat Hable would move the crane or raise or lower it as required. Half of an inch off to the right. Walt and Pat would reposition the crane guessing at the correction.

"Too much, bring it back a half of an inch." To match the mounts to the attachment points was a lesson in how to pray.

Too high, too low. Over and over we would try. All this time, the engine was towering over Jack and I, who were standing off to the side as far as possible. Jack's homemade chain sling was attached to the engine by three half-inch bolts. If the bolts broke and the -29 came crashing down, I wondered if the cement hanger floor or the engine would break.

"Hold it," said Glen suddenly. We were lined up and had one huge mounting bolt was partially inserted. Then two were partially inserted, then all four. They were binding. The engine mount was cockeyed, twisted or maybe just out of line in its construction. Ever try and wiggle a twenty-eight hundred-pound engine? Jack assumed the crane, which was still attached, held the engine slightly cocked upward.

Jack picked up a board and a three-pound hand sledge and placed the board against one bolt. Glen winced as Jack gave the board one healthy blow. The binding bolt slipped into its shoulder. The process was repeated three more times and the bolts were in. In a matter of minutes, the bolts were torqued down and safety wired. We were still hooked to the crane. Jack had Walter and Frank build a simple tower of crisscrossed timbers up to the prop shaft with a stout platform on top. Our neat little red jack was dusted off and the weight of the engine now rested on the jack by its propeller shaft. The chain sling and crane were removed. We returned the crane to Mark Clark. We were going to owe Mark a lot of favors.

The shiny stainless steel firewall had been preserved for years by being covered with oil leaking from the engine. If you looked at the firewall at just the right angle, it mirrored the back of the engine with all its gleaming like-new accessories. For years, I would show this to potential members. It was one of those small things that were very impressive once you started to look at details. Every Saturday, Fencel would wipe off the firewall and the accessories. How that man loved the big Wright Cyclones!

I got Jack aside and asked about the exhaust stacks being mounted and he said we should wait until after the new ignition harness is installed. Those damn things will always be in the way.

As a last comment on the exhaust stacks, Jack added, "Before I forget —- the exhaust stacks from time to time will crack. You can tell if they're cracked by tapping them with the wooden handle of a screwdriver. They will have a dull sound if cracked instead of a ringing sound. If you find a cracked one, you have to replace it. They will have a tendency to crack from the pressure of the exhaust and break apart. Once they're gone, the hot exhaust will burn off the bump out in the aluminum cowl for the exhaust stack. If you don't think you have flame coming out the stack, watch them at night. There is a good two feet of flame blasting out the of the end of each stack with a hell of a lot of pressure."

Jack continued to work up the engine for the starboard side and did a little plumbing, electrical, and cabling while waiting for parts. When fall came, we had two engines mounted. Jack gave us things to do over the winter and we agreed to have him back the spring of 1988. Same price. We removed the engine cans and, eventually with two engines mounted, we had some good floor space at long last.

One of the first things Jack had told us to do was to get the props to a prop shop and preserve and store them. All six blades were okay as were the hubs but props were expensive. Just laying around exposed was not good for them.

There was a FAA advisory on some old warbird props and ours fell into this category. A DC-3 had thrown a prop blade from its hub and gone down. The story went that the prop broke at the round shaft inside the hub. When the FAA accident investigation team examined the prop, they found the blade shaft was corroded and pitted. Water seeping past the prop shaft seal caused this. All props had to be pulled and inspected and a new state of the art seal installed. One year later, the prop would have to be pulled again the shaft examined and a new seal installed. Our prop shop advised us to wait as long as possible to install the overhauled props as, the day they were hung, the clock would start to run on the second mandatory inspection —- which would cost four thousand dollars. This cost included pulling the props, transporting, checking them, new seals, transportation back, and installing them on the prop shafts. This was the time to be in the prop business.

With the engine attached to the engine mount it was facing up which was the wrong way to bolt it to the airframe. Hanson attaches a stout rope to the prop shaft to lift the engine and we all cross our fingers.
Will it hold? If we get it a few feet off the hanger floor we would have to rotate it so the prop was parallel to the floor. Pat Habel to the left and Frank Serrano right.

Rotating the engine successfully it now rests on a cradle of wood pallets that it instantly crushed with its weight. The looks on the faces of the three Weary Warriors tells the story. Left to right Hanson, Habel and Walter Wild.

With many bolts missing from the stress plates covering the bottom of the two fuel cell compartments the wing spars could not support the weight of the engine. To prevent the wing from twisting the little red jack and a precarious stack of wood blocks helped carry the weight of the engine for several months. Note the cockpit canopy has been removed and the rivet work in progress on the nose hood. The forward hatch with its step extended is at the bottom of the fuselage. The front of the engine cowling is temporarily installed.

Months later with all the stress plate bolts in place the jack supporting the engine was removed. The front of the engine cowling is off in preparation to installing the individual exhaust stacks. Serrano, lying on top of the wing, makes some final checks of connections. Note the size of the engine cowl flaps.

Lou Fulgaro

This photo taken from inside the cockpit shows how close the engine is to the cockpit. The engine nose cowling is back on. The exhaust stacks can be seen protruding just in front of the cowl flaps.

Our First Air Show
Robinson Is Back

Comes 1988, most of us are still at it. Over the winter, we did some plumbing and cabling: Hable was a whiz at the cabling and Walter worked the plumbing. Glen and Frank did everything. Tatelman was just about done with the tail. We prepared pulleys, brackets, and tube hangers for Jack. We have miles of wiring and a good city block of new aluminum tubing. Everything Jack would need, we had ready.

On the down side, Gaden found a girlfriend. We saw him at a 1989 air show and he introduced us to his new found love. We never saw him again, as far as I know.

Butler had to tend to his machine shop business and, years later; he was flying a Stearman out of a small field in Harvard Illinois. He showed up, so I heard, at an annual meeting of Weary Warriors in late 1992.

In spring, 1988, we had $164,000 invested in 06, not including the thousands of volunteer man-hours. On the up side, we still had money in the bank and enough to get Robinson through another long summer season with us —- and we had a lot of parts.

Robinson was suggesting we have at least two spare engines. They did not have to be zero-timed since overhaul. Mid-time was okay. The point was that if we had a real engine failure (not just a bad cylinder), it would take months to get an exchange engine or get the bad one repaired. It was nice to have one on an engine stand that would be ready to be installed. We would give that idea some though. Years later it would prove to be good advice.

Spring and early summer saw some real results as wiring, cabling, and the plumbing started to come together. In my opinion, to start from scratch and "plum" one engine was a nightmare: it was an incredible maze, almost to the point of being inconceivable to the human brain. But wire-by-wire, pipe by pipe, and cable by cable there was progress. Everything that went in was new, tagged with a simple notation as to what it was, where it was going, and where it came from. Each frame station was taped with a number that related to the number in the airframe manual. As an example; "at frame member 29, install junction box, wire loom 8... through two-inch access, punch out 5... cables to elevators through three-inch access, punch out 6, hydraulic return line attached with clamp at position holes between punch out 5 and 6..." And so on for every single piece.

On July 16 and 17, 1988, 06 and eight Weary Warriors attended our first air show at the Greater Rockford Airport. We arrived, towed by a ramp tug and were positioned some 1000 feet from our hanger. To our right was a B-26 and to our left was a B-17. We were in good company.

For being less than half an airplane, we looked good. Months earlier, Mark Clark had showed up at our hanger, kicked a tire and asked if we wanted to sell our sorry looking B-25. We gave him the usual answer.

It was pay back time. He was coordinating an air show that was, if I recall, going to feature the Blue Angels. He would like us to be there.

"Us!"

"Yes you."

Many of the people of Rockford were German-born skilled tradesmen who, during the last months of the war, had been prisoners of war held in Rockford. After the war, the government showed them movies of a bombed-out Germany and tried to talk them into staying. Most stayed in the heavy-industry city where they had found good jobs and begun to put down roots. Mark felt that many of these people would be interested in seeing the mechanics of a warbird being restored and he needed planes to fill up the warbird line. I jumped at the chance. What better place to "sell" a warbird than a warbird show? Walt and Glen held back as they were not into that sort of thing. Just maybe, though, we could create some interest.

I looked over 06. Let's see —- about ninety-five percent of the fuel lines were in, sixty-five percent of the hydraulics, fifty-five percent of the wiring, and about sixty percent of the cabling; and it all looked good. We were minus our outer-wings, tail, and props as far as looking like an airplane. We had no glass in the cockpit but we did, at last, bolt on the fuselage. Within a few weeks, Glen would be putting in his masterfully restored panel. The cockpit floor console was ready to be installed. We looked, mechanically, like a showpiece. But, on the outside, 06 was filthy and dingy-looking from years of dust, dirt, coffee stains, bloodstains, and paint over-spray.

She needed a good cleaning up. Show or no show, it was time to do just that. No wonder we were no longer attracting members: our B-25 looked like hell! We were so used to it we did not notice. A complete outside cleanup was in order. There was little enthusiasm to clean.

Four weeks before the show, I started on the engines. While parts at the rear were clean, the front of the engines suffered the same dirty fate as the top of the center section and the inner wings. Jack would not let me spray down the engines with a solvent, as there were still too many openings. I went to work with rags and long brushes soaked in solvent and, as the hours passed, the engine started to look, well, clean. I spent one Saturday on each engine. Fencel joined in on the second Saturday and recleaned the back of the clean engines. The rest of the crew could not be bothered with a petty thing like cleaning —- I guess once again they were just too skilled to do such mundane things. It reminded me of the months of paint stripping.

The crew's indifference to getting 06 ready for the show was ticking me off. What the hell was the matter with them? Were they so narrow-minded they could not realize the opportunity Clark had given us? They broke for lunch the second Saturday and, when I did not stop for lunch, I told then to go get screwed. They left without me.

June of 1988 was the beginning of a record for heat and drought in the Midwest. Our floor fans were on full speed and we drank iced tea like we were in a desert. The crew returned from lunch and Pat brought me some fresh iced tea as a peace offering. They had talked it over at lunch what did I want them to do? I said that, with 06 opened up the way she was, there would be a lot of people poking around and we needed to clean all those inside nooks and crannies. Pat got the vacuum and went to work.

On the next Saturday, I rolled up the engine stand to the nose and started to wipe it off. Dirty shop rags were used first to cut through the dirt on the top side, then a rag with thinner on it to cut the stuck-on film of dirt, then a dry rag to buff up the shine on Glen's new sheet metal work. It might not have gleamed, but the difference was substantial and very evident. The nose took me two hours.

Walt went to his car and produced a bundle of clean commercial shop rags and mentioned to Glen that there were some nicks on the landing gear that should be touched up. Glen began to touch them up, then started on the nose gear. They had tool nicks from years of putting 06 back together. Some of the new bolt heads had a slight film of rust, which was cleaned off and protected from future rust.

The next Saturday was the last before the show and I started it off by asking in a very loud voice, "anybody for dirt?" They all got the bug and, suddenly, the anticipation of taking a Saturday off and just laying back to enjoy those who were enjoying our warbird bubbled to the surface. Maybe the fact that Clark dropped over and gave us our line passes and a box of free show passes helped. Instantly, we were important.

Jack was smiling as he began to clean out his tools and hundreds of odds and ends from the interior. It was his job to make 06 tamper-proof. He did things like wire the landing gear down locks in place. I did not want 06 to flop on her belly in front of thousands of people.

Walter and Frank started to scrub the top of 06 and Hable and Fencel went to work on cleaning up one full cowling for the starboard engine. I wanted one engine fully cowled and the cleanest of them opened up. It was a real problem to figure out which cowling went where and, once they fitted it together they had to clean off forty years of sand and weather to get it to look presentable.

I had acquired one 75MM cannon shell and asked Fencel to clean it up and paint the projectile of the shell. Fencel had fifty-caliber ammo and I asked him to fit together a thirty round belt, handed him our best ammo box to clean up for the nose and told him to make a simple pair of wheel chocks.

I advised Walter I was having some display signs made up and wanted him to build a three sided metal stand to display them. I gave him the dimension of the signs and made a sketch. While he was doing that, Frank took on the bottom of the tail cone, which was the cleanest part.

Glen would tackle the panel and just tack it in and mount the floor console. The throttle quadrant was already in place. There was a lot of inner energy that Saturday.

I helped Frank clean the bottom of the aft fuselage. If I'd thought the bottom was the cleanest, I was not looking at the tail cone when I said it. It had been splattered from the paint stripping days and hung low in its cradle. We did not see the bottom. Once bolted on, the error of our ways years ago was now evident.

The faithful worked hard all that day. As the day ended, 06 was looking real nice: we had all had put a lot of energy in to our cleanup effort. Mark pulled up and gave the 06 a once over.

"Very nice guys, I will raise my price ten dollars. Joke, joke. Be ready promptly at 8:30am next Saturday," and he was gone. He was a man with a lot of things on his mind.

We were not going to make it. I had envisioned 06 at a certain state of readiness and she was not there. Walter, Fencel, Glen, and I decided to come in Friday, the day before the show's start day. Fencel would take everything home and work on his varied assignments. Walter and Glen would install the one low profile air intake that was not installed. I would pick up the posters from Mrs. Chamberlain, the managing editor of the Downers Grove Reporter Progress, my town paper, who championed our cause now and then on slow news weeks.

On Friday at 4:30pm, 06 was ready and gleaming. Walter had painted the three-sided stand for Chamberlain's posters and the two-by-three foot; attractive posters were mounted on them and encased in plastic to protect against the weather. One panel carried 06's specs, one spelled out who Weary Warriors were, and the third panel presented a little history about the not-too-well-known cannon-nosed B-25s. In addition, she printed up about thirty information sheets that would be given to anyone who met our criteria (warbird nut, had money, and walked erect) for membership. I attached my business card to each sheet and we used them all up over the weekend.

I knew that we were a rag tag-looking bunch and that would not change for the show. I had to come up with a way to identify us from the spectators. Chamberlain made up pin-on buttons about four inches across and on a white back ground in upper case letters was printed WEARY WARRIORS. She gave me a treat and mine said WEARY WARRIOR # 1. There was no charge for all her work and time. Thanks again, Carol.

As we rolled the hanger doors shut Friday night, one last glance at 06 told us that we had overlooked something. One big job remained. Boxes, crates, steel drums, ladders, toolboxes, hoses, wires, and loose lumber blocked in 06. We were tired and it would take considerable effort. Walter and Jack volunteered to come in early Saturday morning and clear a path.

Warbirds had been arriving all day and the sounds of their engines drifted down to us. We all wanted to run out of our hanger for a look but we resisted. We had things to do. Come Saturday and Sunday, we would look and listen all we wanted to. When we left that night, we walked the lean-looking warbird line. We bumped into Mark who asked if we were ready. Most of the warbirds would arrive Saturday morning.

As he drove away he shouted "Thanks guys —- it's appreciated."

With Walter coming early, Fencel would come with me. Fencel did not like to drive as his eyesight was failing. In familiar areas, he was okay but he resisted strange places. I was between him and Rockford. Could he drive to my house? Yes, he would drive the twenty-some miles. Fencel advised he was all ready and couldn't wait 'till I saw the wheel chocks.

Fencel arrived on time and all of his work looked good. He went all out on the wheel chocks. He painted them yellow and, in contrasting black he had stenciled our serial number, 43-4106, and B-25. They really looked good. I gave him a pat on the back and we were off.

As Fencel and I arrived, the airport was a beehive of activity. Our first problem was the cop would not let us get to the hanger. It was our dumb mistake —- our passes were at the hanger. We talked our way past him by showing him all the ammo and the ammo box.

I pointed to our hanger and said, "That is our B-25."

He thought about it and, with a wave of his hand, let us through. Walter and Jack were there and a neat path had been cleared for 06. The tow bar was hooked up and we were ready to go. We waited and more Weary Warriors showed up. Fencel and Walter popped for some donuts and we waited some more. I handed out the pin-on buttons and, as expected, I knew who exactly would resist pinning them on. Most did but two slipped them in their pockets.

I said, "You guys should be proud of who we are and what we are doing."

We agreed on a few simple rules. No one goes up the hatches unless accompanied by a Weary Warrior. Chamberlain had made up two stick-on signs to mount at the hatches. They said, "DO NOT ENTER, THANK YOU." I was worried about lawsuits stemming from an injury, as we did not have any liability insurance. The next rule was that there always be a Weary Warrior present: we would not leave her alone during show hours. Hable and Seranno arrived. They could not come Friday as Pat had to work and Frank had school. I had also made some seventy-five copies of an article from the European magazine Fly Past. My now good friend, Dave Graham, had written a splendid article about our restoration project and that would become a handout also. I was all set to sell 06. I don't know what the others had in mind but they all knew that, when Jack left us this fall, we would again be broke.

Things were happening and warbirds were arriving like pigeons to scattered peanuts. It was now 9:30 AM and no tug. Of course, Mark said to be ready at 8:30 — not that we would be picked up at 8:30. I asked Fencel, our chief scrounger, if he would go see what he could dig up for us. Ten minutes later, a tug came around the corner of the line of hangers and Fencel was standing on a fender, he had done it again.

We hooked up the tow bar to the tug and we were off at a walking pace. Fencel was on the tug, balancing the heavy poster stand and all of us carried something. The new wheel chocks hung off the engine prop shafts and swung gently as 06 moved along. She was feeling the warm sun on her back for the first time in about six years. The young tug operator sensed that he was towing something special and crept along at a snail's pace. Maybe it was just that he'd never seen so many old duffers in one place and he figured this was about as fast as we could walk.

Mark Clark met us about half way and directed the tug operator to our spot in the warbird line. I began to get an inkling how things would go when other warbird owners started following us and began taking photos. With one perfect swing, the tug operator positioned us and, with a wave, he was gone.

Wheel chocks in place we hung new red "remove before flight" ribbons so spectators would not bump their heads on the gear doors or bomb bay doors. I did not notice it earlier but Walter and Jack had hung the two bottom hatches along with their retractable ladders. Nice touch, it would help if someone wanted to step up into the interior. Just to look inside, a person could stand on the ramp and the upper portion of their torso was inside. The tow bar was stowed inside the rear fuselage and we were just about ready.

Chamberlain's signs were about six feet in front of the nose and next to the nose gear were the cannon shell and the nose ammo box with Fencel's glistening belt of ammo. The kids over the next few days could not resist touching the belt of ammo or the cannon shell. We would have to keep an eye on them so they did not disappear. We set up our lawn chairs and, as Robinson turned to leave for the hanger, I grabbed him by his shirttail and asked him to stay. He was going to have a paid day off. The little black boxes he was going to work on could wait till Monday. He had the biggest smile and I think that small gesture produced a happy, productive mechanic.

When the gates opened, we were all set and we were immediately overwhelmed with people. The crowd around Chamberlain's posters was at times six feet deep. There were more photos taken of the posters than there were of our B-25. They moved around the three-sided sign, pointed, took photos, probed into 06, and then came back and read some more. Mark was right. The people of Rockford wanted to know. By Sunday afternoon, the people of Rockford had adopted us. One did for sure; we got our paint expert and pigeon racer, Jerry Macomber, who met all three of our three membership criteria.

It was obvious that, while we stood wing-, prop-, and tail-less, the air show patrons wanted to look deeper than paint. In the dazzling afternoon sunlight, 06 literally bristled with her new plumbing, cabling, and wiring. The contrast to the interior OD paint was so marked that people could not take their eyes off the brilliant mechanical scene in front of them. Everyone had to touch and 06 seemed to like the caresses. The most popular place was the bomb bay and the adult men zeroed in on the back of the one opened-up engine and the mirror-like stainless steel firewall. It was fascinating to them. At times, there had to be twenty people standing in the bomb bay or standing on the cement under the bomb bay.

Questions flowed and we were in our glory. Egos were massaged beyond belief. All of the Weary Warriors that showed up that day were relaxed and actually smiling. Tatelman was the only Weary Warrior that could not make it and I wished he could have shared this day with us. He also needed to be softened up and mellowed out.

Out of nowhere, Claude was suddenly seated next to me. I had not seen him for four years.

He simply said, "I am here to check up on my investment."

I replied, "You're losing your shirt."

As the Weary Warriors got buried in the crowds, I noticed that the two holdouts were wearing their pin-on buttons. Some wives showed up to take a look at what their husbands had fallen in love with. My wife referred to the B-25 as "Fulgaro's Iron Mistress".

Whenever a prospect showed up and he looked promising, he was channeled to me and we would get acquainted. Most would have loved to join us but, as expected, few had the money. Camera shutters clicked as what must have been a thousand photos were taken of 06 and the posters. Everyone had to look down the gaping hole in the nose where the muzzle of the cannon someday would protrude. Every child had to be held up to take a peek inside.

The Southern Lake Michigan Wing of the CAF arrived and placed their German JU-52, a tri-engine transport from the late 1930's, in front of us and off to the right. They set up their PX tent and tables in front of us. About ten CAF members showed up dressed in detailed German uniforms and set up perimeter guard posts. They really looked sharp with their German rifles and were a nice showpiece with the JU-52. I could only imagine the nostalgia there was for the many Rockford citizens that were POW's and decided to stay in the USA. Weary Warriors —- well, we looked like hell compared to them. Fencel approached me and said we should have at least worn uniform caps. I agreed and suggested that he and Walter come up with some ideas to present at our annual meeting.

I was keen on the Great Lakes Wing of the CAF, as they had, through Fencel, invited us to join them in their hanger at Gary, Indiana. They had a large hanger and wanted warbirds to join them and share the expense. Fencel was —- well, in bed with them and wanted us to base our B-25 there. It was close to Fencel's house. Gary, to most of us at that time, was one big ghetto that had been an industrial giant at one time but was now a dying city. With the Japanese imports of steel, the great, miles-square steel plants on which the economy depended had just closed their doors and folded. The Commanding officer of the local CAF wing joined me and we had a long talk. I advised him when the time came it would not be my decision to make and all of us would have to make that decision. But that decision was years away.

At our first air show 06 stood tall on the flight line. She was missing her tail, wings, props and a lot of other things. The white cumulus clouds soon turned black and the storm came. Photo Ted Koston.

This photo by Frank Serrano shows the interest that many people had in 06. She dominated the tarmac.

At our first air show the signs made by Carol Chamberlain were looked at as much as 06 was. Note the ammo belt on the ammo can, the four holes in the hood for the machine guns, the low profile air intake on the engine to the right and the individual exhaust stacks. The engine to the left shows the bump-outs for the exhaust stacks.

At our first few air shows we displayed one ammo box with a short belt of 50 caliber rounds for the nose machine guns and one 75mm cannon round. Later versions of the cannon shell were much shorter in length for ease of handling inside the confined interiors of the fuselage. Also, the distance from firing point to target was considerably less than a field artillery piece. Note the restored nose landing gear. Photo Ted Koston.

Rain, Rain Go Away
Come Back Another Day

If I were to pick the most rewarding time for me in my association with Weary Warriors Squadron, this weekend in 1988 would have to be the time. I think it saved Weary Warriors. It gave us a glimpse of the future that was getting closer by the day. We all needed the uplift and it renewed our efforts to reach our goal. It certainly tied a lot of unknowns together for me.

Noontime had passed and it looked like the summer thunderstorm could miss us, but black clouds loomed on the horizon. A few Stearmans cranked up, as did some P-51's and a couple of AT-6's, on they're way across the field to Mark's hanger. The storm was going to hit Rockford and the word on the warbird line was that it contained hail. We were concerned but the tug had disappeared, so it appeared we would have to ride it out. We got plastic sheets and tarps and tied them over the glass-less cockpit and the opening for the top turret and waited.

We watched the lighting and listened to the rumbling thunder as the storm advanced across the Illinois prairie. It was getting bigger, it was getting closer, and it was black. We were worried about the wind, as 06 had no brakes. All that would hold her was our new, small, wheel chocks.

Typically, in the Midwest, when cold, heavy air comes in contact with hot light air on a hot summer afternoon, the results could be violent. The coming storm promised to deliver the usual result. The blast of cooler air with the pungent smell of damp air came first and the temperature dropped about twenty degrees instantly —- which was a welcome change. As the black clouds, some four miles wide, came rolling across the airport boundary, we could see the curtain of rain at the base of the black and dark green clouds. We were going to get clobbered. The ammo box and cannon shell went into the fuselage and the three-sided sign was on the cement protruding up into the bomb bay. Ice chest and lawn chairs were stacked on the inside of the main wheels. We were ready.

Preceding the advancing rain and black clouds, dust and stray paper blew in erratic, swirling, confusing directions. The wind was right on the nose of 06, which, if you had to have a big wind, was the place for it to be. We were tempted to join the line of people scurrying for cover, many of whom took refuge in the line of porta-potties behind us.

The first few drops of rain fell and pinged on the skin of 06, a sound that most of us had never heard before. The drops of rain were big, cold, and refreshing. The Great Midwest Heat Wave and Drought of 1988 was about to come to an abrupt end.

We went from sunshine, to gray, to black in a matter of minutes. The storm broke on 06 and Weary Warriors. The rain now fell with a vengeance and we had a full-blown thunderstorm on our hands. Not one Weary Warrior abandoned 06. We grew concerned as, within minutes, the wind was clocked at sixty-three MPH. The rain was now being blown horizontally and we were all taking a beating. I think we all prayed that the wind would stay on her nose.

It did. We had lucked out. Glen suggested we move the front wheel chocks and pair them up with the rear wheel chocks. It was a good idea and two Weary Warriors stood by each wheel in case the chocks, that were meant for show not blow, decided to blow or float away. Two passersby joined us in the bomb bay and Fencel, who had scurried up the rear hatch with the ammo and cannon shell, stayed there. Smart man, that Fencel.

Visibility dropped to a scant two hundred feet but it was good enough to watch the CAF's tent go flying, dragging its poles tables, merchandise, and counters with it. If we'd had a starboard wing attached, it would have all hit our wing.

The faint female cries for help from the porta-potties, which had been blown over on their backsides, drew our attention. We watched the doors opening up that were now pointed straight up and people climbed out into the driving rain. The porta-potties had not been a very smart shelter choice to make. We watched some women struggling to get out and were about to go (with reluctance) and give them a hand when a couple of hero-types helped them out.

The water on the pavement was a good two inches deep and a few lawn chairs went bouncing by when I noticed our ice chest floating away. My camera case was on top of it. Frank made a dive and got the ice chest but the 35mm camera in its leather case continued its wind-blown journey along the current. Jason, Walter's grandson was after it and retrieved the water-soaked camera.

Speaking of soaked, we were all soaked. 06 leaked like a sieve, but we knew she would do that. In World War II, B-25 pilots hated to fly in the rain as they came out of the lightest of showers drenched. All these years in the hanger and the first time we take her out she ends up in the middle of a granddaddy of a thunderstorm. I wondered if she was doing her thing again.

The wind slowed, the black turned to gray and the rain let up. Within minutes we had sun and pleasant weather with blue skies. It was over. Over two inches of rain fell in less than an hour and there had been no hail. The storm had given our B-25 a real good power washing, courtesy of Mother Nature and she had never looked cleaner. She had a pewter-like glow about her.

The airport came alive. There was no real damage, just a lot of huff and puff. The porta-potties were tilted back up on their bottoms and the German troopers retrieved their tent and most everything that went with it. Fencel climbed down the hatch. He was wet. The air show was delayed, but it went on late in the afternoon.

We had survived our first air show day. With our first air show experience under our belt, we all looked forward to Sunday. The Air Force Thunder Birds were going to perform and Mark had mentioned that advanced ticket sales indicated there would be over ten thousand people on hand. We were ready and 06 was ready. With assurance that security would keep an eye on 06, we left her out for the first time. We left with soggy shoes, wet clothes and a camera that would end up in the shop.

The tent that blew away. In the background, the row of porta-potties that were blown over. Frank Serrano.

Lou Fulgaro

Air Show Sunday

When Fencel and I arrived Sunday morning, Walter and Jack were busy talking to individuals that were asking, by now, routine questions. By noontime, 06 was buried in a sea of people and I saw some friends that I had not seen in years. On Sunday, there were eight Weary Warriors present plus Jack. We were all kept busy. Pat brought his kids, Hanson his wife and later his son. Gaden came with his girlfriend and Claude with his wife. Weary Warriors had another positive day. We talked, we laughed and had fun. The air shows volunteers, especially the gals on their golf carts, kept us in a steady supply of cold drinks and hot dogs as the temperature again climbed toward ninety degrees. They treated us like royalty, which was very nice. A lot of Glen's airline pilot buddies showed up and Glen was beaming. I was not sure if he knew how to have fun. I do know he was very proud of our B-25 and the workmanship.

Some of the many pilots who had first looked at 06 years before were now interested; but when they heard the new buy-in amounts for 1988, they just melted away into the crowd. We had no regrets. 06 cost money. It was a very simple fact. From the air show, I had four names in hand and two of them joined us. Macomber joined right away and a pilot a few months later.

Late afternoon came and the crowd dwindled to a few diehards as Fencel went to fetch a tug. We were pleasantly exhausted and tired; not from hard work, just from being outside so long and doing nothing. As we pushed 06 back into the hanger, I had just two regrets: that Tatelman could not make it and Chamberlain did not see the thousands of people who read her posters. Tatelman would have enjoyed talking to all the World War II B-25 pilots that showed up and poked around. He would make our next air show.

I could write a book about our three air shows.

"Three air shows?" you ask.

Yes, we did the same thing in 1989 and 1990. Sorry to say, we were still being towed to the warbird line for both shows, but the people of Rockford got to watch "their" B-25 come together. This was getting embarrassing, already; but each year there was progress and by the 1990 Rockford Air Show, it was a complete, partially painted

B-25 that was presented and we were at the stage of working out the bugs.

Out of some forty-eight photos I took at our first air show, only a few survived the water. As Fencel and I piled into my Sterling for the ride home, Fencel asked if I had seen Dick Lambert. With regrets, I said I had missed one of our founders. Fencel mentioned he looked good. I wondered what he thought of 06.

On the way home Fencel gave me the pitch. He was a good pitchman. Our paint scheme should represent a real B-25 not a Weary Warrior. If we looked authentic we would be invited to more air shows and they would pay our way.

"You're never going to get all those cheapskates we've got to pay for all the gas and oil that thing is going to burn," he said. "We don't have enough people with big bucks to support that gas-guzzler."

Fencel had a point. "What do you have in mind?" I answered.

"You ever heard of R.T. Smith, the Flying Tiger ace?"

Yes, I had.

"Well, he flew a cannon-nose like we have. They were a small outfit that saw combat in Burma. They had about ten cannon-noses. His ship was called BARBIE III and it was very colorful. We could have a real winner. All the crew is still alive."

"Sounds interesting, Jerry. If you want to go that way, you have to convince some people."

"No, all I have to do is convince you. These guys will do anything you say. You can talk them into it."

"I am flexible on this subject, Fencel. I got what I want and that is the cannon-nose, low profile air intakes, and the exhaust stacks. You have to sell what you want. If you want, I will put you on the agenda for our next annual meeting and you can make a presentation."

"Barbie had all the stuff you like. You're the President. How are you going to vote? They will follow you."

"I probably will not vote as I feel the President should vote only to break a tie. My job is to conduct meetings and appoint committees."

"That's a bunch of crap," muttered Fencel.

"Yes I know, but it gets me out of the middle."

What Fencel did not know is that Glen had also approached me, as he wanted a polished aluminum B-25 and wanted it to be VFR equipped. What Glen did not know is that Tatelman had approached me and he wanted a full IFR B-25.

Fencel said, mulling it over, "I suppose Tatelman wants it to be a eight gun-nose and named Dirty Dora."

"No, Jerry. He never brought it up." I wanted to get Fencel off this subject.

We were on the Illinois Tollway, speed limit sixty-five, and, as luck would have it, a sports car went passed us at about ninety. I was at a safe seventy-three. Fencel watched the little car pull away.

"I bet that guy has his foot in the carburetor to pass you like that. You going to let him get away with that?"

The chance to get Fencel off the Barbie subject presented itself.

"How fast does the German JU-52 cruise?" I asked.

"I dunno, about one hundred-ten I guess. Why?"

"I will let you know when we hit its cruise speed." I mashed down on the accelerator and we were on our way. No cops behind us. No overpasses in front of us and the guy in the red sports car was blazing the way for us. I had a safe shot at it.

With the windows rolled down and the sunroof open, the Sterling hunkered down. As we swept past one hundred, the wind was blasting through the sunroof and the open windows with hurricane force. Fencel hung on and did not say a word. One hundred-ten came up and I pointed at the odometer. Conversation was impossible with the windows rolled down and the beat of the tires across the tar strips of the cement roadway was soon lost in the roar of rushing air. At one hundred twenty-three MPH, we flashed past the red sports car and continued on. We were nudging one hundred-thirty and the Sterling was just about wound out. I was rushing up on a gaggle of cars ahead of us and I let the Sterling coast down. I enjoyed the rush of speed. It ended a perfect day, provided a state trooper did not have his radar crosshairs lined up on my spinning wheels.

I looked over at Fencel. His profile reminded me of a boxing prizefighter that has had his day. It was a tough looking profile, ruddy and healthy-looking for his seventy-plus years. It was a little beat-up looking and he did not bother to push his swirling hair from his face. He was silent. I looked again. Yes, he was still alive.

These moments of silence were so rare that moments like this one should be carved in stone. I reflected on the last two days and the short run of speed had matched my enthusiasm. The tires picked up their rhythmic beat on the pavement. I was snug and safe, strapped in my seat and comfortable with myself.

Fencel drove a boat of a car, a 1974 Buick. The few times that I drove it out to Rockford from my house when it was his turn to drive, I was impressed by the size of the hood. It looked like it was eight feet wide. It was so large that, as I looked across the expanse of sheet metal, it reminded me of an aircraft carrier deck. It seemed to fill up the entire width of a traffic lane. Even though it had a big three hundred-horsepower V-8 under the hood, he would not let me drive over 65 MPH.

The silence was short lived.

"Nice car," was his first comment. "Are those real wire spoke wheels?"

I nodded yes.

"Nice leather. Is this car is made in England?"

I nodded again. We crept past those drivers that, I guess, obey speed limits.

"I never have been in a car going that fast. You never struck me as being the type of person that would do such a thing. I can't believe we were going that fast. Do you fly the same way?"

"Yes, I do."

"You're a crazy Italian."

"Yes I am."

"Goddamn it, don't ever do that again! You scared the crap out of me."

"Would you like to do it again?"

"No, damn it! And if you're going to fly the B-25 like that, I am not going to fly with you. You're crazy!"

"I guess so, Jerry."

We approached a tollbooth and Fencel reached in his pocket and came up with the change. This had to be a first.

As we pulled away from the tollbooth he said, "You know, that was fun."

"Well, Jerry, we will just have to do it again some day."

There was no reply.

This was the air show where we let everyone know that 43-4106 was going to fly as Barbie III. Fencel had the color scheme print made up and I contributed the photo that R. T. Smith had given to me. It is just above the Barbie III print. A portion of that photo appears in this book. The air show patrons fell in love with Barbie III.

Lou Fulgaro

Odds and Ends
We Close Out 1988

In September of 1988, with the air show behind us, we are back to our Saturday routine and Macomber has joined us. He fits in nicely with his laidback way of doing things. He is a steady, solid person. He is a refreshing addition to our work force. We talk about paint and we all know that, in a year or so, he will lead the paint team. He is nonchalant about painting 06.

"Just tell me what you want and I will do it."

He pitches in and does everything that is asked of him. We all like him.

Jack Robinson has dusted off two never used but old batteries and charged them up. We all wait and wait.

"Not yet, maybe after lunch."

We came back from our lunch and he was smiling. He announced "we are ready" and he threw some switches and 06 jumped and hummed to life. Glen's instrument panel glowed, fuel boost pumps roared vibrating 06's frame, and electric motors whined. We were getting close. She was looking and acting more like an airplane every day.

Weary Warriors had purchased over four thousand feet of the best copper wire we could get — we would never have considered the much cheaper aluminum wire. I would never attempt to understand the maze of neatly tied bundles of wire that went from switches to bus bars, then to circuit breakers, to boxes of all sizes then to their intended destination. The wires went out, up, down and then came back.

While we all listened to the hum of life, I could not help but admire the hundreds of feet of new aluminum fuel and hydraulic lines that mingled with the new white wires. At this time in our restoration, on the human side, Jack Robinson was the best thing that could have ever happened to us. He was a real find. He never let us down. Thank you, thank you, thank you.

October 20, yes, I know the exact date. Fencel and Walter contact a CEO at an aluminum firm, Fencel tells one of his famous tales and ends up with a piece of round aluminum stock that is about three feet long and five inches thick. It has a two-inch hole bored down the center lengthwise. When I arrive at the hanger, Walter and Fencel are smiling and beaming to the point that they are glowing.

I ask, "What the hell is that?"

Walter places two blocks of wood in the cannon opening in the nose of 06. They both carefully place the aluminum stock in place and voila! We have the muzzle of our 75MM cannon. I am elated. We all are elated. What an idea!

Walter explains that he will have to bore out the hole to the correct size. He will then machine a sleeve from steel to insert into the bore so the cannon has its lands and grooves and the correct twist (we are sure all the "experts" will reach up with their fingers and check for the lands and grooves.) We will have to find a 75MM cannon and take measurements. We figure it will take a trip to the Air Force Museum until someone suggests checking out the local American Legion Posts. Many have this famous artillery piece mounted near their flagpoles.

The bottom half of our cannon-nose looks good with the muzzle of our "cannon" protruding. If you look at it from certain angles, the "cannon" muzzle squares off her receding chin. We leave the "cannon" sitting in the nose until Walter is ready. I have a surprise in the trunk of my car but will keep it there for another day. I did not want to take away from the "cannon". It was not the time for one-upmanship.

One of my best traits is patience: without it, I would have gone berserk with this project. It gets more complicated by the day. One of the things that helped me to keep my sanity was "shopping" for all the neat little goodies that were not essential but dressed up 06. I had three of them in my trunk.

November 5. Yes, this day was also carved in stone in that stuff I got between my ears. It was another benchmark of sorts as it pertained to our restoration. The hydraulics were about one hundred percent in. On a dreary day at 10:00 AM, we were ready to give the gear a try.

Hable was up in the cockpit and Walter, Fencel, Macomber, Robinson and I were in the hanger standing clear. Frank was starting to miss a Saturday here and there and Glen could not make it. I was outside the hanger, poised with camera in hand to record the milestone. Jack would direct as he was the only one that really knew what to do.

Our B-25 was balanced like a Prima Dona on her borrowed three hydraulic jacks. Her presence towered above us. As I waited, I could not help but think she was one mean-looking machine. I would have hated to be on the receiving end of her killing ability.

Robinson instructed Hable to turn on the master switch and things started to happen. Hydraulic pumps to the low side and the whine of electric motors disturbed the quiet of the interior of 06.

"Bomb bay doors first, Pat."

"Clear bomb bay doors" came from the interior.

Robinson replied, "Bomb bay doors clear."

Pat activated the bay door switch and they snapped shut instantly without hesitation. They stayed closed and did not sag open. They were closed and tight.

"Open the doors, Pat."

"Bomb bay doors clear."

"Clear!" and they snapped open locking in the full open position.

We had operating bomb bay doors. It would be a nice feature for flybys at air shows. We were all grinning from ear to ear.

It was now 11:00 p.m. and we wanted to retract the gear before lunch. With the usual "clears" and "switches on", Pat shouted from the cockpit that he had only 600 pounds pressure and we needed a minimum of 800 pounds.

"Try it anyway," Jack replied.

With the usual "clears" and "switches on", the port gear moved about six inches and stopped. It would go no further. Pumping the hydraulic pressure by hand or by motor produced no more than 600 pounds. We had a glitch somewhere.

"Gear down!" yelled Jack and nothing happened. Jack gave it a good shove with his foot and the gear, with a loud metallic sound, locked in the down position.

Somewhere, we had air in the hydraulic lines or a valve was stuck. We bled the lines and what a mess we had with the sticky expensive hydraulic fluid! We still had 600 pounds. She was doing her thing again. I was concerned as Jack was set to leave for the year and it would be nice to have the gear operating before he left. We broke for lunch and some hot chili.

"We will have them up by five," Jack remarked as we pulled away from the hanger.

At lunch, we mulled things over. We enjoyed lunch in the cooler weather as it got us out of the cold, damp hanger and it was a time for relaxed fellowship. The restaurant used to set us up in a corner far away from their normal patrons. The help took turns with us, as we were generous with our tips. The waitresses took all our good-natured, off-colored remarks with ease.

We were back and gave it another try. We were missing something. The floor flowed with hydraulic fluid; bomber blood as Walter called it; and we had the stickiest tools you ever put a hand on. We caught and saved what fluid we could. The time was 5:00 p.m. It was dark and the gear retraction was not to be. Jack advised he would stay another week. The gear would retract by next Saturday or he would stay and work at no charge until it did.

As I drove home that night, Walter's words, "bomber blood", reminded me of our first few months in our hanger. He called it that back then. God, we had come a long way since those days. I also noticed that Walter and Fencel had a falling-out of sorts and I wondered if Fencel hit Walter with the Barbie III concept. Fencel no longer showed up with Walter and during the winter —- he missed a lot of Saturdays. When he did come, it was with me.

November 12 was a sunny Saturday and a little warmer. I was a little late, as I had to wait for Fencel. When we arrived, Jack had a smile on his face and I just knew he had the gear up during the week. He would not admit it.

"Got your camera ready, Lou?" I was poised and, with the usual formalities, watched the gear retract smoothly and, without a sound, tuck itself away. The gear doors swung shut. Then the bomb bay doors slammed shut. Our Mitchell was once again flying six or seven feet above the hanger floor. She was beautiful. She was streamlined and elegant-looking with her gear tucked away. For Walter and me, this was a magnificent day.

"Hey!" Walter yelled, "Did you get some shots off? I saw no flash." In my excitement, I had forgotten to shoot some photos. I stood there feeling stupid.

It had been some seven years almost to the day, give or take a week or two since she did the same thing on Lambert's farm in 1981.

"Okay, let's do it one more time for our day-dreaming leader."

The flash went off once and then the flash stopped working. I checked the batteries. One metal contact was rusty and the other had rusted off from the soaking the camera took at the one air show. So much for getting the camera serviced. I shot the rest of the photos with no flash.

We all sat back in wholesome enjoyment and watched, transfixed, as the gear swung up and down. It was a delight and I wish I had a better command of the English language so I could express the sheer joy of this event.

Pat yelled, "Are we planning on wearing it out before we fly it?"

The batteries were getting low but Jack had one more surprise for all of us. While we stood wingless, we still had the inboard flaps. Robinson went up the forward hatch and mumbled something to Pat and Walter and, to all our surprise; the flaps came down to their full down position and then went back up. What a super day! The heat risers to the carburetors also were now working. While the batteries had just a little juice left, they were back on the charger with just enough juice to slowly spin the starters. Each engine, with unconnected old spark plugs loose in their holes, were slowly spun so all cylinders went through their cycles. Then the batteries gave out. We also had brakes.

Robinson advised the hydraulics were now one hundred percent complete and one hundred percent operational. The wiring was re-estimated at eighty percent installed and cabling at seventy five percent. In three to five more months, we should be ready.

Annddd- while all of us were now in a good mood, he had a delay in his next job start date and he could stay until December 9 before he headed south for the winter. We had just enough in the checking account to extend his pay. We would then again be broke. We had one winter to put together some sixty thousand dollars for our next spring, summer, and fall, assault on 06.

The following Saturday, it was time for my surprises that had lain in the trunk of my car for weeks. The first was the turret collar roller ring, a hard-to-find circular ring that the top turret rolled on. It had a flat flange bottom and vertical sides, not the easiest thing to form into a circle. It would need a little work.

Next I had two of the same. I brought just one out and gently laid the heavy steel object on the wing that we used as a workbench. I would guess it weighed about twenty pounds was small about ten inches long maybe seven inches high. The flat topside of heavy steel sloped from the front upward toward the rear. No one could guess what it was. I brought out the second one and laid it alongside the first. Nothing.

"Glen, your "G" did not have these but our "H" did

Glen studied them and I positioned them, as they would be mounted.

"Bullet deflectors," uttered Glen. "They're bullet deflectors without the fairings!"

Glen was right. They were mounted just aft of the top turret machine gun muzzles so the turret gunner could not accidentally send a volley of 50 caliber slugs into the back of the tail gunners head. On Glen's "G" model, the turret was mounted further aft and did not have a tail gunner. We would eventually mount them but never did find the fairings for them. Glen talked about some day hammering out some fairings; but, naked, they fit the mean look of 06 and we just left them as is.

We had a winter to catch up on a lot of odds and ends and once again get ready for Robinson. This winter, I started skipping a Saturday here and there. It was so cold that many others did the same. It could be that we had stopped giving shares of 06 a few years earlier for hours worked or we were just cold and tired. Those of us that labored on 06 just had to get away for a while. A few of us needed a break.

The aluminum stock that would some day become our cannon. Wild, Tatleman and Robinson.

The bomb bay doors swing close during our early testing. Note the tree patches on the bay doors and two on the fuselage bottom. The large patch on the bay doors is where the "fourth" wheel protruded.

Top: Early gear retraction test. Flag is to warn visitors away from the sharp corner of the gear well door. Bottom: A small sample of the new plumbing in the fuselage.

Pompous, Arrogant;
I Don't Think So

With our annual meeting in March 1989, this chapter may stray away from our progress with 06 for a few pages. A few pilot types would join us and we get no real workers out of the new members. But that is okay — our checkbook would be, once again, way up in the black and we would be ready for Robinson.

At the annual meeting required by Illinois law, I am once again elected to lead this great bunch of guys and one gal for no other reason than that no one else wants to do it. They either want to work on 06 or pilot 06. Other than how we spend our money, some lose interest quickly.

This evening, everyone showed up as, on the announcement of the annual meeting, I had placed an agenda of what would be discussed; where to base 06, her paint scheme, her name and her instrumentation. There was some talk about basing her in Florida for the winter. Whether or not to install the bottom half of the turret was a big nut to crack. With our growing number of members, we would need room. Should we install small jump seats behind the pilots and co-pilots seats? Notice I said, "discuss." We did not have to make any decisions, as it was a little early for decision-making time, but all our members had to get used to the idea that there were growing differences of opinion.

The meeting started at 7:10pm in the conference room of my office. It would adjourn at 11:40pm and there were a lot of words in between. As I called the meeting to order, I could not help but think if I blew it tonight, the last item on the agenda was the election and these people would not hesitate to throw me out. There was a lot of money involved. Some members were shy and retiring and some plain aggressive and loud. I would look out for the shy ones.

They were all mature and well mannered. We had to get these items discussed and, unpleasant as it may be, it was time and it was not going to be easy. Looking out at the members, I could see that most were leaders and not followers. This would complicate things. A lot of them were used to doing things their way and only their way. If they were dumb, one could sweet-talk them but this was not the place for a snow job. They were intelligent and fast-thinking individuals and to lead them all in the same direction at the same time would be a task in leadership. We were all in the same choir, so to speak, but not on the same page. The interesting mix of people was, in most part, civil and polite; whoever had the floor would not be interrupted. We always respected the other's input, let him have his say and then, in turn, responded. Once we had beaten a subject to death, we moved on to the next subject, related by a small link called a B-25. It was still there and all ours.

One hour; two hours; three hours; we took a short break. The members broke into small clusters during the break with think-alikes in each group. I was sure it would be give-and-take the next hour. Back at the table, I advised each member they would have three minutes to discuss whatever subject had been discussed. As Walter was the senior member, he led off the discussion.

Walter said that the membership knew we were going to name 06 Weary Warrior, the color scheme, the decision to mount the cannon-nose and so on; but he also thought that those decisions had been made by three of us a long time ago and that it was, perhaps, not fair to the rest of the members. He liked the idea of Barbie III and could live with it. He also could live with polished aluminum but he was not going to polish it. He suggested that we leave the seat and pedestal of the turret out, as we would need the room; but install the bubble.

Tatelman said, "Let 'Dirty Dora' go, but let's keep the eight-gun nose in case we ever want to modify our configuration. The only reason I would like an IFR (instrument flight rules) ship is so, after an air show, we do not get stuck someplace for days. I am too old to wait out days of bad weather in some small hotel room, waiting for the weather to clear up. Some of you mentioned the expense, which could reach $25,000. I will purchase the equipment and pay for the installation. The IFR package will be mine and, if we sell the B-25, I will remove the IFR package."

Tatelman concluded by saying that he would not vote on this subject and would let the rest of the membership make the decision. What a gentleman.

Glen took a pass on his bare aluminum and VFR (visual flight rules) desires. He did remind us that he had joined under certain understandings. He also would not vote and would let others make the decisions. Glen was hurt inside.

We worked our way around the table and many did not want to comment any further. What had to be said was said. To end on a high note, I advised all that Aero Traders were going to make up a few top turrets. They would be delivered primed and with glass. The price would be at least $4,000 and it would take about a year and a half. It would cost a couple of thousand up front. All agreed. That is how it went to adjournment time.

We all opted to settle the questions once and for all. The BARBIE III scheme got the nod and we decided to try the jump seats. The turret seat and pedestal would be left out and Barbie would go to Florida for the winter months. If Tatelman wanted to pay for the IFR package, that was fine but we would have to hide some of the new electronics in 1943 radio and navigation boxes. There would be no tinted glass in the cockpit and we would keep the eight-gun nose, just in case.

Some three months later, at the July 1989 Rockford Air Show, we let the world know 06 was going to fly as "BARBIE III", in honor of the mount of R.T. Smith, the Flying Tiger Ace. Fencel paid to have a beautiful full-color poster made up that we displayed at the '89 show on its own stand next to Chamberlain's posters. The show patrons fell in love with "BARBIE III".

When Smith heard about us, he tracked me down from California. He and his crew were thrilled. From R.T. Smith, I received the famous photo of him and his crew standing alongside their mount when they were flying combat in Burma. We had the photo professionally matted, and mounted. We attached it to Fencel's poster.

For me, the contact started an ongoing letter and phone relationship with Smith that lasted for years.

"Lou, did you know that she flew without a co-pilot's seat? We had twelve ships and none of them had the seats."

"You're kidding."

"Are you going to have one or two seats?"

"Two seats and you're going to sit in one of them."

"You're going to take me for a ride?"

"No, you're going to take me for a ride."

"Hell, Lou, I don't think I can climb up into that piece of iron anymore." "You let us worry about that. We will get you up the hatch."

"I have a question for you. The photo you sent me looks like BARBIE was OD all over. Some of artist's renderings show her with a gray bottom. Which was it?"

"Hell, Lou, I don't remember. I will have my crew chief give you a call. I just kicked a tire and drove her around and hoped everything worked."

BARBIE III helped us maintain a positive self-image and was the source of pride for all of us. It provided the avenue for many of us to leave the fragmented, frustrating, mind-boggling, technical world we lived in. We would submerge ourselves in a simple, straightforward world of nuts and bolts. Our task was uncluttered, with very little pressure, no hurry and now in a phase where we had the ability to see and touch our project going from a fantasy to a dream to reality. Out of thousands of hours of labor, at times under miserable conditions, coupled with hundreds of thousands of dollars, our B-25 emerged.

Our efforts had produced, in gleaming metal, a prize beyond comparison. Our combination of unselfish participation and generous, but costly, contributions was paying off in self-pride that could not be measured. We were indeed a unique consortium of individuals, accomplishing as a group what none of us could achieve as individuals.

It quietly crept up on us and we did not realize it until the '89 Annual Meeting. We had, without knowing or realizing it, crossed an invisible line. We had sacrificed, worked hard and long and found solutions to problems that would have taxed the best minds. We had given up much to bring BARBIE III, our very own warbird, to where she was today. Many warbird lovers were not willing to do that. They were not willing to work and sacrifice and were too lazy to find solutions. They would rather go on vacations, buy that new van, sleep in on a cold Saturday: they would rather buy a carton of cigarettes than a carton of nuts and bolts.

We began to resent those who would come to share, to touch, and to sit in BARBIE III. We did not like those who came to be in her comfort zone and thrill to her touch and were not willing to put themselves through what so many of us had put ourselves through.

They did not go out and get a small personal loan like one of our members did so he could join. They would not get up at 5:30am on a cold February morning like Walter did or rivet ice-cold metal like Glen and Frank did. They would not neglect a business like Mike did or rent a truck like Tatelman did and on and on. We labored on those cold days, cutting our skin on jagged pieces of metal. We were so numb from cold that we did not realize it until we saw the rusty colored droplets of blood on the bare aluminum. We wondered at not knowing we were bleeding.

We did not want to share; we had worked too hard and for too long. There were too many that wanted a free ride, a free touch. There were too many who opted to watch their interest grow in a savings account than spend fifty-five dollars for a generator brush. We were getting protective and clannish; we did not want to entertain those who would not entertain themselves. "BARBIE III" was ours and we did not want to share her. Stuck up, pompous, arrogant; I don't think so. Maybe it just appeared that way. At times we were just too busy to take the time to be nice.

On the other hand, there were many that visited us who we thought were arrogant, pompous, and impolite.

It was not just one-sided. They smoked in the hanger and in the cockpit, dropping their ashes and crudding up the cockpit with a film of tobacco smoke. They arrived with coffee in hand and sloshed it all over the place. They did not have to clean it up — we did. They stomped up and down hatches with hard-soled shoes, dragging belt buckles and keys across our precious paint, let their children have the run of the place and, in general, did things that none of us would do. We had too much money and time invested to ignore infractions of common courtesy. It was easy for us to understand why many warbird owners were perceived as arrogant. To be friendly was to invite unintentional abuse to your warbird.

There was only one place we would welcome such people and that was at any air show. We came prepared mentally to receive the novice and the curious. We would shepherd them around as well as we could and let them touch our prize. In spite of these efforts, I can't tell you how many crumpled-up paper cups we found up in our wheel wells, or how many teenagers pushed Popsicle sticks into those neat vent pipes that protrude from the rear of the nacelles. They really had to reach to accomplish this little trick. Then there was the six year-old doing chin-ups on a fragile gear door-actuating arm and the youngster dropping pebbles into the openings of our wheel rim while the parents watched. The chewing gum stuck in the weirdest places and hot dog wrappers tucked away in our bomb bay always provided nice touches. One teenager used the oil cooler intakes on the leading edge of a wing as a place to practice his graceful hoop shots, using a crumpled-up piece of paper as a basketball. He did have good form but it was the same mentality as the litterbugs that abused our roadways.

At an air show, we tolerated that, but it was not okay in our hanger

Wing and a Tail

In early spring, 1989, we all decided it was time to hang a wing. Once again, I approached Mark Clark, this time for the use of his hand crane.

"Are you planning on attending the '89 air show?" he asks.

Yes, I tell him, we are.

"Good," he says, "it will be in July this year."

Walter retrieves the crane and, once again, hauls the crane over to our place. It takes all day to tack the wing on. As we work at hanging the wing, we talk about a bigger hanger.

Walter and Frank had worked out a method to get the tail through our hanger door opening, which was tall but not tall enough. When he and Frank threw a strap over the tail of the fuselage and pulled downward, the nose came up about eighteen inches. While Frank held the strap, Walter placed a block of wood alongside the nose strut between the stationary and sliding strut flanges. The nose stayed up, the tail was down and the tail could now pass under the beam of our hanger door. Glen and I did not like the idea, as the "what-ifs" were very obvious, especially if the tail was under the door beam.

What we needed was a bigger hanger. I put the word out and made some inquires. Mark Clark gave me a call. He knew of a hanger just across from him. The hanger was large, could hold at least four B-25s and the landlord was looking for a mechanically inclined tenant who could keep the large hanger doors operating. They were old and needed constant attention. The landlord had heard of us and yes, he thinks we could be just what he is looking for. We check out the hanger and, in its day, it must have been a palace. The landlord asked if we could also work over the toilets and keep the floor drains open? Yes we could. We could not beat the price.

Macomber, of all things, knows the guy who installed the doors and, for years, maintained them. He comes and takes a look. He proposes taking the best from four doors and working the hanger with just two automatic doors. We talk to the landlord and propose using two of the doors as a wall where we will set up shop. Other aircraft can work around us. He buys the deal and we invest a few hundred dollars with Macomber's doorman —- along with a promise of a ride in Barbie.

We do a lot of the mule work. We set up the two bad doors so they can be operated by a system called arm strong power. Walter and I work over the toilets with new gaskets and so forth. We won't worry about the heat. If and when the landlord gets tenants we will have to watch our tools and start locking them up. Tatelman is overjoyed that we are moving. The new hanger is like the Queen Mary compared to a river garbage scow. The tail is ready and will be on its way. We silently promise ourselves that the tail will be on as will the wings complete with wing tips. We all commit to the goal that, at the '89 show, the people of Rockford will see progress and more or less a complete aircraft.

Robinson arrives and goes back to work. As we approach June, the big moving day arrives. We rent a truck and borrow a tug. One of the first things to go into the truck is the starboard wing. It takes a lot of beef to lift it. We are all once again pressed to the limit. Walter will take Barbie across the airport by tug and the rest of us will go around the airport by truck and car. We will have to work just as hard to unload the wing and place it on its cradle.

We all watch Barbie trundle off. She looks wrong with only one wing mounted, no props, and no tail. We all meet at the new hanger and tuck her into her new home.

Mark applauds from across the ramp. "Welcome to the up scale side of the airport."

We spend all day moving all that we have accumulated over six years. It is a long day and Robinson works the hardest. Late that afternoon, I notice that some of the "skilled" Weary Warriors are on Barbie, doing their things. The rest of us are still doing the grunt work, hauling and settling junk. At the end of the day, as President, I get the privilege of sweeping out our old hanger with my broom and my shovel and load up my garbage can. Walter helps. It was a good day and we all worked hard. The new hanger seemed to give every one a good shot of happiness.

As we took a last look at our dingy old hanger, I remarked to Walter that it was such a dudgeon of a place that I don't know how we lasted as long as we did.

"The Mitchell kept us going, Lou and we were determined to beat the museum. You and I started here and it is fitting that you and I be the ones to end it here."

"You're right, Walter. I started here cleaning the floor and I ended here cleaning the floor. That doesn't sound so good."

"Yeah, kid; but a lot has happened in between."

I had to know and now was the time to ask.

"Walter, what do you think of BARBIE III paint scheme?"

"I like it Lou. I would have liked to have seen our serial number on her but she's going to be nice."

To end an era that few cared about anymore, Walter took the photo of the museum President off the wall and wiped an oily spot on the floor with the museum tee shirt. The photo and the tee shirt are the last to go into the garbage can.

"Always wanted to do that, Lou."

Tim cruised by in his jeep, shouted to take care and wished us luck. Little did we know that, a month later, Tim would have a catastrophic fire in his row of storage hangers. Many warbirds and hundreds of thousands of dollars in parts and equipment were melted. Tim was specializing in rebuilding Sea Furies. Both of his jeeps were lost. We saw very little of him after that. He just seemed to disappear.

New hanger keys for everyone.

June was a fabulous month. Warm weather and our new hanger was incredible pleasant to work in. Glen showed up during the week as did Macomber and Frank. Glen completed the work on the bow strip of our windshield and Walter, Glen and I spent frustrating hours installing the new "glass" along with the eyebrow glass. We must have passed the windshield up and down over a hundred times to try and fit it. Cut this, grind here, and file there, over and over again. The problem was that the glass was not only too big overall it was too thick to fit under the trim securing strips. With the glass being too thick, the mounting screws for the trim straps were too short.

The eyebrow glass fit where the windshield went from the vertical and rounded off to the horizontal. Many B-25s fly today with that piece tinted. Tatelman advised that we would regret not having it tinted as the sun will just burn us up. We laughed at his remark and advised him to wear a baseball cap. As always, he graciously backed away from a subject we were not to keen on. This was very considerate of him as Tatelman was now the biggest shareholder of

Barbie and he could certainly get his way if he pushed anything. He was also named our chief pilot: Glen would become our senior pilot. Glen was a little hurt by this but he was also a man with great character and went with the program. The closer we got to flight, the more Tatelman and Hanson would influence our decisions.

I had picked up a new, never installed top escape hatch for the cockpit and, once again, Glen made it fit perfectly —- it operated flawlessly. Walter and I installed all the side glass: I showed up one day and all the top glass was in. Tatelman's tail arrived and it was like new.

Hable took on the tail as Walter and I finished off bolting on the port wing. Each and every bolt had to be torqued. Walter worked the top of the wing with the torque wrench and I the bottom of the wing. The leading edge and trailing edge of the wing were hard to get to and we spent many frustrating hours working the wing nuts and bolts in these locations. Once the port wing was secured, Glen gave us the okay and we mounted the starboard wing.

The '89 show was a few weeks off and more and more Weary Warriors showed up to finish off the details. We were excited about this show. Barbie was going to look like a B-25.

I talked to Tatelman to try to give him a good lesson in mellowing out. He had to learn how to enjoy people and share his B-25 with appreciative show patrons.

"You can't hide in the middle of your citrus grove the rest of your life, working in your shop and only come out as the chief honcho at your Air Force reunions or when you go to the bank. Forget about your damn lettuce and carrot diet and come up and eat good old-fashioned, artery clogging Chicago hot dogs and drink ice-cold chemical lemonade with the rest of us peons. Don't you want to see your tail mounted and look over Barbie? Come on up and get your nose sunburned with the rest of us. Most of these guys are going to be your crew and they don't really know you and you don't know them."

I would pick him up at O'Hare and he would stay at our home. My wife and I turned over our master bedroom to him for his stay.

Robinson did his thing with wires and cables and spent a lot of time with Pat getting the tail rigged. I mentioned it would be nice to have the wing tips installed but there were things to do and we were nowhere near ready to install the wing tips.

"Can't we just tack on the tips like we did our one wing when we brought her over to our new hanger?" I said one Saturday. "Three screws on the top and three on the bottom. Just enough to hold them in place. We still have to sell our B-25. We need pilots and their big buy-in checks. Come on, guys, let's do it."

The wing tips were tacked on the day before the show. Much to my joy and future well-being —- and with no prodding from me whatsoever —- everyone pitches in and cleans up and wipes down Barbie. Each in his own way was proud of her. There was no doubt who she was and where she was going. Under the dust and very little grime, the luster from the previous year's nature-induced power washing still gave her aluminum a pewter-like glow. As Walter manned the tug and took her away across the airport we all admired her. I wondered how she might look if we kept her in bare aluminum like Glen wanted.

Since our 1991 annual meeting, we had found out "H" models did indeed ply the war in the Pacific with no paint. In fact, most did not have paint. Tatelman had produced an intelligence photo that showed a bare aluminum "H" beating up a Japanese airfield on some remote, unnamed island. The "H" was photographed from above while flying a few hundred feet above the ground. Those who wanted 06 painted insisted no "Hs" flew in combat in bare aluminum. It was a strong point in their favor and the keystone of their argument. They were wrong and Glen won a moral victory. He was right. He had done his homework but was too much of a gentleman to push the point. Like Walter, he could live with Barbie. I sent Tatelman's photo off to Dave Graham of Fly Past and he published it, asking if anyone could identify the photo and tell us about it. There were no replies.

Tatelman enjoyed the air show and was so hyped up that we damn near had to sit on him to hold him down. He was everywhere and he made sure that every kid that wanted to got to step up the forward hatch. He ate hot dogs and drank lemonade. When I dropped him off at O'Hare, he thanked me for the best few days he ever had. I had often thought his primary interest was to just pilot Barbie and take her to his yearly Air Force reunions. This weekend, a new dimension of Tatelman's involvement had been added.

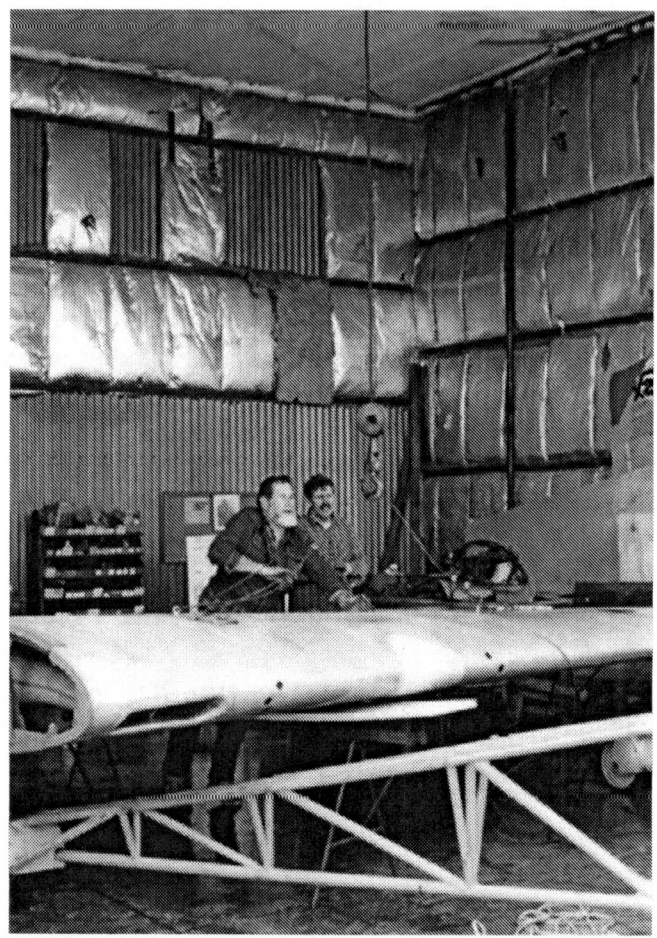

Jerry Macomber and pat Habel rig the outer wing minus the wing tip in preparation to hoisting. The wing not only had to be raised to the proper height but also turned to mate with its attachment points. Once again we had to borrow a crane.

With Wild working the hand crane, Hanson looks on as Habel guides the wing into place.

Tacking the wing in place. Hanson, Habel, Wild and Macomber. The oil cooler inlet is just above Habel and in front of Hanson. The openings above Wild and Macomber are inspection stations with the inspection covers off. The white elliptical object at the top of the photo is the protective covering on the landing light.

Our first move and Jack Robinson contemplates the heavy starboard wing and how to get it out of the rental truck. We got it out the same way we got it in and that was muscle power.

06 was backed into her new hanger with one wing tacked on and looking lopsided. The two openings in the nose above the four machine gun openings are for the hood latch access.

Tatelman at work in his home shop, makes some final adjustments on the vertical stabilizer. Tatelman is extremely neat and orderly and his work reflected this.

Once again with a borrowed crane we hoist the horizontal and vertical stabilizers into position. The elevators and rudder have not been attached. At this time we were getting to be experts at working the hand crank crane. Photo Frank Serrano.

The twenty-three foot long horizontal stabilizer has been safely tacked to the fuselage. Habel poses on the borrowed work stand and wants to know why I was so worried that we would drop the "thing." Photo Frank Serrano.

Habel at work on the tail attaching rudder and rudder trim cables. Note that the rudder has been attached and the front tip of the eight-gun nose in the background.

The fire at Tim McCarter's hanger complex destroyed many aircraft. Shown are his two jeeps. The fire gutted the interiors of the hangers and the temperature was so high that aircraft actually melted.

Who? We Grow

A Change in Plans

"What's that name again?" I was on the phone with one of my favorite people beside Tatelman and Walter. R.T. Smith was barking some words over a static-filled phone line from California. "Enloe. Doctor Cortez Enloe. He was our flight surgeon over in Burma. He wants to come out to your place and meet you guys, see the ship, shoot some photos, and give us a report at our next reunion. Can you help him?"

"Certainly, give me his number and consider it done."

I waited at the train station in my hometown of Downers Grove Illinois and was anxious to meet Doctor Enloe. He was coming from Maryland and would stay in Chicago. With several phone calls to each other under our belts, we found each other mutually intriguing. He had always wanted to ride the Burlington Railroad and the local run from Chicago would be just fine. When the train arrived many people got off and there, with his original leather flight jacket and his officer's cap complete with insignia, was Enloe.

He was a dignified, loveable character with an Eastern accent and was intelligent beyond belief. He started asking questions about cruise performance, range at different altitudes, etc.

He fell in love with Barbie and must have shot two rolls of film of her from every angle. On the way back from our visit, I was so intrigued by this man that I drove him back to his hotel in Chicago instead of letting him take the train.

As we became close friends over the next few years, it came about that he was putting together a manuscript about the death of Major General Orde Wingate.

"You know, Lou, he died in a B-25 crash and I, as flight surgeon, was involved in the body removal at the crash site. Today I have a lot of questions about it. He always carried a rifle with him and some people speculate that he committed suicide and took the B-25 crew and his aides with him. We could never figure out where he was going that day. The crash site and the route of flight were between nothing."

"Gee whiz, Doc, I cannot imagine a general going somewhere and nobody knowing where he was going."

"Lou, we were a weird bunch of officers back in those days. They took a lot of people that did not fit in and we ended up in Burma out of the brass' hair. Lou, what does the term "British Cruise Rules" mean?"

"It has to do with fuel, Doc. Fuel was a commodity that was hard to come by —- it all had to come by boat. To save on fuel consumption, the British set up mandatory cruise settings that saved fuel. They went so far as to set climb power settings."

"We had the same problems Lou. Most of our fuel came by air and in drums. Do you know those settings?"

"I just happen to have something that is titled 'Pilot's Notes by Order of the Air Council', which was part of the Air Ministry. Got a minute, it's your dime."

"Okay Doc, just the highlights. I will send you a copy. Here we go."

I summarized from the booklet. "Climb in, weak mixture 29.5 inches of manifold pressure and 2100 rpm at an indicated speed of 150 MPH. If the boost drops to 23.5 inches, put the super charger to the high side. Out bound, 29.5 inches and the rpm set to maintain 175 MPH. Coming home, rpm to maintain 160 MPH. The higher speed outbound is because they're loaded up with munitions and fuel. Once weapon stores and fuel are consumed, you can fly slower as you are lighter."

"What is the fuel consumption at those settings Lou?"

"29/21 according to the British is 183 gallons an hour up to 10,000 feet. 188 gallons at 15,000 feet. The problem, Doc is you don't know the weight of the ship and the rpm settings to maintain that speed. For an example, full rich and 38 inches and 2400 rpm, she will suck up 336 gallons an hour. With 31.5 inches and 2100 rpm it drops to 250 gallons an hour. So you can see the variance. But if the rules were followed, I would use 185 gallons an hour. We will cruise Barbie at 120 gallons an hour and when we want to show off it will be about 160 gallons an hour. We'll get a good turn of speed because we are very light. You can squeeze every drop at 20 inches and 1700 rpm and consumption is only 88 gallons an hour."

"Lou, I am thinking of mounting an expedition to go back to Burma and locate the crash site. Would you like to go? I will need someone that knows the B-25 and has investigative skills like you have. Someone who can tell me things like is there any fuel? Are switches on or off? Power settings —-things like that. Are you interested?"

"Yes I am and I will pay my own way."

"The problem back then, Lou, was that the investigation was more of a body removal and confirmation of death than a crash site investigation. I will keep in touch. We cannot go now because of government politics."

Old Doc Enloe really turned me on to his cause but it was back to my own project in Rockford.

We would also move a second time. In a nice hanger and looking like a B-25 (although still unpainted) Barbie was an easy sell now. In fact, she sold herself. All I had to do was unlock the hanger door.

Between 1989 and 1990, we had attracted within a few months, some pilots and the money that went with them. One was named Jim Porter. We set up a meeting at his posh country club about mid morning. Over a cup of coffee we shared our mutual love of flight and his growing interest in Barbie. We both talked and we both listened. If I recall he was a stockbroker of sorts, a pilot, and he dropped a very nice size check. Chad Koppie, an airline pilot who owned a stagger-winged Beech, came along and also dropped a check. A fellow by the name of Hracek, who, of all things, was a private detective like me, owned and flew a light twin joined.

There were a few others that came along but their duration with us, for one reason or another (anything from divorce, to bad times, to "my wife found out"), were not around for long. Weary Warriors, Inc. would buy them out, in a sense, giving them their money back. We more or less kept our original target of fifteen active, dues-paying members. We always had a nice balance of pilots who, in most part, did not do a lot of grunt work but put their talents to work creating and standardizing flight operation procedures specifically for Barbie as she neared her operational flight time.

Doctor Cortez Enloe, Flight Surgeon for the 1st Air Commandos Burma 1944, dropped in for a visit and caressed our cannon. I was really impressed with this grand individual. One of the most intelligent persons I ever met. Above his World War II officers cap complete with insignia is the nose jacking point. Over the authors left shoulder is the cannon muzzle compartment vent to release gasses when the cannon was fired. Note the patch on the fuselage side.

Clear The Props

October 1990. Jack was again talking about heading south and brought to my attention that we soon would have to find a mechanic that had a certification as aircraft inspector. Some referred to them as A.I.'s. Jack's work was about done and it would help in the aircraft certification process, as the FAA would, as a rule, go along with the ultimate designation of mechanics. He should be knowledgeable in the certification process and paperwork that goes with it. The FAA would simply come out give her a visual once-over, listen to the engines run, see that the props cycled correctly, watch the gear go up and down, see that controls moved in the right direction and take the A.I.'s word on the weight and balance calculations and just about everything else.

There were a lot of small glitches that had to be worked out and tests that had to be completed. I got Jack off to the side and we talked about the feasibility of an engine run-up before he was gone for good. Jack was not going to come back. This made some of our members happy as they thought strongly that he was milking us while others thought he was God's gift. No matter. Jack solved the problem and we would not have to resolve it. He could have the engines running in two weeks, but the problem was the prop overhauls.

We could not run the engines without the props mounted and the props would not be ready on time, due to the illness of the owner of the prop overhaul facility were the props were stored. The estimates had gone from, "You'll have them in three weeks" to three months. I was stalled so many times in my endeavors to bring key components together at a predetermined time, that no amount of prior planning would make things happen on schedule. There were so many in the warbird support field that was just not good business people. The prop overhaul was costing nine thousand dollars. You would think they would want to get the overhaul completed and the advisory satisfied and collect their money.

Robinson mentioned that Mark Clark had two prop assemblies from a B-26 hanging on the wall of his hanger that would do nicely (yes, Mark, we will be at the 90 air show). I got Jack off the airframe and on the engines. Glen went along with the program. We got the word out that we were targeting October 27th for an engine run-up. It took Jack a day to get the props and another day to hang them. We needed fifty-six spark plugs and, at they were now $12.50 each that came up to a $700 price tag. I advised Jack to use our old ones and clean them up as best he could.

We directed Jack's efforts to the engines and now nailed down a Saturday afternoon in October. Fencel was out and about looking for a drum of engine oil at the best price possible to be delivered to our hanger. Jack advised that fifty-five gallons divided between the two engines would be enough to run them on the ground.

Insurance now became a prime concern of the Weary Warriors board. We needed liability insurance and it became a major concern to have one million dollars in insurance. The board was open to litigation if we were negligent and something happened. Each Weary Warrior member was assessed four hundred dollars to start an insurance fund for ground and taxi insurance now and flight insurance later. As expected, only four of us came up with the money but it was enough to pay the thousand-dollar premium.

I guess Fencel was right when he said, "You're going to have problems getting money out of those cheapskates."

October 27th was an overcast day and cold prevailed. With an insurance binder in hand and a cold Tatelman up from Florida, we were about there. Walter was up on the tug and, with our trusty tow bar hooked up; Barbie angled toward the hanger door. Her new tires made squeaky sounds as they made their way over the painted cement floor. We had measured the hanger door opening when we towed her to the air show and she would fit through with ease. With two wing walkers, Barbie eased through the hanger doors, this time with props. If you looked closely, you could see that the props were in the full-feathered position. Most did not notice that the positioning of the prop blades was wrong for a startup.

We set her up facing into the wind, borrowed some large wheel chocks, and put the parking brakes on. After a short wait, the fuel truck arrived along with the fire truck we had asked to be on hand just in case. Everyone had a camera, a video camera or sound recording equipment. The airport police showed up just to see what was happening.

Some Weary Warriors noticed that the pilot's side of the windshield and the eyebrow glass had been removed. Those of us that had worked on the glass did not like the end result, had dismantled it and then ran out of time. Barbie would have been more photogenic today with all her glass in but it was not to be.

With Walter up on the wing supervising the fueling and Tatelman watching Walter and Fencel watching both of them, Barbie swallowed up two hundred gallons of gasoline. At $2.47 cents a gallon, we got acquainted with the expense of fuel. Down deep, we all waited for the fuel to come running out from somewhere but, happily, none did —- not a drop anywhere. She was dry and free of gas fumes. With all the fuel pipe and hose connections, this was truly amazing. Thank you, Jack Robinson.

Tatelman was in the left seat and was the only current-rated pilot we had for our B-25. Anybody, even a non-pilot (like a mechanic) can run an airplane on the ground but it was nice to have a rated pilot in the left seat. It was a way for us to thank Tatelman who now owned the biggest individual piece of Barbie. Jack would join him in the cockpit and would orchestrate the first startup.

Because we were not sure what was going to happen and when it was to happen, the rest of us were on the outside looking in, so to speak. Jack did not want the narrow short flight deck of the cockpit crowded with gawkers. This smoked some Weary Warriors butts but Jack was right. For this show and tell, he was the boss and it would be his way.

The starboard engine would go first. This was normal start up procedure for a twin-engine aircraft. Since the pilot in command (PIC) sits in the left seat and really cannot see the starboard engine, he must rely on sound to "read" the engine during start up. Once this engine is on line, in our case with the related roar, he then has to visually check the port engine during the start up. Also most twin-engine aircraft that have only one generator always had the generator on the starboard engine to help the batteries get the remaining engine started. Barbie had two generators but still the generator on the port engine does nothing until that engine is running.

We had our fingers crossed. The starboard engine was now our old port engine and it had not run a lick since her first week at the museum in 1981, about eight years before. When Jack built up our one engine from the scrap pile, the built up engine was on the engine stand. To free up some working room on the stacked engine side of Barbie, it was mounted on the port side.

The time had come. Some of us had our fingers crossed. Jack was the only confident one. The borrowed auxiliary power unit was on line. I could not help but think that we were always borrowing support equipment and we owed a lot of people. Someday it would be payback time for us.

From the cockpit, someone shouted, "Clear the props!" and the prop swung to life. We waited and counted prop blades as they passed a fixed point. Now —- do it now! From the start position turn the mag switch to on position to send the hot jolt of electricity to the correct spark plug at the correct time. So much could go wrong!

"Come on Barbie. Do your thing," I whispered to myself. We had a lot of Weary Warriors present today plus a potential pilot member with a thirty thousand-dollar check in his pocket. He would join us once both engines showed the gift of life.

Catch! The exhaust stacks cracked to life sent their sharp message of thunder and the engine spun and fell silent. Robinson was leaning over the copilot's seat looking out the copilots window watching every sign, every subtle message the -29 was sending.

Catch again then, with blurred spinning prop blades, fall silent.

"Come on! Get going!" I heard Tatelman talking to Barbie.

Walter glanced at me and we both crossed our fingers. We had close to three hundred thousand dollars invested in her at this time and this was not the time for her to do this. She wanted to run but could not get the hang of it. The optimists among us were beginning to wonder and the pessimists were growing more confident by the second.

She was close. The staccato bark of her exhaust lasted a little longer each time and the -29 would roar to life run a few seconds, hesitate, deciding whether she liked this new experience, and then fall silent. After many tries, belching dense clouds of white smoke, the -29 decided to give life a try.

I heaved a sigh of relief. She was running, actually running. The fire-breathing mass of swirling, pounding steel called a Wright Cyclone R-2600-29 roared to life and said hello to all of us. They kept the starboard engine at what I would call a fast idle and turned their attention to our port engine. I would soon realize the starboard engine start up was a piece of cake compared to the port engine's try at life.

With deep, convulsive coughs from the very heart of the -29, Barbie attempted to coax her port engine to life. The shaking, twisting engine appeared to be trying to tear itself from the engine mounts. It would catch; roar to life belching heavy clouds of deep blue smoke from her exhaust stacks and, with an airframe-jolting shudder, come to an abrupt stop.

Silence. The seconds passed and seem like minutes. We all watched, waited, and wondered. The two in the cockpit would get squared away, the prop jerked to life and the process would start again. Tatelman was counting blades again as the prop blades arced past the cockpit window. To hold our attention, there would be interludes of magnificent, jagged sheets of flame exploding from the exhaust stacks and the air intake scoop.

Wait! The flame coming out the intake scoop during her spectacular backfires was a different red! The flame would be sucked back into the scoop in the blink of an eye as the engine continued to run. There it was again—-the red, just a flash. The third time we saw it for sure. It was a red mechanic's rag being spit completely out, then being sucked completely back in. The -29 had an obstruction in her throat and was trying to cough it up. You never heard so many "hold its!" "Cut its!" or saw so much arm waving in your life. The engine was secured and Walter and I were up the mechanic's stand in a flash. Having the smaller arm, I reached down into the air intake system, fished around and came up with the red mechanics rag. I had stuffed three clean mechanic's rags, sprayed with a light coating of oil, into both intake scoops about a year ago to keep dust, moisture, and debris out of the air intake system. This was my reward.

Walter was raising hell with Fencel, who had been assigned to clear the intakes of the rags while Barbie was still in the hanger. Fencel had missed one rag. Back to the start-up. To make sure none of us spellbound Weary Warriors dozed off; the -29 actual ran backwards a few times just to hold our interest. The novices among us, and there were many, were impressed. I envisioned the -29 tearing itself from the wing, (I never did trust the four puny bolts holding the engine mount to the airframe) and crashing to the cement tarmac. But that did not happen. With a few more gasps and belches, she caught and was on line.

Robinson had pulled it off. From a pile of scrap engines and parts, he built up one hell of a set of deafening-thundering engines.

The blue smoke from the exhaust stacks turned to white and then disappeared as the engines reached operating temperature. This was a very good sign. With both engines at a very fast idle and every Weary Warrior wearing a wide grin, Jack came down the hatch. Holding his hat on with one hand, he braved the prop wash, examined the back of each engine and was back up the hatch to give the engines a faster rpm as they wore in. They were now sounding smooth and confident. They ran nowhere near cruise power setting where they ran smooth as they wore in.

Robinson was back down the hatch. He walked up to me, said, "She's all yours, you can run her till the tanks go dry," and stepped back.

Jack was done. His three-year affair with Barbie was over. He would remove the props and return them, pack his tools and be gone in a few days. I would never see or hear from him again. He left his mark, though: a throbbing, breathing, B-25 and a rag-tag collection of smiling Weary Warriors.

Glen was looking at me anxiously. I gave him the nod and the same to Walter. They both followed my pre-startup instructions on how to approach and board Barbie to the letter. Our years of working around Barbie and the endless repetition of tasks had formed some bad habits. We were not safety oriented. We now had to become aware of the spinning props. I wanted no one to walk into a prop.

I told Glen to start a squawk list and handed him the clipboard. Over the next hour, those who wanted to play pilot did so and Barbie was shut down and started up several times. I did not board Barbie that day. I was busy lifting Fencel's spirits, thanking Jack, and talking to the potential pilot member who had thirty thousand dollars burning a hole in his pocket. Jim Porter made a nice fly-by in his two-seat jet trainer with the "V" tail. It was a foreign-made jet and had the most annoying whistle during engine idle and in taxi mode. He pulled up and parked just as we packed it in for the day. Of all things, he noticed our cannon, now mounted in the nose.

Once the "We did its!" were over, I got our board together off in a corner and talked while Barbie was being tucked away and cleaned up. Our landlord had experienced a change of heart and now wanted a thousand dollars a month for rent. Further, we would have to foot the bill for snow removal on his driveway, the parking lot, and in front of the hanger doors. He was not sure but he might also add the utilities. It was evident that he felt the doors were now just fine and that he did not need us anymore. Nice guy. We were being held up without a gun and all of us balked at the proposition. We were getting it stuck to us again. What our landlord did not know was that Macomber, along with the doorman on occasion, tinkered with the doors just about every Saturday morning.

While the board gave the matter some thought, I advised them that it had been brought to my attention that an A.I. had opened up a shop some eight hundred feet from our first "TEE" hanger and was looking for customers. I had spoken with him and, if we wanted to work on Barbie in his shop, the fee was seven hundred dollars a month. He would give us a corner, we could paint Barbie in his shop, and he gave us a graduated hourly rate for his services. The more he worked, the less his fee. He had no experience on warbirds but had extensive experience on twin Beeches that had old-fashioned round engines like Barbie; but at four hundred and fifty horsepower, they were small compared to our -29s. He was sure that, with our help, he could bring us to certification.

Tatelman commented, "He is the answer to our prayers. This could not have happened at a better time, Mr. President, I recommend we do just that, not negotiate with our present landlord, and move out at the end of the month which is just a few days off. We post a letter to him one day before we move out, advising him we have vacated the premises."

The board agreed. We would delay the move one month as we had already paid the November rent and the A.I. would not be ready until the middle of November. We gathered the Weary Warriors that were still around, curious as to what the board was discussing. They all agreed and the last word was from Macomber.

"The doors won't last two weeks once we are gone and I will make sure the door man never sets foot in this place again."

On November 25, two days after Thanksgiving, we made the move on a forty-degree day. Hanson, Fencel, Macomber, Wild, Hable, Walter's grandson, and I would once again start loading a rented truck and begin the process of moving all over. I was pleased that we had a good turnout of the doers, considering the holiday season. From 8:00am to 5:00pm, Barbie and her support systems worked their way around Greater Rockford Airport. We left the plush, but old hanger, better than we had found it: the plumbing was working and two doors worked.

At the end of the day, it was still forty degrees, cloudy and windy and we were all tired and cold. We would now have to get to know our new mechanic and landlord.

It would not take long for many to dislike him and the same group that mistrusted Jack did not waste much time lining the new guy up in their sights. He was not warm and friendly like Jack. Mysterious in his ways, there was no way to get close to him. They took their shots and planted the seed of paranoia. I could not help but think he was a man with a lot on his mind. If he did not lighten up, he would not last as a businessman. His mannerisms alienated people and, unaware of this, he did not know how to relate to paying customers. On the good side, he knew his stuff and went by the book.

It was a good size hanger; neat, clean, and well maintained. The faithful went back to work. Hanson and Macomber also worked during the week. Most, however, worked on Saturdays when our mechanic had his day off —- which was the best thing that could have happened.

Wild on a borrowed tug and with borrowed props on the engines 06 is pulled from her upscale hanger for the first engine run-up. Jerry Fencel is the starboard wing walker. With all the borrowing we did we owed a lot of people a lot of favors.

Barbie III and Company

With our first fueling underway we all waited for gasoline to leak out of 06 but not a drop was visible. Wild leaning on the fuselage, supervises the process and Fencel looks on from the hole where the top turret would go. This is the day we realized when it came to feeding 06 she had an insatiable appetite. Note the inner and outer wing flaps in the down position.

With a puff of smoke the port engine coughed to life. It was not an easy start. Tatelman is at the controls. Note the borrowed auxiliary power unit on the other side of 06 and the patch on the bomb bay door.

The port engine is at idle speed and Jack Robinson braved the prop wash to examine some connections. Note the patch just behind the cockpit. The shine on the tire is from oil blown out of the engine.

We Try Again

The overhauled black props with their yellow World War II stenciling glistened like new in the darkened hanger as Gene, our A.I. and landlord, cautiously backed Barbie through the hanger doors. To fit through the opening, we had to once again remove the wing tips when we brought Barbie over. Morris was walking her starboard wing and Koppie the port wing. We had about five inches of clearance on each wing end. Barbie slipped through the door opening on the first try.

I was standing with Hable and Macomber at the rear of the hanger as we watched our majestic warbird glide slowly and silently from our dark corner of the hanger and into the light of a gray overcast sky. This early afternoon, I was hoping it would warm up and get sunny but it was not to be. The wind continued to blow and it was a miserable, damp, raw, cold day.

Clearing the doors, Gene backed her into a broad curve. One wing end was pointed at the hanger wall and the nose was across the hanger door opening. Midway through the turning maneuver, I remarked to Hable that she was one mean-looking machine. She was crisp, neatly tucked together, agile looking, and seemed to have a nice balance to her. She was well put together and the cloudy sky gave her bare aluminum that pewter-like glow that I liked so well. Every time she was outdoors, I could not help but think that Glen was perhaps right in his thoughts not to paint her. Macomber must have been thinking the same thing.

"It's a shame to paint her —- she is so pretty."

Hable said, "She will still have the classic lines. That will never change."

It was time for our second engine startup. All morning, fourteen Weary Warriors sat in the cold, damp hanger as we went through our annual meeting. It being a Saturday, Gene was reluctant to turn on all the lights and did not want to give us too much heat. It was nice of him to come to work on Saturday and it must have cost him a fortune to heat the place. I could not blame him for trying to keep his utility bills within reason.

While the meeting went on, Gene tinkered with Barbie to prep her for the start-up. The temperature in the hanger was about fifty degrees and we were all cold and uncomfortable. We were just sitting and talking, and the cold was getting to all of us. Tatelman was suffering the most. He did not know how to dress for our lousy weather. When I picked him up at the airport, I had a warm Chicago-style coat for him and gave him one of those wool pullover caps. The last ten minutes of the meeting, I was so cold that my hands were shaking and I envied everyone else that had their hands tucked in their pockets. As I waited for adjournment, we were deciding to go forward on our certification and the only thing that remained was the FAA observation of an engine run-up, complete with cycling of the props, and an observed gear retraction test. Macomber advised that we would paint as soon as the weather was warm and stabilized, hopefully by June. In another bit of news, it appeared we would have to run about five hours on the engines before Gene would certify to the FAA approval inspection.

I was always up front with our people. They were adults and should handle bad news. I prepped them that Gene also advised that the starboard engine had three cylinders with low or bad compression. He hoped it was stuck valves. This would have to be corrected.

Walter and Gene made up some concoction to free up sticking parts and Barbie swallowed her W&G cocktail like she lived in a bar. I hoped it worked. Gene also advised the starter on the starboard engine was turning slow. It may have been from our long grind last fall. He also found that the timing had to be adjusted by seven degrees. We adjourned for lunch and Morris and Taylor, our electronic wizards, stayed behind to correct some engine-wiring fault that Gene had come across.

At 1:45pm, Tatelman went up the hatch followed by Walter and Jim Porter, who was getting acquainted with engine start up procedures. He would just observe. We got off to a bad start and had no standby fire extinguisher. I yelled at Fencel who was closest to one and he set it up for the starboard engine. It should have been twice as big. The airport police arrive.

I was apprehensive about the start-up and irked about the lack of protocol pre-start procedures. Gene stood by the borrowed auxiliary power unit wanting nothing to do with the cockpit procedures. Smart man.

I banged on the side of the fuselage and looking up at the cockpit asked, "Who the hell was in charge up there?" Nobody seemed to know.

Tatelman offered, "I guess I am, Mr. president."

"Good, what's the first thing on the pre-start check list?"

They rummaged around and I heard muffled voices.

Tatelman leaned out the cockpit window and said, "Fire guard in place and standing by. It will never happen again Mr. President."

The fire truck arrived.

Gene started the APU and let it warm up.

The same police officer and the same three firemen who had arrived at the first start up were on hand again.

I leaned against the police car fender with my back to the wind. Damn, it was cold! I wondered if the oil was fluid enough at this temperature but I was sure they would use the oil dilution system if need be.

I waited patiently. I wanted the run up to go successfully. Gene got the APU warmed, looked at me and I gave him the nod. He looked at the cockpit, raised his hand above his head and moved his hand in a circular motion, with the forefinger raised, indicating it was time to go. Gene was just as apprehensive about this start-up as I was. If any other Weary Warriors felt the same, they were keeping it a secret.

Like magic, the blades of the prop on the starboard engine jolted to life. Smoothly, they traced a blurred black invisible arch with a yellow edge. I was happy that Morris and Taylor had finished their wiring repair. The APU puffed a black load of smoke from its exhaust as Barbie's starter drew a heavy load. The APU was being strained to its limit.

Twelve blades passed a fixed point and it appeared, as I counted softly to myself, that the blades appeared to be slowing down. Thirteen, fourteen, fifteen, blades swung by. Nothing. I pictured a disaster. Either they were slow with switches on, did not know how to count, or the -29 was not getting the message.

A light puff of smoke followed by another and then another. The prop was spinning faster. More puffs of smoke, spinning faster and the -29 exploded to life. She was on line. Gene looked at me and made a sign of the cross in thanks. I acknowledged.

Well we had smoke, we also had oil, sheets of it and chunks of I guess carbon being blown out of some of the exhaust stacks of the troubled cylinders. Smoke! I could not believe the amount of smoke. The exhaust stacks on the problem cylinders were belching blue-white smoke like the stack of a steam locomotive going upgrade, pulling a heavy drag of loaded cars. After about ten minutes, our starboard engine was still polluting the hell out of Rockford Airport. One of the cylinders was lightening up and getting with the program.

Gene was up in the cockpit. He wanted to watch and listen to the engine for a bit and wanted the cockpit crew to hold off on the port engine start-up a few minutes. Gene walked over to me. We conferred. If the cylinders would not correct themselves with this run up, he would have to pull at least two, maybe three cylinders. We watched together as he pointed out odds and ends and explained the sounds coming from the engine.

He wanted a full power check. If we were lucky, it would shake something loose. He would not take the responsibility if it blew up on us. He wanted my okay. I gave it and he was up in the cockpit again and told the crew what he wanted. Walter looked at me and I gave the nod. What choice did we have? Power came up and the tail vibrated like hell. I recalled Tatelman's experience during World War II. The tail was going to be one shaky place to go along for a ride.

The full-bore run-up was no longer than sixty seconds and nothing blew up but she coughed out smoke like there was no tomorrow. Back to a fast idle, at least two cylinders were still belching smoke and, to my dismay, raw oil. It was time for the port engine. Now I wished we had listened to Robinson. We had no spare cylinders and it would take a month to exchange them.

Even our good friend Frank Howerton had said, "You have to keep good cylinders in your inventory. In time, you will become experts at exchanging cylinders. Take a spare cylinder with you on a trip unless you want to limp home."

The port engine, the one I had all the confidence in, would not start. It caught, spun, and then clattered to a stop. The backfires were magnificently spectacular. The sharp, jagged sheets of flame would explode out of the air intake opening with a loud, crisp report of short duration that echoed off the wall of the hanger, then the flame would be sucked back in. It would have been perfect for a Fourth of July celebration.

Remembering, one of the firemen turned to me and said, "you guys don't have another rag stuffed up there do you?" I replied that I hoped not.

At exactly thirty seconds, they gave up on the port engine and let it rest. Good. They were going by the book. We would have a five-minute wait.

Fencel walked up to me asking, "What the hell is the matter with that thing? Is that the engine that Gene changed the timing seven degrees? I bet he screwed it up, it ran good last time."

"Oh I think it's in the cockpit, Jerry. Give them time. It could be a lot of things. To me it sounds like not enough prime, they're starving her." Fencel walked away and talked to the Quatrines.

They played with the starboard engine, did a mag check that sounded good and the prop went from takeoff setting to cruise setting nicely as someone in the cockpit exercised the prop from full increase to full decrease. The cloud of smoke extended across the airfield and cars on the perimeter road began to stop and watch.

I imagine everyone in the tower had their binoculars on us and their comments went like this; "Nothing to worry about, it's that weird bunch with the B-25."

Porter watched intently. I admired his level of intelligence. He would be a good pilot for Barbie. He never questioned anything we did. He also had a boyish, mischievous way about him and I knew he would be one of the first to be cited by the FAA for cutting up. It would be nothing too serious: just a little too low or a little too fast. He would have a little lack of restraint resisting the charm of Barbie and her awesome power.

When Tatelman got current in a B-25 about a year or so ago, he came up for a visit and with the towers permission gave us a fly-by down the runway. It was executed with maturity; carefully thought out; at a good height and a conservative speed. It was well done and impressive. Porter, on the other hand would have come full bore, mowing the weeds with the prop tips.

The five minutes were up and the crew in the cockpit began to set up for the start. I smiled to myself as Walter alternated the position of his head as he read from the start checklist. Looking through his bifocals, then looking over the bifocal lenses as he glanced at the panel, caused his head movement.

A forlorn Hanson looked on. Glen was on two crutches and his right foot and ankle were in a heavy cast-like affair. While the ladder up the forward hatch was a short climb, the ailing foot was no match for the ascent. I watched Tatelman and Walter as they went through the start-up. They both had to be seventy plus years old. Tatelman was, perhaps, a few years older than Walter.

Old reliable lefty was swinging her prop again as if nothing had happened. She was online and running like a sweetheart. Tatelman and Walter had gotten it right the second time around. For some reason, the cylinder head temperature decided not to work, oil pressure was low, and there was no response from the prop control. They would keep an eye on the oil temperature and, if it climbed, they would have to shut down the port engine. Suddenly, the oil pressure came up and we assumed there had been some air in the line that went to the oil pressure gauge.

A full power check came off with out a hitch. Both engines were cranked up to a cruise mode of 2100rpm, manifold pressure of twenty-nine inches, and a full rich mixture. For the first time, I was aware of the awesome power of the -29's.

Conversation within three hundred feet was impossible. I now realized the true meaning "the B-25 with short stacks was the noisiest aircraft of World War II to see combat in all theater fronts" The cement tarmac was trembling.

The three guys in the cockpit between the thundering monsters had to be taking a beating. The huge props, with their twelve-foot-six-inch reach, beat the air inches from their heads without mercy. Porter, I think, was simply overwhelmed. None of them had headsets on and they were not wearing earplugs that I could see. Gene kept them online. The starboard engine was still throwing smoke.

Gene approached me. "What are the climb power settings?"
"Thirty inches and 2200rpm."
"Initial takeoff power?"
"Thirty four inches and 2400rpm."

He wrote them down on a pocket-sized sheet of paper and was up the hatch ladder. The engines were backed off to a fast idle. Gene was holding the piece of paper and explaining that he wanted power settings for a takeoff run, then a climb run, a cruise run, and then a let down run. Tatelman was nodding in the affirmative. Gene was down the hatch, constantly walking around Barbie, watching everything. He may have not been Mr. Personality, but he was good.

And the people! They came from nowhere and we had a good-sized audience. Barbie went through her fake takeoff, climb, cruise and landing and Gene motioned to the cockpit crew to shut her down. They continued to go by the book. Throttles at 1500rpm for thirty seconds, then 1000rpm to idle cutoff. The silence was overwhelming.

We had some repairs to make.

Weary Warriors were elated and once again spirits soared. Only a few of us realized this engine run-up had more problems than our first. I talked to Hable and theorized about the vibrating tail and wondered if we had shaken anything loose. He did not think so, as everything was safety wired or had self-locking nuts; but when he had time, he would take a look-see.

The damp cold crept back as the excitement of the engine test run slipped away. I thanked the firemen for their assist and Gene tucked Barbie back into her corner. Those that remained manned the rags and we started wiping down Barbie's oil-streaked skin.

We discussed the failure of the prop to cycle and decided to get a new propeller feathering pump and a propeller governor on an exchange basis. Gene felt it would be better and there would be less cost involved than attempting a repair. Morris and Taylor would address the cylinder head temperature. They felt it was the sending unit, but would check it out. Gene, on a high, agreed to tinker with the two cylinders that had acted up.

Lou Fulgaro

Gene our mechanic and landlord carefully backs 06 out of his hanger. We had to once again take off the wing tips to fit 06 through the hanger door opening. There was no charge for tug and auxiliary power unit use. Photo Ray "Doc" Hillson.

Gene our mechanic waits patiently beside a borrowed auxiliary unit as the flight deck crew climbs aboard. We had new batteries but felt they were not up to cranking over the –29s for an anticipated troublesome start. The police car is behind the power unit where I spent the entire engine run leaning on a front fender. It was a deep penetrating-cloudy-cold-damp-day. Photo Ray "Doc" Hillson.

Lou Fulgaro

The reluctant port engine, with a few encouraging belching clouds of smoke, staggered to life after a five minute rest from the failed first engine start attempt. Photo Ray "Doc" Hillson.

With her brakes locked up tight 06 hunkers down at 100% power. The inadequate fire extinguisher is on the tarmac to the right but we had a fire truck present just in case. We had more mechanical things go wrong with this engine run than we did with the first. Photo Ray "Doc" Hillson

Two visitors Earnest D'Angelo and Louis Virgilio. This photo is included, as a rumor had spread that we were using imitation fiberglass gun side packs. It took years to find authentic aluminum ones and they show very clearly in this photo. Note the muzzle flash deflectors and that we always prime painted mating surfaces to prevent unseen corrosion.

Bad Times

There were the telltale signs. The fragmented beginnings of a division of our members was forming. I noticed certain members lining up with Fencel, who was now beginning to turn sour on us. He was being rebuffed and did not like it. Walter and Glen avoided Fencel, as they found him annoying with his constant talking and advice that was not solicited or wanted. Our new mechanic soon got wise and told Fencel to get lost, which really lit Fencel's fuse. The mechanic would not take directions from anybody but Fulgaro, Wild and Hanson. In fact, he did want to talk to any members for any reason. Fencel sulked at home and talked to many members that he had attracted to our group. Many, like the Quatrains, considered Fencel a long-time friend and listened to him as he planted the seeds of mistrust and mismanagement. I spent a lot of time on the phone talking to members and trying to sort things out for them.

Where we would base Barbie on a permanent basis and flight insurance were now the concerns of the board. The question of whether she could fly had been answered. It was now assumed that she would fly. We had to plan ahead to have sufficient funds on hand to meet our anticipated expenditures. We needed a simple, old-fashioned budget and had to plan ahead one year. Fencel, who was the only one to volunteer, was to scout out locations and their costs. I would take on the insurance question. The prorated insurance costs and hanger rent would become fixed yearly costs, part of each member's yearly assessment.

I began to realize many of the agents soliciting us were using the same parent insurance companies that insured warbirds. There were not that many. The difference in rates seemed to be tied to the amount of the commission the agent wanted. The first quote for one million dollars of liability insurance [the minimum for air shows] came as a shock. For one year, with only a crew of three at any time on board and not including hull insurance, the premium was nine thousand dollars. No passengers would be allowed. If we bent our bird, the repair was our nut to crack. Adding hull insurance would jump the premium to between fifteen and seventeen thousand dollars.

I sat across the table, buying my insurance agent (who had insured my aircraft for years) lunch.

He explained, "It's a bad market for warbirds at this time. There are about nine hundred warbirds that are insured at an average premium price of three thousand dollars a year. This includes many trainers and many do not carry one million dollars. Some are like a car —- one hundred to three hundred thousand liability or maybe a half of million. Nine hundred warbirds bring the insurance company $2,700,000 in premiums. Take out the agents' commissions and they have a little over $2,000,0000.Two dings and they're in the red as far as warbird revenues go. Light aircraft, at $900 a shot times ninety thousand aircraft, brings in $81,000,000 and therein lies the success of one category and the failure of the other."

"Lou, a lot of warbirds are sitting right now or they get a short-term policy for a few days. The price varies. The thing that has the insurance companies running right now is that there are no caps on settlements in the United States. The settlements for band-aid type injuries are outrageous. Have you ever noticed how many warbirds sit out the actual show itself? They sit because they don't have the one million-dollar policy, which, by the way, may go to one-point-five shortly after the jet warbird crash in California. That was a real bad one. The secret is, you perform; but let the pros do the actual show."

"Now, you did not hear this from me. You arrive early and beat up the local town at legal heights. No fancy stuff. The idea is to tweak the interest of the citizens, get them to want to come to the air show. The day of the air show but before the actual show, you work over the town again and do a low fly-by at the airport to keep the people's attention and make them feel they are getting their money's worth. Do not violate the two-by-two rule when you make a run down the runway."

"Two by two rule?" I asked.

"No faster than two hundred miles an hour, no lower than two hundred feet. Only make one pass. Do the same thing when you leave. You have to sell the show promoter. You have one of the rarest and noisiest warbirds around. It is perfect for this role. Offer to send the promoter a couple of photos, you write the captions. You know your bird. Take a few reporters for a ride. You will find many will go for it and you get the same gas and perks as the air show performers, but you do sit out the show. Also arrive with low tanks. They will top you off when you arrive, no questions asked. Why arrive with your tanks half full? Let them pay the gas bill."

"Anyway the insurance picture should change. The warbird demand is a growing market and the more warbirds, the better price-wise it will get. Soon some company will try to capture this market by offering attractive rates. Almost all warbirders belong to the War Birds of America I don't see why the EAA does not put the arm on the insurance company that they are associated with to include warbirds."

Now, let's see, I thought. Nine thousand in insurance, six thousand in hanger rent divided between fifteen members comes to one thousand dollars each not moving the airplane. There were at least four that would not or could not pay this tab. Then the rate per paying member jumps to just under 1400 dollars each and that would eliminate another one or two and the domino effect clicks in.

It became apparent to me that, in time, maybe six or seven of us would have to foot the dollar tab and the rest would contribute like amounts by laboring on the maintenance end of Barbie, which would be significant. If I could only get four to come up with the ground insurance assessment of four hundred —- thousand each would be unheard of! We had time to work this angle out. First, get people used to the big numbers while there is still no commitment.

It was now close to a year since we assigned Fencel to explore locations for our next home and it was the subject on the floor. Fencel was giving his report. The only requirement was that Barbie had to be hangered. It would be nice if she were hangered somewhere in the middle of the area that we all lived. It was not to be. Fencel came up with only one place and that was, as some of us suspected it would be, the Confederate Air Force hanger in Gary Indiana. They had a tug, cranes, and a lot of equipment to support a warbird. The rent was cheap —- three hundred dollars a month.

After the motion and discussion, the motion carried and it was done. For me it was about the same distance but in the opposite direction and a lot of traffic. It was close for Walter, Hillson, Fencel, and a few others. It was very far for Glen, Frank, Koppie, and a few others; a good four to five hour round trip drive. But that is not the end of this saga.

Many of us were invited to tour the CAF hanger, which we did. It was big, old, dark, and dirty. To get to it, we had to drive through miles of slums and junkyards. Most of us were not impressed.

A great bunch of guys, the CAF but what a neighborhood! The terminal was closed and run down although the field had an operating Federal control tower and the controlled air space that went with it. There could not have been twenty aircraft based there.

One CAF member stated, "We have the whole field to ourselves. I don't think ten aircraft come and go a week."

While he was trying to sell his location, I could not help but think what a waste of money. I now knew the true meaning of living out of the Federal pork barrel.

Porter had a business associate and friend who was possibly interested in joining us. Sitting in his office at his plant, he was as articulate and well-mannered as Porter. He did not join us and went off to buy and restore a P-40 World War II fighter. However; during our conversation, he mentioned that his home base at Aurora, Illinois was looking for warbirds and was offering attractive rates and discounts on gas to warbirds. The city fathers realized how many gallons of gas warbirds consumed and saw a windfall in gas taxes. Porter's friend opened the door for me and, within two hours, I was sitting in the business office of Lumanair Aviation in Aurora, Illinois.

Aurora was about as close to being in the middle of all of us as you could hope for. The field, a small controlled airfield with new hangers, had been rebuilt since I had flown in many years ago. It was new looking and well kept. The manager showed me around. The hangers were large enough to easily house our B-25; he would tuck us away in a corner of a hanger and we could have our own corner workspace. They could roll us out and put us back in with their tug and their personnel with a phone call. Yes, we could install our own phone. The rent was four hundred eighty-three dollars a month, including utilities, and we could come and go as we pleased. There were clean restrooms, vending machines, and a meeting room or two. What a find!

"I don't know how our man missed this place. He was exploring locations for us," I said.

"Lou, I think I talked to him months ago and told him the same thing I told you. There were two of them and they owned a B-25."

"Can you describe them?"

"I can do better than that I have one of their names in my contact book. I called the number for a follow-up call but it was a bum number, let me look it up—- Fencel was the guy's name."

"Do you know the other fellow that was with him?"

"Sure; he purchased a twin and bases it here now."

I thanked the man for his time and consideration, gave him my card and asked that he give me a few months.

I walked away seething and could not believe Fencel would pull something like this. It explained why the member who had just purchased a twin did not show up for the meeting. He did not want to be part of Fencel's sham.

Okay, good for him but, how the hell do I get this thing back on track? Aurora was the place for us to be. There was no doubt about that. It was perfect. We had a meeting coming up and I would address it at that time. I had my secretary purchase an updated Robert's Rules Of Order, advised her of my problem and told her to research it and give me an answer. A good secretary always makes her boss look good.

Days later, she came bouncing into my office with a smile and the book in hand. I knew she had the answer. She sat down and I gave her my full attention.

"There is a time limit," she began. "It has to be brought up at the next meeting and the person that made the motion has to bring the motion back to the floor for review."

"That's no good. Fencel made the motion. He will never do that."

"If that happens," she said, "the person that seconded the motion can bring the motion back on the floor." That person was a fellow by the name of Pat Hable.

"Here is a copy of the rule and I typed your last meeting's minutes for you."

"Thank you."

"You're welcome."

With that tucked away it would all come down to Hable. It was important at our meetings that we do things right as we were a registered corporation in the State of Illinois and taking short cuts could get us or me in trouble. It would be one hell of an interesting meeting. The subject "Hanger Location" was listed under old business on our agenda for the next meeting.

Meeting time came and I took every one by the hand through the scenario. I would like the motion brought back on the floor and both locations be considered by the membership. Fencel was furious and refused to bring the motion back on the floor as he thought that the CAF was still the best location for us. He then made a mistake.

"You dummies don't know what you are doing and we need the CAF." Walter damn near came out of his chair.

Walter shouted, "I regret ever bringing you to our hanger."

I halted the hostilities "Walter, you are out of order and, Fencel, so are you. Mr. Hable the question to bring the matter back on the floor for discussion is up to you."

Glen was so mad he was turning red. Tatelman did not care where we went, seeing he was from Florida.

Hable said, "Mr. President I am not sure. Are we still going to discuss both locations after the motion?"

"If you word the motion correctly, we will open both locations to discussion provided your motion has a second." Pat was in the middle on this one and was not comfortable. But, Pat was a gentleman and a man of honor and I felt he would do the right thing and he did.

The motion was made and there were so many seconds I cannot recall who actually made it. The vote came after heated discussion and we would be going to Aurora. Fencel damn near went berserk, threatened to sue us, promised he would tie us up in court, said we would never get that thing off the ground if he had his way and left. It was the only meeting I ever taped and the next workday I asked my secretary type it up word for word just in case there was litigation.

Fencel's conduct was discouraging to many and morale sagged. Most of all, mine. I did not need this. I promised myself the day we were ready to fly I would walk away from the board, pay what had to be paid every year and fly a B-25. I would see her through to completion.

More Odds and Ends
Anybody for Paint

Late 1989 through late 1990 was a good time for us overall. Fencel mellowed and life of a Weary Warrior was upbeat. There were a few bad days, but it was a good time.

The decision to paint 06 with the scheme of the First Air Commandos had been made: it would replicate R.T. Smith's mount. We purchased the reproduction machine guns, mounted the two gun packs on the starboard side, mounted the "armor plate", installed the muzzle flash plates and, after waiting a year and a half, the top turret arrived. The like-new, now correctly stenciled props had been hung. We were lovingly involved with all the items we had accumulated over the years, including bomb shackles and some look-alike, fiberglass 500lb bombs a fellow by the name of Al Heinze had made up for Fencel.

The 50 caliber machine guns and some barrels were so authentic looking that, laid on a bench, you would think they were real. The only way you could really tell was by picking them up. Made out of aluminum, they weighed a light fourteen pounds each. I think everyone on the airfield came to see them. We got so worried they would get "lost" that we all took some home until the day we were ready to install them. When a Saturday came and we were going to install two as an example, we only brought two.

I asked Glen to concentrate on the armor plate and the two muzzle flash plates, as once they were installed, Macomber was ready to start painting. The armor shield for the cockpit windshield would not be installed as Hanson and Tatelman felt the "armor" would block the field of vision and be unsafe when in flight.

A heavy piece of aluminum sheet stock was purchased and Glen went to work. It would be mounted under the cockpit window on the port side. The outside edges had a bevel about two inches wide and the idea was that it had to look like the original armor plate. It also had to be fitted to the fuselage profile. Glen labored for weeks and was proud of the finished product. It really looked good. During the beginning of the installation process, Fencel pointed out that it was not right. The original had square corners and the now-completed armor plate had round corners.

Fencel was right. We all looked at some photos of the original armor plate and it had square corners. The muzzle flash plates had round corners. Glen took it in stride and we would use the "spoiled" armor plate to make the flash plates. He would have to start all over again. Glen apologized for the error, as the aluminum stock was expensive. This he did not have to do and it was not necessary, especially when you consider the thousands of dollars I flushed down the toilet.

We got the plates installed and we were so fussy that we primed and painted the fuselage area and the back of the plates where they mated. We did not want any corrosion to form between the two surfaces. With a magnifying glass, we counted the number of bolt holes and their proper locations on the old photographs so we got all three plates mounted correctly. The end product was a masterpiece.

It was Mark Clark again. "Lou are you ready for the 90 air show? Think you can taxi that thing or do we have to tow you again?"

"We could taxi it," I answered, "but we're going to start painting soon and we don't want the "thing" splattered with oil as she is pretty clean now."

"Got the guns mounted?"

"Nope but we can tack some on for the show."

"Good —- those guns are gorgeous and people like to see and touch guns. We will damn near place you in front of your hanger. Can you guys push that heap of aluminum to your slot?"

"If there are enough of us we can.""The "heap" is very heavy."

"Hell, by the number of hot dogs you guys eat every year, you should have a small army."

"We will set it up ourselves," I said.

"Thanks, Lou we are counting on you guys. The people of Rockford love your warbird and look forward to seeing her progress every year. One of the first things one of the gals on the show committee asked was if the guys with the B-25 were going to be here."

"Nice to know we're wanted."

The show came and went. We had six guns mounted. To the uninformed, Barbie was all set to fly. The Air Show patrons poured over her and we took their good wishes with gratitude. We began to realize during those two days that, in theory, with our overhauled props hung, all we had to do was gas her up, point her blunt nose down the runway and go. She was that ready. But it was not going to be that simple, that easy, or that quick.

Paint, very expensive paint was the next job. At one hundred eighteen dollars a gallon plus a gallon of this, a half gallon of that, and a few ounces more of something else for a total yield of three gallons of paint. I was impressed as I peered into the five gallon mixing bucket. The fumes wafting out of the bucket were overpowering.

Macomber was smiling. "What's the matter boss, can't you handle that stuff?"

I did not reply.

Macomber readied his equipment. The green-brown concoction was the exact shade of paint the real Barbie flew with, thanks to the folks at the Archives in Washington. The 1990 Barbie would exactly match the OD-flat non-gloss paint that the 1943 Barbie had. With her flat paint, she would not be as glamorous-looking as today's, restored, high gloss, painted warbirds, but the only ones she had to impress was us. We did not care if she was not photogenic and most of the warbird magazine photographers would pass her up to shoot the shiny warbirds. We would present her as she was and if they preferred to shoot the Hollywood types with their glamour paint jobs, so be it.

This was the day that all of us had looked forward to. Barbie was poised and ready. Today was Wednesday: the Saturday before, Macomber, Habel, Ralph and Elaine Quatrine, Wild, Fencel, and I had readied the tail. It was scrubbed clean and dried. It was then etched to help the primer grab the bare aluminum. In the late afternoon, Macomber set up his equipment and applied two coats of primer. Why we did not use the stuff that was the primer and finish coat at the same time, I do not know. Macomber was the pro and, at this phase of our restoration, whatever he said was the way it was going to be. Macomber cautioned that the prime would only hold to next Saturday and we would have to apply the finish coat, at the latest, on that Saturday.

Our mechanic, the landlord, changed his mind and told us to paint the tail outside. He did not want to put up with the mess in his hanger from overspray. We could live with that this Saturday, but next Saturday rain was forecast. Putting our heads together, Macomber and I agreed on Wednesday as the day we would begin to apply the finish coat. The mid-week date was hastily thrown together and I took a vacation day. There would be five of us for the tail paint project.

Murphy's law prevailed and the paint party ended up with two of us instead of five. It was 8:00am as Macomber and I went over the tail with sticky tack clothes removing all the dust from the primer coat. As we worked, we patiently waited for the Quatrines and Fencel. We were ready to paint at 10:30am. Barbie was pushed by tug about fifty feet out of the hanger and we set up to paint. Where in the hell were Fencel and the Quatrines? We needed them.

We decided to go ahead without them as the paint life was measured in hours and it was time to do it. With two mechanic's stands in place, a couple of ladders and a few benches, Macomber set up his schedule and route to paint. I would be below him keeping the lines free, moving the rolling stands, and keeping the five-gallon paint bucket moving. The air was hooked up with, if I recall, a low pressure of thirteen pounds and Macomber was up the first stand. He started with the port vertical stabilizer.

The green/brown spray of paint was impressive as the rudder turned OD before our eyes. The green overspray was also impressive. The light wind swirled it around as it drifted downward, assisted by gravity. I had brought a paint shirt and promptly covered my head and shoulders. With me being on the bottom, this was going to be a bad experience.

Up on the stand, Macomber did his thing, immersed in a cloud of green spray. He seemed to thrive on the stuff. He wore no mask, no hat, and I watched his teeth turn whiter as his complexion turned greener. He barked orders and smiled as he worked his way around the tail. I cursed Fencel for not showing up and there was a constant flow of profanity flowing between Macomber and I. I worked my head off catering to his needs and following his direction. I also was turning green as the paint drifted down onto me.

Macomber was down on the tarmac and I held the spray gun for him as he fiddled with the paint bucket. We looked over the now-painted tail and we liked it.

He was back up the first stand with the comment; "It's time to cover the first wet coat with the final coat."

Again, my mind wondered as I sweated in the hot July sun. If Fencel was here, I would have stuck the paint gun up his butt and pulled the trigger. The sun was frying Macomber and me. Of all things, he was the one who wanted it painted this way and he was nowhere around.

I would later find out that Fencel did show up at my house for the paint detail. We got our signals crossed. The night before, I had called him and advised him we had to be at the hanger at 8:00am. He would call the Quatrines. Fencel called me back to say he would be a little late and would arrive about 8:30 am. I say fine. I wrongly assume he will ride with the Quatrines. At 8:30am Wednesday, Fencel arrived at my house where my wife advised him that I had left at 6:45am. Fencel and the Quatrines turned around and go back home, not realizing that they were supposed to be at the hanger at 8:30am.

As we moved around the tail, people were already admiring the "camouflage" paint. Barbie was looking like a real warbird. Macomber's sputtering spray gun caught my attention as I peeked out from my now-green shirt.

Macomber was down the ladder. While I held the spray gun, he disconnected the airline, unscrewed the lug screws that held the top of the paint bucket secure and totally sealed.

"Damn; we are out of paint."

It meant nothing to me; I assumed it was supposed to be this way. We had about a half-gallon left in the mixing bucket and I retrieved it while Macomber wiped off his equipment.

Macomber held the filter as I poured the remaining paint through it. My fingers were sticking to each other and the sides of the mixing bucket from the substance on the impregnated tack cloths. With the gray primer paint from a few touch ups here and there a little earlier, then green paint mixed with sweaty dirt, we were each a mess. The mixed-up batch, I was informed, should have been enough for two full coats on the tail. The wind was carrying some of the paint away.

Macomber was back up the ladder and, in five minutes, the paint was gone. I mentioned to Macomber that it was 2:00pm and we were way overdue for lunch.

"No time, boss," shot back Macomber, "we got to mix a new batch fast to finish up the wet coat. You see those clouds building up? We may have one of those famous Rockford summer storms."

I was up so early that I'd had no breakfast and my stomach lying on my backbone was not helping my disposition. If Fencel had showed up, there was no doubt in my mind I would have put my hands around his scrawny neck and wrung it.

Macomber and I must have set a record for hand-mixing paint. We hurried but did it right. Into the paint bucket, via a paper filter and all hooked up, we were back in business. As Macomber went up the ladder, my eyes followed him and rested on a rudder. It was a different shade of color; it looked wrong. I pointed it out to Macomber and he could not see it. Back down the ladder he came.

The fabric rudders and elevators were sucking up the paint like a sponge. While they had been primed twice, once by Tatelman and once by Macomber, we would find that the fabric needed five to six coats while the aluminum took two.

So much for the wind theory.

Jerry Macomber silhouetted against the threatening summer sky started painting with a vertical stabilizer and rudder. I watched him turning greener by the minute. As his face took on Barbie's color his teeth showed up whiter and whiter. Several months later we had the most gorgeous paint job imaginable. 06 was an exact duplicate paint-wise of her namesake Barbie III. Her flat olive drab paint was perfect.

Lou Fulgaro

From Bad to Worse

The clouds were building up and the threat of rain was coming closer. I wet down the pavement (to prevent the overspray from sticking to the cement) for the umpteenth time. Macomber was up the rollable mechanic's stand for the umpteenth time and started laying the paint to the rudder.

"Lou, move me back around a foot or so," he said.

As I rolled the stand around the back of the rudder so Macomber could get to the other side, the paint hose from the bucket to the spray gun caught on the stand structure. I was watching the rudder as all I had to do was ding it with the stand and there would be hell to pay.

Now, the paint bucket had small, hard wheels and would roll somewhat. Murphy's law kicked in. One of the wheels caught in a crack in the cement and over went the bucket. The bucket was sealed, so that, in itself, was not too much of a problem; but as the top of the bucket pivoted to the cement, it came to rest on the paint hose and one of the pointed locking lugs promptly punctured the hose. The result was a twenty-foot high geyser of OD paint with the gentle wind forming a nice horizontal rooster tail. We both scrambled to right the paint bucket, which promptly changed the direction of the hose and its geyser. As it spun around, it got both of us. Macomber disconnected the airline and the geyser dwindled and stopped.

I washed down the pavement and got rid of most of the paint but some of it is probably there to this day. We taped the hose but it would not hold. We cut out the perforated portion of the hose with a hack saw and, from our vast supply of odds and ends, patched the hose using some automotive hose clamps as a temporary fix. None of this seemed to faze Macomber, who went back up the stand to continue on. The temporary repair held. Remarkable. Almost unbelievable.

It was now late afternoon. It looked like we would beat the rain but I was completely unprepared for our next problem. As I listened to my stomach complaining about its lack of nourishment, I found solace in the thought of ringing Fencel's neck.

The blue squad car came up fast —- it was not making a social call. The young officer reluctantly left the sanctuary of his air-conditioned car. He was polite and we had talked before. They had received a complaint about our painting. It was not permitted on the ramp and we would have to stop. We would also have to clean up. I advised him we would comply but we would be finished in about five minutes. Could we finish up? He checked with his base and they said okay and the officer left. I advised Macomber to start painting. Whoever turned us in was probably watching, would soon make a second call and the officer would be back. Macomber uttered some profanity that only another retired painter who raced pigeons could comprehend.

I suspected that the local paint shop made the call as they had showed up at our hanger after seeing Fencel's photo at one of the air shows and solicited us for a paint contract. To prep and paint they felt would take two weeks. The cost would include all the paint, primer, etch, and all materials. The price they quoted was $16,000. After today, I thought it was a good deal.

A few minutes passed and I watched as the police car returned, coming right at us. I told Macomber to keep on painting and pretend he did not see the officer arrive. I would try and stall him.

"How long to finish?" I asked Macomber.

"About two minutes, boss."

I eyed the cruiser, closing fast on us. "You got the bail money?"

It was a fast stop on wet cement he slid and almost spun out. A very angry, embarrassed officer untangled himself from his seat belt. In his haste, the seat belt got caught in his microphone cord, which did not help the young man's composure or disposition. He came bursting out of the car and informed me to stop painting immediately or face arrest. Before I could respond, he pulled a small notebook from his shirt pocket. Opening it, he asked my name and address and I slowly spelled my last name for him. I could hear Macomber's spray gun going.

When the young officer realized Macomber was still painting, he started yelling and there was no doubt in my mind we were past the point of taking names and kicking butts. Macomber stopped. He was finished. The officer watched us disconnect the paint equipment, tuck Barbie in, and wash down the ramp.

Barbie was starting to look like a real warbird.

We both blamed Fencel for our day, perhaps unfairly, but with at least three it would have been so much easier and someone could have gone and gotten a few sandwiches and cold drinks. Macomber took me to his favorite out of the way watering hole, a very old brick storefront about twenty-five feet wide and a hundred feet long. Talk about long and narrow! I had the best hamburger at the best price of a lifetime and the draft beer was drawn at the perfect temperature. It would soon become our favorite lunch place.

The next day I called our landlord and advised him we would be painting inside from now on as that provision was in our contract with him. There was no argument. He had seen and heard the police officer.

Lou Fulgaro

If It Was A Horse
I Would Shoot It

Throughout August and September 1990, Barbie wore her coat of more-brown-than-green paint. She was not done but she was close.

We had reluctantly exchanged the two cylinders. One had a cracked exhaust valve and the other had a cracked piston ring. Pulling the cylinders and crating them took a week: shipping took another week. The exchange took one week at a facility in Oklahoma where Robinson used to work. Check up front, please. Return shipping and installation took another week.

How time flies when you are having fun. Gene was now doing engine run-ups on his own. We had eight hours of running time on the big Wright Cyclones and they were doing fine —- or so we thought.

Unknown to us, the third pump for one prop would only cycle partially. Gene also was draining a small amount of oil from each engine after each run-up. As it drained, the oil was passed through one of Macomber's paper paint filters and Gene would check for metal particles. The starboard engine was shedding metal like a dog sheds hair and there was more each time. The port engine was just fine. We explained it away as a result of the new cylinders and convinced ourselves that it should lessen in time. Gene would date each filter and keep it. He advised us he could not certify the engine if this continued. This was hard to take, as the engine seemed to be running like a champ.

The fellow at the pump station for the prop insisted it had to be the prop itself. The prop shop said no way. Gene volunteered a solution: he would switch pumps and see what happened. We agreed as our shop bill was continuing to go through the ceiling. On the next engine run-up, the port prop cycled perfectly and the starboard engine prop malfunctioned.

It was the pump. Walter and I were on the phone with the stubborn pump shop and, after threatening bodily harm they agreed to send off another one yellow tagged —- but only after they received the exchange pump. The price for this small pump that fit in your hand was $600 and Fencel was sure the pump shop did nothing but flush out our old one, clean it up, and paint it. More weeks went by. The fourth pump worked.

Through all this, Macomber kept on painting. I could not find a drip or a run in the paint. His painting skills were extraordinary and he did most of it on his own. Every Saturday when we showed up, more was done. You could not tell were he had left off for one day and started the next day. The fuselage, the top of one wing, and the tail were now painted.

At one of our air shows, a young artist approached me with a sample of his work and volunteered to paint the name "BARBIE III" on both sides of the fuselage. There would be no charge and he was sure he could duplicate the original. He would consider it a privilege and would use some photos of his work to attract other sign painting contracts. I gave his card to Macomber and if Macomber approved of his work, let's do it.

Gene had called me and the metal debris was heavier than usual on the last run up and he was not going to run the engines anymore unless I was present. He now had five filters with metal debris. Glen was worried about the engine metal and if Glen was worried we all were worried. I could no longer talk myself into the idea that the exchange cylinders were shedding a little casting flash and some loose odds and ends. We cleaned all the oils screens, drained the sumps a little and Gene backed Barbie out. We enjoyed a forty five-minute engine run up with forty-five seconds at full power. It was a perfect run up. The -29's and the props could not have performed any better. There was over ten hours running time on each engine. The old reliable port engine was now certified as airworthy.

Weary Warriors did the draining and filter routine this time as Fencel had once again proposed that Gene was pouring metal into the oil so he could have more work. I trusted Gene as I had trusted Robinson. I think most of us did. Those that had taken cheap shots at Robinson were once again doing the same thing.

A chill ran up my back as we looked at the overflowing thimble-full of granular metal. I was no engine expert but I had talked with enough people the last six years that I had some very limited knowledge.

"See those bright looking slivers?" I asked Walter and Glen. "If that is silver we have a pending master rod bearing failure."

On the older -29's, they coated the master bearings with silver as that was what was available, given the shortage of metals used in manufacturing during World War II. I had also been informed that the shelf life of a bearing coated with silver was about ten years. The bearings would then have to be replaced, used or not. Long-term mechanical life was not the main concern during World War II.

The master rod bearings were the heart of the -29. Like a human heart, if it stopped so did life. If the bearings went, so did the entire engine. It was referred to in the warbird circle as a catastrophic engine failure. The -29 would not limp along when this happened. It was not like a cylinder or two that failed. It would literally blow up, tearing itself to pieces.

I needed a second opinion and called in a -29 "heart" specialist. By phone, I advised Al Heinze what we had and asked if he could take a look.

In about a week Fencel and Heinze turned up. He advised the slivers looked like silver and, if they were, we were facing a major engine failure within the next twenty hours of engine time. To make sure, he took an eyedropper of acid and tested one of the silver flecks. The fleck disappeared: it was silver.

"Sorry guys, she's going on you."

We were all devastated. We had prepared ourselves for the bad news but it was still hard to take.

That morning, if I'd had a gun and Barbie was a horse, I would have shot her on the spot. Her hydraulics were acting up again and refused to work. Gene was baffled. Fencel went into a shouting performance, blaming all our mechanics over the last few years. Heinze assured him that it had nothing to do with our mechanics. Machines break and the older they are, the more often they break. The matter was put to rest.

What to do was not the question. How do we do it was the question. Tatelman got the news and called for a board meeting. On September 8th we met and discussed our dilemma. An engine overhaul would run us $28,000, plus freight of $1500. Added to that was the cost of labor to hang the engine and install our accessories. We were looking at a bill of $35,000 and we had $19,000 in the bank.

After about twenty long distance phone calls, I had two options for the board's consideration that we could afford. First, there was a mid-time -29 in Texas with logbooks but no guarantees. The owner would run it for us for two hours. It had 325 hours on it. His price was $10,500. Heinze said he would go down and look at it but we would have to pay the airfare and lodging.

The second choice was that I had located a -29 case with new bearings (which was our problem). The gears were good and mated. We did not need the gears; they just came with the package. It had the correct serial number logbook. The owner did not want the case. He had removed the accessories and cylinders. His price was $4,000: $2,000 up front and, once we were satisfied, $2,000 to finish. The freight bill of about $400 was ours to pay. We had the cylinders and accessories. It could be a good marriage.

Unfortunately, Gene, who had overheard Fencel and his cheap shots, refused to work on the engine. I could not blame Gene. He wanted Fencel banned from his shop. Fencel did not show up for months. I had to maintain the armament that was mounted on Barbie, which had been his assignment.

Gene had hired a mechanic to assist him and they spent much of their time with other customers. Slowly, over a year the hanger filled up with other aircraft. Some were rentals and some for inspections or other maintenance.

Gene had not billed us for two months and I asked him to make up the invoice. Gene would give me a day-by-day summary of his time and materials. Like his work, they contained a lot of detail. When the invoice came by mail, the total was $13,000 for some sixty-three days of work and two months' rent.

There were a couple of Weary Warriors that had heart attacks over this and the "he is ripping us off!" started all over again with a couple of "double billings!" thrown in for good measure. Macomber, who spent a lot of time at the hanger, advised that when he was there Gene was working. Glen felt the invoice was an honest one but Gene was not familiar with the hydraulics and time was wasted while he tried to sort things out.

I met with Gene on November 8th, advised him of our financial situation and told him that he was not to proceed on the mechanicals. We had some rent money for a few months. The turret, paint supplies, engine problems, hydraulics, gas, oil, freight, and Gene's two-month bill would literally put us in the poor house once it was paid.

On December 1, we had a meeting called by some of those that were not happy. Fourteen Weary Warriors got together and vented their frustrations with the appropriate profanity. We were so close. The meeting started at 1:30pm and ended at 5:00pm. The members advised Glen, Walter, and me to "cautiously" proceed with whatever we thought was best, considering our financial status. I felt really beat up at this meeting and, once again, reminded myself to walk away as soon as she was ready to fly. My second retirement was on schedule and Barbie was not. It was that simple. We would pay all our bills.

We rolled the dice and chose the second, -29 case route. Weary Warriors would work the hydraulics. We did not have much choice. The case arrived and Heinze felt the bearings were good. The mated gearing would stay with our replacement case. We would do most of the labor of bolting our cylinders and the accessories on to the replacement case. Anybody for skinned knuckles?

We would remove a cylinder from our problem engine and would immediately mount it on our case. Done this way, we would not loose track of what went where and how. Gene gave us a lot of advice and I knew he checked our work when we were not around. Thank you, Gene.

Fencel's engine stand was worth its weight in gold. To myself, I wished he would come back. I missed his idle chatter. While his chatter irked many, I would let it bounce off of me. The same thing three times, though, would strain the moment.

Barbie sat in the corner of the hanger with her nose turned into the corner of two joining walls. She looked like a naughty little girl that had been sent to a corner to reflect on her behavior. She was pouting and had her back turned to me. Sitting on beat-up yellow hydraulic jacks, her gear dangled. Her tires were a few inches off the cement floor. We had made some very nice large trays on wheels that sat under each -29 to catch the never-ending dripping oil — Gene did not like a dirty floor.

God, she looked beautiful, even in her rather leggy, awkward stance. Macomber had completed one first-class paint job, a lot of it by himself. It was an enormous task and we had spent thousands of dollars on paint. The name "BARBIE III" was in place, the diagonal stripes were incredible as were the American Stars and Bars. She was now carrying R. T. Smith's serial number on her tail. She was all dressed up and had no place to go. We now had just over $389,000 invested and tens of thousands of volunteer man-hours. We were a far cry from Walter's prediction in dollars and years.

The engine came together, was mounted, and it ran just fine. After Gene's new dictum of ten hours of running time, Gene certified it and we sent the man his remaining $2,000. The FAA wrote off the engines in their progressive certification. All that remained to do were the hydraulics and we would have a legally flyable B-25.

I started to again explore the insurance market and Tatelman started to make inquires also. The warbird market insurance had, in a few years, improved dollar-wise and pilot experience qualifications decreased. Don't get me wrong; it was still expensive but it would be obtainable. Insurance companies had begun to realize the money in warbirds and they were scrambling for business. This would drive the price down as they competed. My insurance agent was right; they would soon ask us if they could insure our B-25. Weary Warriors would eventually luck out with our insurance quest.

In 1991, the most expensive B-25 around had an asking price of $325,000 dollars. It did not take a rocket scientist to realize we had one hell of an expensive B-25 and it had a lot of old used parts.

It would have cost us some $425,000 when we finished in early 1992. We estimated that every dollar we had originally invested, was now, in 1991, worth about sixty cents. Not a good investment dollar-wise.

Someone had told me that, in 1943, a brand spanking new B-25 cost $73,000. In the year 2002, as I write this book, there are two mint glass-nosed B-25's on the market. They are zero-timed, have operating turrets and are original. The asking price on each is $1,200,000.

I gathered Glen, Walter, and Hable around me and we discussed the hydraulics. Why would they work and then not work? When something was in a certain mode; say, like the flaps down; the gear would not go up. If we raise the flaps, maybe the gear would retract. We all had our theories but, somewhere in the thousand feet of hydraulic plumbing, something was hooked up wrong. All we had to do was find it. We would have to trace every line, label each line and, with manual in hand, track it down. I also felt it could be a ten cent valve somewhere in the system that was corroded.

Money, money was on my brain. I talked to Tatelman and Porter. I had come up with the idea that we loan Weary Warriors some money instead of buying shares like we had been doing. The dollar value was no longer there in 1990 and, when we sold the B-25, we would recoup our loans in full before we divided the pie, so to speak. The "pie" would be divided by number of shares outstanding into the dollar amount of the sale (after we'd subtracted the interest free loan money). This way, we would not lose money on the loan but it would take away from the per share value. We would each throw in, say, five thousand dollars to keep us going. Tatelman and Porter were agreeable. Now I had to sell the idea to the members, whose value-per-share would drop.

Every time the nice young man came for a look, his wife was with him. He was a corporate pilot for an outboard motor company in Wisconsin. He wanted to buy in and, since we needed the cash, the board let him put a few thousand up front to hold our last open slot, giving him his requested five months to come up with the balance. His time was up and we had a second pilot interested in joining us. I made the call. He told me he could not raise the balance due and I said yes, we would return his money. Our arrangements were that we would have just as much time to return his money as he had been given to pay his balance. His wife must have called me every week demanding their money back.

We needed money and it got to the point that I was not sure where our next month's rent was going to come from. We got a short reprieve when the yearly dues came due and we had a few thousand in the bank. Some members just decided to buy more shares in Barbie and I got rid of the nagging wife. We also decided to put Gene back to work on the hydraulics but kept him on a tight leash, money-wise.

Eventually, we found the hydraulic problem. Two lines were crossed and there was some corrosion on a valve seat. Again, the question —- who crossed the lines and when? With the confused lines put back in their proper places, we were, at long last, certified and began to prep for the test flight.

Macomber masked off the famous five stripes with tape and gave the project a lot of thought. The stars and bars would go on at the same time. One of the bars had to notch into the last stripe while the star was on top of the side escape hatch. One of the bad points of the B-25 was that if it was bellied in, the two belly hatches were useless. The front crew had an escape hatch in the top of the cockpit canopy. Note the open bomb bay doors.

What many Weary Warriors forgot was that Macomber was a master painter for one of the largest car manufacturers in the U. S. and painted all their show and dream cars. For us he was a real "find." His painting skills were extraordinary.

Lou Fulgaro

Barbie III and Company

Sometime in late 1990 or early 1991, I received a phone call from War Birds of America, a division of the Experimental Aircraft Association, both of which I belonged to. Someone had seen or heard of us at the '90 Rockford Warbird Show and it was evident we were a unique organization with a unique warbird. Would I write a descriptive article without the usual razz-ma-tazz; come from a different perspective for the warbird magazine? I sent off the article within a week on a disk. Three months later, they called to ask when I was going to send the article. I advised them that I had sent it. They had it and must have misplaced it. No, I would not rewrite it.

Ten years later, I found the old-fashioned five-inch backup disk at the bottom of a box and had it transferred to a modern three-inch disk and, viola! The ten year-old article comes back to life. It is printed here as it was written in 1991.

REMEMBRANCE
"REFLECTIONS FROM THE 1990 ROCKFORD WARBIRD AIR SHOW"

She is our gift to remembrance; a tribute to our heritage from World War II; a unique instrument of war from the past. Her twin tail design is from a bygone era. Her dynamic stance and compact well-proportioned design draws the eyes of all who walk by. She is admired by all. The novice and the expert alike are drawn to her side.

I sit, relaxed under her wing, escaping the searing July afternoon sun. The hours slip by and thousands "Ooh!" and "Aah!" as they walk by. Inquisitive fingers touch this and that. Glancing at the open bomb bay, I count ten pairs of legs from the hips down. The bomb bay doors hide the torsos. I wonder who is attached to the legs. A young boy counts the machine guns.

"There's twelve of them!" he shouts to an adult male.

A woman asks, "What's that in the nose?"

"A 75MM cannon," one of my partners remarks. The rest of the conversation fades and is lost as they walk to the other side of our cannon-nose B-25. I smile to myself: the prettier the woman, the more attention she gets.

An elderly, gray-haired male is heading our way with a determined walk. In tow, I would assume, is his grandson. As he nears, he is telling his grandson, "This is what Grandpa flew when I was younger than your daddy."

The gentleman is visibly excited. He points and pats the cannon muzzle explaining it is a 20MM cannon. He is a little off in muzzle size but that's okay. He exaggerates the speed of the B-25 to a woman (who must be his wife) as she catches up to them but that's all right, too. He has tears in his eyes. He is special. We will let him up in the cockpit and we advise him to come back around six o'clock after the show.

Camera shutters are clicking all around us. Two of my partners busy themselves as adults and children line up ten deep to step on a wire milk bottle crate and poke their heads up and inside the forward hatch. We don't charge them to look, but we don't let them inside either. We give no paid tours.

As president of this crazy fourteen-member bunch known as The Weary Warrior Squadron, Inc., it is my role to day to meet and greet, then grip and grin. The more money you may have, the more I talk the talk. We own this smoke belching, fire breathing cannon-nosed sweetheart and we are looking for one well-heeled pilot with a fat checkbook.

A second gray-haired gentleman walks a wide circle around our B-25, eyeing her up from all angles. He is telling hair-raising war stories. He is off by himself and poses for some photos and then approaches me. I invite him to sit in a lawn chair next to me, which we keep open and call it our "sit and get" chair. That is; when you sit in it, I try and get your money.

The questions start.

"When was she built, how much to restore her?"

"In 1943, serial number 43-4106. She was the second cannon-nose B-25 built and is very rare. To date, our restoration has cost us $389,000 with 22,517 volunteer and paid man-hours. We are still counting dollars and hours. Business cards are exchanged. He flew B-25 G's H's and J's in the Pacific. How I envy him. Curiously, today, he envies me.

"How did you ever get involved in such a project?" he asks. He is watching a black oil droplet clinging tenaciously to a corner of a cowl flap.

I wanted to avoid the long answer, but he persists. He skillfully dodges the elongated drop of black, sixty-weight engine oil bobbled by the summer breeze as it journeys to the hot cement. I decide to give him the short answer version. The love of warbirds brought us together and this warbird keeps us together.

From a dream, to a desire, to realty took some forty-five years for me. When we started about seven years ago, we faced formidable obstacles; we simply hunkered down and defiantly refused to cave in or give up. In between, we had to have the willingness to work and make difficult, expensive decisions. Our odyssey would strain relationships, enlarge our vocabulary of profanity, and, with maturity, learn to put aside petty differences. It was precarious at times but we persevered.

The gentleman stands up, straining to look over the heads of the people milling around us. He has our fact sheets in hand. He asks about my personal thoughts. I am sixty years old this summer and my boyhood dream towers over me. Sometimes her presence is frightening, overwhelming. Her massive engines develop an awesome, combined 3400 horsepower. She is forty-six years old but acts like she is sixteen.

Climbing up the forward hatch into the top turret compartment is a step back in time to forty-five years ago. The stark, sterile nakedness of a combat machine fills your vision. Exposed wires, cables, hydraulic lines, fuel lines, brackets, pulleys, handles, and valves contrast sharply against the bare stark interior. One well-placed bullet could blow the whole thing to hell. Your senses are confused by the ever-present mixed odor of sweat, fuel, oil, and hydraulic fluid. The hotter the day, the more overwhelming the pungent smell is. There are no creature comforts. It is, in reality, an expendable killing machine. It was its only purpose to exist.

I tell our guest that sitting between the two thundering -29's is an encounter only a few can experience today. Mentally, when I enter the cockpit, I always salute the many young men that died in a cockpit just like this one.

"The picture on the poster shows the name BARBIE III and strange markings," he notes.

"They were part of the Tenth Air Force," I answer. "They called themselves the First Air Commandos.

"Never heard of them." commented our visitor.

"Few have." I commented back. "That is one of the reasons we chose Barbie. No one ever heard of us either."

We shake hands and he hustles off with a backward glance and gives a civilian type salute. Adjusting the lawn chair for deeper shade, I sit back down. The voices of my partners drift over to me. Three of them are in their seventies, two in their mid-sixties. At age sixty, I am the youngster.

A gaggle of young seventy year-olds is headed our way. Cameras dangling, bi-focals in place, baseball caps off-center. It is easy to spot the leader of the group. He has gold braid on the visor of his cap. They approach with their eyes fixed on our B-25.They approach in a ragged skirmish line. The same story will be told again. I wonder if it gets better with each telling.

The rewards and self-satisfaction on a day like this are very evident. Egos are at an all time high. We belong to a very exclusive club but do not flaunt it. There are no smirks on our faces. At long last, our B-25 looks like a B-25. The camaraderie, though strained at times, is easy today. I always did like to talk warbirds even though I am a solitary person by nature. Barbie makes me very special. I know the rest of the Weary Warriors feel the same way. We are proud of her and delight in showing her off. She is almost like a grandchild. We welcome all who come to touch and inquire. We are not arrogant pompous, cold, or indifferent. We are humble warriors today in the presence of our B-25 and thankful to those who come to share in her magic.

The line of seniors has arrived. The leader approaches me with an extended hand and a smile. Skillfully, he dodges a drop of black engine oil, a good sign. I rise to meet and greet, grip and grin. I wonder if he can afford thirty thousand to buy in. Immediately I begin to measure him and access his potential. He is well groomed which spells money. He has a small EAA pin on his collar, which could mean pilot. I talk the talk and give him my full attention and put forth my best manners. Time will tell. It is a good way to end the last hour of the last day of a good air show.

At our second air show the most looked at and investigated component of 06 was the bomb bay. People were mesmerized by the dazzling mechanical display. From my viewpoint seated under a portion of a wing, it was literally a sea of legs and feet. I always wondered who was attached to the legs. They all poked and probed leaving behind their chewing gum, pop corn bags and soda pop containers. We learned to live with it and cleaned up after them.

Lou Fulgaro

Retirement and the "Ding"

The year 1991 came and I was ready to retire a second time - this time for good. I will hang up my private detective licenses for four states and walk away: it was time to get out of the rat race and the stress related to running a business. There was one small glitch. Barbie was not ready. She was close, very close, but still not there: there were hydraulic problems again, this time with the brakes. I tried hard to bring the two events together at the same time, but it was not to be. I was on schedule and, as always, Barbie was not.

My wife and I decided to put our home on the market and, once sold, give us two to three months to clean things up and walk away. We would leave family, friends, and a very good income. It would come to be that the income part was like falling off a financial cliff.

Many years earlier, Dee and I had fallen in love with the Great Smoky Mountains National Park in East Tennessee and, after several visits, decided it would be a nice place to spend our last years. Believing in the three big P's of management [Prior Planning Pays], we had purchased two parcels of land that bordered the park. Here, someday, we would build our retirement home.

As time passed during Barbie's build up, I realized the B-25 was a rather selfish indolence on my part and I began to think family. My wife loved old wooden boats with their rich exotic woods, classic lines, and varnished bright work. In the winter of 1984, we purchased an old wooden motor yacht with an overall length of forty-one feet with a fourteen-foot beam. We had hired an independent surveyor who examined the boat for us, declared it would need six to eight thousand dollar's worth of work to replace some rotten wood and into the shop she went. I had one happy wife. We named the boat after her. Two years and sixty-five thousand dollars later (so much for estimates) we had the most pristine classic wooden boat you ever saw. I also learned restoring wood was just as expensive as restoring aluminum.

As we plied the waters of Lake Michigan, we fell in love with our boat and decided that, when we retired, we would take the boat with us, moor her on one of the TVA lakes near our property and live aboard her while we built our retirement home. It was a nicely thought out plan and it was now time to execute it.

Our home was sold and in mid-1991 it was time to pack up and go. Barbie was less than thirty days away from the big day and operational flight procedures, check lists, rules for flight crews and passengers were being formulated.

I conferred with Vice President Tatelman and Walter Wild. Being a hands-on type person living some six hundred miles away, I felt I should pass the torch and resign from the board. I wanted to take a back seat as I had promised myself to do when we reached this stage. Anyway, it was time to build that new home that my wife and I had designed. Tatelman and Walter would not hear of my resignation and insisted I stay on. The reason was still the same —- no one wanted the job. With tongue in cheek, I kissed Barbie goodbye, advised Weary Warriors they were on their own for better or worse. It was a sort of a "don't call me I will call you" thing. I felt that there was a lot of talent and intelligence in our group and the step from restoration to flight was an easy one. Many things were already in place, including the hanger space in Aurora. I advised Tatelman, who lived twice the distance away as I did that, while it bothered me, I would not be a candidate for office at our next annual meeting.

Absentee leadership is not a good thing. People being people, the first thing that happened in my absence was a final falling out with our mechanic, Gene and the resulting loss of hanger space. The delicate balance of getting along was soon trashed. Relations with Gene came to a not-too-pleasant end. Barbie was out in the cold, so to speak. Weary Warriors found a new home at Rockford and this put my mind at ease. What was to come up next floored me.

I was relaxing on our boat, admiring the warmth of the teak deck and the phone rings. It is Tatelman, who is thinking of buying out Hanson's shares. Hanson had visited him and wanted out. In a matter of days, Hanson, our first real B-25 pilot, is gone.

He had worked so hard, taught us so much, given years of his time and shared his wealth of experience that it was hard to comprehend. In the back of my mind, I searched for some reason for his departure. We were within weeks of flying: why now? The reasons were subtle and I think they just piled up. He was a very sensitive man and did not take to making close friends. Very few could get close to him. There could have been other reasons and there probably were.

The democratic process, being what it is, contributed to his leaving —- or at least made it easier. Tatelman and Hanson were both being considered for our top slot of Chief Pilot. Weary Warriors chose Tatelman who was simply more likable. Hanson got the title of senior/instructor pilot and was, I thought, deeply hurt.

Then, suddenly, Barbie was going to become a full IFR ship and just bristle with modern-day antennas. Tatelman would purchase and loan a complete IFR radio package —- and have it installed. Our low and slow, look-and-see style of flying went to hell: it was not as our B-25 was intended to be. Glen held firmly to this original avenue and I sympathized with him. Glen's original beautiful instrument panel that he worked so hard to complete would soon be cluttered up with little black electronic boxes and look like the panel of an airliner capable of transatlantic flight.

Next on the list was a real heart breaker. Barbie was being tweaked for her big day, which was now one day off. At long last her time had come. The commercial hanger where she was housed had a peaked roof in the center of the doorway, which would allow her twin rudders to pass through easily. One of the landlord's employees was backing her through this opening without wing walkers and struck the steel door opening. One rudder and its stabilizer impacted with such force that the twenty three-foot horizontal stabilizer was permanently twisted.

It was a major disaster for Weary Warriors. All of the truck rentals, the year plus of Tatelman rebuilding the tail, Habel's months of installing, Robinson's weeks of cabling, wiring, and rigging, and Macomber's painting was a shambles. It was going to be a major repair and would delay the first flight by seven months. Once again, the rudders and elevators would have to be disconnected and removed, then the two vertical stabilizers and, finally, the horizontal stabilizer.

Tatelman again made arrangements for a rental truck and most of the tail was on its way to Florida, but two things are different this time. First, the landlord's insurance company, straining relations further, will pay for most of the repair. Secondly, the tail goes to Tom Rielly's B-25 complex in Kissamee Florida for repair. Tom is a longtime friend of Weary Warriors and during the build up of Barbie, he visited several times.

Weary Warriors, because of their falling out, for whatever reason, with the mechanic, new landlord are between a hard place and a rock. They were supposed to be in Aurora by now and there is no space at Rockford to hanger Barbie. She stands outside in the weather for the entire winter of 1991/1992. Walter assures me she is well tarped over the cockpit, tail end, and engines and that most of the guns have been removed. I am really irked at the turn of events and, in my mind, I envision our precious pristine warbird, battered, broken and left neglected and abandoned to the elements. No one had worked harder than I to make sure that she would never be in such a position. When I remember all the time I spent smoothing over relations and personality clashes between our landlords, hired mechanics, and some of our members, it is too much for me. I only look at the result, do not like what I see, and it is the last straw.

I blame everybody and I blame nobody. Two months before my term expires, I send a note to Tatelman. It is my letter of resignation as President of Weary Warriors and I remove myself from the board. I had let Barbie down. I failed to follow through and broke my promise to her. I blamed myself.

Early spring 1992. Tom Rielly, true to his reputation has completed a well-done tail rebuild. Out of two bad ones, he and his crew build one good one. Tatelman, living close-by, visits Rielly's shop on several occasions and assures Weary Warriors it is a first-class piece of workmanship. The tail is better than new. Rielly comes to Illinois, installs the tail, and adds a few shims to get it rigged just right. He takes Barbie down the runway to try her out lifts her a few feet off the ground for a hundred yards or so, the tail does what it is supposed to do and he sets her back down.

He advises Weary Warriors "Why don't you guys go fly your airplane?" and heads back to Florida.

A short time later, the official first flight day comes. It is May 1992, some fifty years after our war with Japan. The place is an airport in Northern Illinois. A few people gather to witness and photograph a meticulously restored cannon-nosed B-25H prepare for its first flight in eleven years. Her colors are flat olive drab paint exactly as it was when R.T. Smith and his crew drove her around the hostile skies over Burma in the early 1940s. On the vertical stabilizer, the yellow serial number 34380, the same serial number as R.T. Smith's mount, stands out. On its cannon nose, just above the muzzle of its cannon, is the Roman numeral I. Below the cockpit in yellow, outlined in blue, is the name "BARBIE III". Five white diagonal stripes adorn the fuselage behind the trailing edge of the wings.

In the cockpit, the Pilot-In-Command is Tatelman. Barbie responds to his touch and like a ghost from the past, thunders off the runway at Greater Rockford, Illinois airport and angles her blunt nose skyward. Her powerful radial engines pull her through the hazy sky for all to see and hear.

Now airborne, it could once again be 1944. The noise, the smells and vibrations are the same. Time cannot change those images that feel. But today, if you look very closely, the pilot in command is bespectacled and gray with age although he still flies with the skill of a master. BARBIE III lives again, thanks to the efforts of many. She flies today as a living museum of remembrance to this magnificent medium bomber, the gallant men who crewed them and to the brave men who died in them.

Weary Warriors have reached the stage where the work theme of "Let's not look forward at how much we got to do, let's look back at how much we have done" comes to an end.

Like at the beginning in 1981, I was not there for the finale in 1992. I was not aware of the flight plans and I guess the old saying out of sight out of mind holds true.

As Barbie rumbles off into the distance, Habel turns to Macomber and makes the comment, "It's a shame Lou is not here to see this."

Macomber replies, "He's up there with her; all of us are up there with her. His time will come — this is only the beginning."

Vic Tatelman and the author. We knew someday Barbie was going to fly and when she did, we could not believe it. Once the hatch closed behind you, you stepped back into a glorious time in history and the good part was yet to come. Photo: Reporter Progress Newspaper, by Diane Alrich.

Barbie Waltzes With the Big Guys
Oshkosh 1997

Perhaps a better title for this chapter would be "Barbie and the Best of the Best."

"BARBIE III" sat proud and tall in the warbird flight line. She was in some real high-class company. She attracted a lot of attention, being one of a kind. She was not a glossy painted cookie cutter warbird. With some paint chipped here and some faded there, she looked like a war-weary combat veteran.

The seasoned Air Force Captain walked around her poking and probing "One hell of a gun ship. Ever been to California?"

He was Capt. "Cujo" Macouso. It was his third trip in the last two days trying to make contact with one of Barbie's owners. He had, at last, connected with Pat Habel. He was looking for a few good men, so to speak. Actually, he was looking for a "good old-fashioned gun ship", as he called it. The B-25H was different and the Air Force wanted to fly our airplane. Yes; they preferred low and slow. It was a straightforward request that was interesting, to say the least.

"Barbie" had never been referred to as a gun ship - this was a modern-day term. A seed was being planted, as the two men talked that meeting would bear fruit in the fall of 1999. Habel took the officer's card and passed it on to Doc Hillson, now President of Weary Warriors. Hillson passed the card off to Tateleman. Hillson felt that, with Tatelman being retired Air Force, he was a natural to work out the logistics and clearances, which would take time. The visit by Lt. Col. Imig, who was operations commander of the test flight school, along with an Air Force airframe mechanic, was a good indication that they were really interested in Barbie.

They came all the way from California to Aurora, Illinois to take a look, talk to Hillson, and have the mechanic inspect Barbie. The Air Force was not about to put any of their pilots in a corroded piece of junk. Once the inspection was complete and the aircraft logs examined, the mechanic gave his approval and some serious talk was completed.

All of her pilots would be F-15 and 16 pilots, male and female, some foreign, and many who had seen combat in the Gulf

War. Some of the pilots would be instructors. But the younger ones did not have a clue what went before them: they needed indoctrination and an appreciation of what combat was like in World War II. They had seen movies and read books but they needed more of the feel of an airplane that a test pilot gets with modern jets.

Barbie would spend sixteen days, fly two hours in the morning and two hours in the afternoon, seven days a week. Sometimes she would fly three times a day with a briefing before each flight. Each flight would have three Air Force pilots on board who would rotate in and out of the left seat. Weary Warriors would fly the right seat, set all power settings, raise and lower flaps, and work the gear. The pilots were not there to learn how to fly a B-25 —- they were there to learn how to feel and deal with control pressures. There would be a lot of note-taking. Non-pilot Weary Warriors would act as flight engineers and observers.

For this, there would be no compensation but O'Donnell, Hillson and Tateleman would get acquainted with speeds in excess of Mach I in an Air Force two place T-38 as a "thank you". All three would break the sound barrier. Tatelman stated that the F-86 Saber Jet he flew in combat over Korea was like a child's red coaster wagon compared to the T-38, which was the jet trainer of today.

The Air Force would pick up the fuel bill for Barbie while she was at Edwards, house and feed the Weary Warriors. They would have to pay their own way there and back including fuel and or repairs. For their country, and nothing but their country's thanks, they would go to this hot, godforsaken, desolate desert and wear the hell out of their B-25, sweat like they'd never sweated before, and cross their fingers.

October 2, 1999 was a typical fall day in Illinois as Doc Hillson gathered his crew together. They were on their way to sunny, warm, Southern California.

Jim O'Donnell, a twenty thousand-hour airline pilot, was a new member. He and Hillson would be the drivers and Morris, Macomber, Taylor, and Habel would make up the crew. The Weary Warrior crew pointed Barbie west by southwest from Aurora Airport and aimed for Edwards Air Force Base in southern California. She was not going for a show and tell. Barbie, in her old age, was going back to work for her country.

Edwards Air Force Base is our country's premier test site center. It is the home to the most sophisticated aircraft in the world, incorporating the pinnacle of state of the art technology. The best test pilots America have call Edwards home.

Barbie would share hangers with some polished, sleek, swept-wing aircraft that cruised more than ten times faster than she did. They could climb to one hundred thousand feet in three minutes. It takes Barbie three minutes to get to three thousand feet, including the takeoff run. Barbie begins to struggle hard at a height above twenty-three thousand feet.

In her mature years, Barbie would once again strut her stuff for her country with some very fast company. She could do one thing that her dazzling rocket-like powered younger sisters did not do. She could teach the best pilots in America how to fly an airplane by touch.

One of the pilot trainers at Edwards told us, "Our guys are lacking some very basic piloting skills. They can strap on the winged rocket, light the fuse, point the damn thing down the runway and enter the world of Buck Rogers and Flash Gordon. What they cannot do is fly by the seat of their pants."

Being young and trained in only modern aircraft, most had never sat behind a propeller and flown an airplane with their muscles. They never strained to move a control. They did not know how to yank a control at one end and have a cable move something at the other end. They did not know how to fly without control boost, or computers, or fly-by-wire technology. Most of the aircraft sitting under Barbie's wing would have the ailerons and elevators moving hundreds of times a minute, controlled by computers, which made micro-corrections, as they cruised at a thousand miles an hour. Pilots sat in their heated/air conditioned complex office and watched their control surfaces flapping up and down while they sat, essentially "doing" nothing.

The basic skill they needed was to be able to fly the airplane instead of managing the airplane as it flew them. No magical electronic help: you fly by looking out the window instead of looking at digital readouts or electronic screens. To round off their test pilot skills, they needed flying time in an old, antiquated, powerful mass of flying iron that was so different from what they were used to that, as they climbed up the hatch, they became novices.

What was power more than a half of century ago was like a gnat on an elephant's butt today. The Air Force wanted to go from an airplane that was a perfect ten to an airplane that was a perfect one on the same ten scale. The only way they wanted the airplane to talk to their pilots is in what the pilots felt "through the seat of their pants", so to speak.

Enter Barbie, the perfect one on the ten scale. She provided the mass, the power, the outrageously slow cruise speed of 250 MPH —- and an instructor pilot who could sit alongside the young pilots and coach them. She looked like a warbird, acted like a warbird, sounded like a warbird, and smelled like a warbird. She was perfect for what they wanted. She was about as original as you could get as the Air Force entered the twenty-first century.

When Barbie entered the magical world at Edwards, she was a flying dinosaur. At age fifty-six, she and Hillson, age sixty, were the oldest working "things" there until Tatelman showed up. At age eighty, that honor then fell to him. The pilots that would fly her and the mechanics that would pamper her were kids compared to her and the Weary Warrior crews with her. They were awed by her history as a killing machine and her straightforward simplicity. No exotic helmets were needed in this cockpit; no strap-tight G suits, no oxygen masks, no lace-up boots, nobody to strap you in, no special nothing.

If you were hot and wanted cool air, open the two sliding side windows on either side of the cockpit. If you were cold, close the windows and the two direct air vent scoops. Learn to sweat or shiver. There was really no comfortable in-between. The young pilots would learn quickly how temperature affects fatigue.

"You're going to sweat so much when you're through, you will want to burn your flying gear."

"Oh, don't worry about the vibration, we assure you the tail is not going to fall off."

"Wow, I took a real beating from the noise while in the cockpit."

"Yes, we know."

Barbie gathered a crowd when she arrived. Her history and reputation preceded her. There were a lot of anxious pilots. They could not wait to get their hands on her. None were born when the cannon-nosed B-25's reigned supreme over Burma and the South

Pacific. At long last, she had arrived and sat on the ramp like she belonged there.

There were a lot of gung-ho pilots and this was going to be a real experience for them. They were aggressive, intelligent, and were about to step into the past. They all wanted to go first. Barbie would soon take the pilots by the hand and say hello. She would let them get settled, get comfortable, feel like they fit in, and then teach the hot shots a thing or two.

It was a meeting of yesterday's craftsmen and tomorrow's technology. She could do something her young modern sisters would not dare do. She leaked oil, like a tobacco-chewing mountain man who did not bathe too often or change clothes who, visiting his high-class sister-in-law in her Manhattan penthouse, did not know where to spit. The contrast was that obvious. The pilots at Edwards would soon be mesmerized by her unique, antique charms.

Tatelman would join the rest of Weary Warriors a few days after their arrival. He came first-class by commercial airline.

He was not about to endure ten to eleven hours in cold weather in a B-25. Not at his age and not with his intelligence.

It was a good choice. Barbie was airborne, about two hours from Aurora, Taylor smelled fresh hydraulic fluid but, after a quick check, everything appeared okay. Five minutes later, Macomber reported fluid spraying out of the starboard engine nacelle. Hydraulic fluid was being pushed out of the system at a thousand PSI. Habel remarked it was raining hydraulic fluid. Three spare gallons were quickly added. The pressure needle continued its downward journey and Hillson and O'Donnel were advised to "slow this thing down and drop the gear and flaps" while some pressure remained.

Down and locked and with zero pressure, they elected to land at Omaha. The landing was good and they swung off the runway and headed for a repair shop. As they approached and applied the brakes, they found they had no brakes, were aimed at two parked gasoline trucks and could not stop or turn. They had an emergency air brake lever but where the hell was it? Never used, its location could be easily forgotten. Hillson's brain clicked in and, on the hydraulic console, he located and pulled up sharply on the small emergency air brake lever, broke the safety wire and then pushed the lever down again. Barbie's brakes locked up, bringing her to a quick and abrupt stop. The stop was so sudden that the crew in the back who, feeling they had it made, had unbuckled, and were slammed against the rear bomb bay bulkhead, followed by tools, parts, duffel bags, and anything else that was loose. They stopped twenty feet short of the parked gas trucks.

The shop emptied their hanger, got Barbie inside and had a look into the nacelle. There was a hairline crack at a hydraulic fitting and, with a simple repair, it was corrected. It was caused by vibration and soon after this trip all fittings would be connected with flex pipe. Now they had to get the air out of the hydraulic lines, which meant bleed the hydraulic system and recharge the emergency air brake system. It would take time and the repair was expensive.

Near Nevada, they started to get engine readings that the starboard engine was ailing. Once on the ground, after close examination of the electrical system by Morris and Taylor, Weary Warriors' electronic geniuses, it was determined that some electrical cannon plugs were immersed in hydraulic fluid from the previous incident at Omaha. It was quickly remedied. Once at Edwards, a fuel pump failed and had to be replaced. Tony and Carl of Aero Traders once again came to the rescue.

There were many stories told as the pilots got acquainted with Barbie. Two of them are repeated here.

To set up a solid feel for the controls, a power setting for a 250 MPH cruise, burning 160 to 170 gallons of fuel an hour was set. To control Barbie, especially when maneuvering, both leg and arm muscle would have to be used. To give the sensation of speed, most flying was done below one hundred feet. Morris remarked that at times they were so low they created a dust trail. Pilots worked up a sweat as they weaved and bobbed, twisted and turned through canyons and arroyos at speeds that made the desert floor a blur.

On one of these rides, the young pilot crested a low mountain ridge at about thirty feet, went down the down slope and speed built up to over 300 MPH. Reaching the valley floor, the young officer leveled off and bored on, straight ahead. On the other side of the valley, about a mile ahead, the up slope of a mountain rose from the valley floor.

Tatelman asked the young pilot, "What are your intentions Lieutenant?"

"Climb up the slope and over the top of the ridge, Sir," was the reply.

Tatelman grinned, "Then you damn well better get started right now or we're going to bounce off that mountain."

With muscles straining, the young pilot held the control column back into his chest. He was damn near standing on the rudder controls bracing himself to overcome the elevator pressure. Up, over the crest. Now push the control column forward, level off and drop the nose so you don't stall out. A lesson well learned, the exhausted pilot let the next pilot take over.

At cruise, a Weary Warrior nonchalantly reached over, put the carburetor heat on and reduces one engine to idle. The yaw effect is overwhelming. The young pilot stomps on a rudder pedal [sometimes the wrong one] and tries to hold the B-25 in a straight line. There was no rudder trim used to help out, just one locked, stiff leg holding one rudder pedal against its stop. In a very short time, the pressure of two large rudders would wear your leg down. With leg and body braced, ramrod fashion, against the seat back, most had to eventually resort to two feet on the same rudder pedal to hold her in a straight line.

That's how it went day after day. It was hot and it was a grind. Some forty-five pilots got a taste of a "you-got-to-work-at-it airplane." As I listened to Hillson, Habel, Morris, and Tatelman, I could not help but reflect that, in 1943, inventory serial number 43-4106 spent all of her military life between MacDill Air Force Base [of one-a-day-in-Tampa Bay fame] and what is now the Air Force Museum in Dayton. She served as a test lab for just about everything the military could come up with. She never saw combat, never fired a shot at the enemy. It was fitting that over half a century later, she would once again respond to her country's request and do what she did best.

****
****

"BARBIE III" passes into the twenty-first century as many of the original Weary Warriors that gave her the gift of life age, pass on and dwindle in number. Eventually, she will indeed outlive all of them. New and younger members take their place, fill in the gaps and carry this rare warbird forward for all Weary Warriors who preceded them. As Barbie thunders into the twenty-first century, belching fire and smoke with her mission of remembrance, she carries the legend of the B-25's and the men who crewed them with her.

Weary Warriors have managed and maintained Barbie well and they do it still with the help of a few friends. Under the guidance and the experience of those that came first, pilots, flight crews, maintenance, and operations learn the magic ways of Barbie through a conduit that carries a smooth flow of information and experience. Some members wear two hats, some three. As the years pass, adjustments are made, changes are implemented, and updated methodologies are initiated: flexibility and awareness are the key. The driving force, the principles, and the spirit that prevailed from the impromptu meetings when 06 was a near-hopeless pile of junk scattered about the hanger floor are still there.

The beginning provides the foundation for Weary Warriors to grow, mature, and live on. They bring 43-4106 with them —-

THE END

Eight years later, this is the after photo. The pilot seat is not installed. The instrument panel, made from scratch by Hanson, was a masterpiece. The long handle at the bottom is the hydraulic hand pump. We all spent a lot of time working this handle when we had our hydraulic problems. The small oblong handle between the pump handle and seat is the emergency air brake. Leslie Hicks.

Lou Fulgaro

The business end of Barbie III. The four ammo boxes have not been installed. Note the top turret.

Dave Morris our electronic genius and Al Heinz a mechanical wizard with the top turret. It was a mechanical master piece and after this photo was taken it was lowered through the top turret opening and installed.

The rusted and corroded gun sight after Milt Gaden restored it to pristine condition. I found it in 1983 and sixteen years later in 1999 we talked about installing it for the 2000 Sun and Fun Air Show.

October 1999. From the piles of near scrap, this pristine, unique warbird restoration emerged. It took ten years, tens of thousands of volunteer man-hours, over $400,000 and some very strained relations. We had the only flying cannon nosed B-25H in the world. Photo by Ray "Doc" Hillson. Tatelman collection.

This frontal view shows her ammo boxes and ammo steel feed chutes. The two protrusions on the top of the nose hood are covers for the hood lock release mechanism. Photo Ray "Doc" Hillson. Tatelman collection.

A quarter rear view of Barbie. Air show patrons are using her as a giant sunshade. Note the bullet deflectors near the top turret under the machine gun barrels. Photo Ray "Doc" Hillson. Tatelman collection.

Photo Leslie Hicks

Photo Leslie Hicks

Photo Leslie Hicks

303

August 1997. Chicago Air and Water Festival. Over Lake Michigan Barbie positions herself to open the festival. Timing had to be just right. As the Star Spangled Banner ended Barbie had to make her low level pass down several miles of lakefront shoreline. Photo by Vlado Lenoch. "Doc" Hillson collection.

Barbie III and Company

Carrying her dedicated crew of Weary Warriors, her nose and tail bristling with machine guns, Barbie thunders by overhead on her way into the twenty-first century. Sixty years ago, over Burma, this is the view that many Japanese had of her during her deadly strafing attacks. Photo Pat Habel.

"——this cannon toting sweetheart was nothing more than a blunt nosed killer. The Japanese soon learned when a cannon shell punctured their slab-sided armor, before exploding, it spun around the interiors, shredding the crew into a bone splintered pulp that clung to the twisted steel and burned-out interiors——"

R. T. Smith

Lou Fulgaro

Where Are They Now Year 2003
Miscellaneous Odds and Ends

BUTLER, GADEN, SERRANO and DeFACCI: Remain on the inactive list. BUTLER and DEFACCI for some twenty years. Weary Warriors bought out KOPPIE and HRACEK when they lost interest.

LAMBERT: Has remained a friend to Weary Warriors. He often shows up at local air shows to touch base with 43-4106.

FENCEL: About a year or so after the Gary/Aurora conflict, walked away from Weary Warriors; regretfully, a very bitter man. Weary Warriors bought him out in 1994. FENCEL had a favorite war story he told me several times and it went like this.

He was a B-24 enlisted air crewmember assigned to German submarine patrol duty over the Atlantic. The incident happened some twelve hours into their search and destroy patrol and they were on their way home. Most of the crew had dozed off, put into a dream world by the endless expanse of the ocean and the monotonous, steady drone of their four engines.

Dead ahead of them —- and submerging —- was a German U-boat. The B-24 crew jumped to life as they lined up for their depth charge run. They came in low and slow, dropping half their depth charges and climbed away. The tail gunner reported the sub was bracketed nicely by their salvo of depth charges and buried in cascading, erupting columns of water. They had executed and completed a textbook bomb run.

They swung around for another run or look and the PIC ordered FENCEL to take some photos for confirmation of their kill. FENCEL, leaning out the port waist gunner's position, took two photos of the floundering German sub as it settled below the surface.

They were the heroes of the day. When the photos were developed, the intelligence officer advised the "celebrating we are feeling good" crew that they had depth charged a large whale. Their hero status plummeted as fast as their depth charges had. They were the only B-24 in World War II to sport a whale-kill painted on their Liberator.

I still regret FENCEL'S departure from Weary Warriors. He had done so much for us. It was indeed sad. He never spoke to me again. I like to think my moving to TN may have something to do with it. Fencel passed away in 1997.

HABEL, MORRIS, TAYLOR and MACOMBER: Still tend to BARBIE III. They are all now B-25 experts and at least one of them is aboard for every flight. They have had so many in-flight emergencies, changed so many cylinders and hydraulic connections, and repaired so many electrical glitches, that they have lost count.

QUATRINES: Purchased their own light twin and lost interest in Weary Warriors at about the same time that Fencel did. They were very close. QUATRINE also had a favorite war story and this is how it goes.

He was PIC of a B-17 and had many missions over Germany. Once over occupied landfall, he would constantly inquire of his navigator of their exact position in case they were shot down. This would enable him, in his mind, to picture an escape route. Mission after mission, every half-hour after half-hour, Ralph would make the inquiry. One day, when Ralph made the inquiry, the aggravated and perplexed navigator responded, "We are six hundred feet behind the B-17 in front of us!" He never asked again. Ralph and Elaine were bought out in 1994. Ralph passed away in 1998.

TATELMAN: Put himself on the inactive list for a year or so. He pilots his single engine, four place for recreation and lives on a private airstrip with an attached hanger to his home. TATELMAN is on his healthy way into his eighties and Hillson still considers him as their chief senior pilot. TATELMAN takes BARBIE to many of his Air Force reunions.

HILLSON: Is now a retired M.D., has been the President of Weary Warriors for about eight years. He is now sixty plus years old. He has accumulated more hours as PIC of BARBIE III than any other pilot and gets a sparkle in his eye when he tells of cranking BARBIE up to a 300 MPH cruise. Even with her blunt nose, Barbie still cruises faster than any B-25 around with the same power settings. The secret is that the props are indexed a few degrees sharper than the norm.

PORTER and SCHIERA: Both are also PIC's for BARBIE III, both active. PORTER owns several warbirds on his own. He authors the Weary Warriors Squadron Newsletter. As predicted, the FAA has taken several looks at his low, fast, and noisy flying. They were some (very minor) finger pointing-type things but nothing ever came of them.

WILD: Is still considered the father of Weary Warriors and remained active to the age of seventy-five. During the first and second test flights in May of 1992, Walter was aboard as flight engineer. He went to work on the first test flight when they developed a hydraulic leak and had to add fluid to the hydraulic reservoir while in flight. Back on the ground, the leak was repaired over lunchtime and they were back in flight. WILD gave directions and Tatelman steered BARBIE III to her new home at Aurora. Walter passed away summer 2002

HANSON: Never really got to pilot BARBIE III. He has been around the patch a few times as a guest of Weary Warriors. HANSON also used to have a tale or two to tell. When on a strafing run, once, his cannonier had the "75" loaded and ready the cannonier would crawl up on to the flight deck a few feet away and link his arm through and around Glen's arm. This way, HANSON knew the cannon was clear and ready to fire. In the early days, the Air Force would not let them throw out the empty 75MM casings, as they wanted to keep the cannons a secret. The empty shells lay on the floor, really cluttering up the floor and making footing perilous. HANSON also used to mention that after two or three 75MM shots during a long strafing run, the cockpit would fill up with so much smoke they could hardly breath. There was also a problem in that, when the cannon went off, there was so much muzzle pressure built up that, at times, the nose hood would be blown open. Once the noses were properly vented, this problem stopped.

R.T. SMITH: With prop failures, engine failures, weather conditions, and what-have-you SMITH never got to pilot our

BARBIE III. It was a most frustrating scenario for all of us. Our namesake quest fell short. My last words from SMITH were when we planned to bring BARBIE III to a First Air Commando reunion.

They were, "Damn it Fulgaro, I got five hundred bucks for you guys when BARBIE arrives and is sitting on the ramp in front of me." Sadly it never came to be. SMITH passed away in 1995.

CORTEZ F. ENLOE: My last conversation with ENLOE was in early 1995 when he advised me that R.T. SMITH had passed away. ENLOE passed away March 1995 just before his 85th birthday. We never did get to Burma. His daughter, Margaret, informed me that he never finished his book and that the Wingate crash preoccupied him to the end. Dr. Cortez Enloe's manuscripts and research notes explore his time in Burma and the death of General Orde Wingate in detail. All materials were given to the U.S. Air Force Academy in Colorado Springs, CO.

HOWERTON: Is sixty-seven years old as we enter the 21st Century. He sold his B-25 Fairfax Ghost in 1996. He and I still talk. We see each other once in a while at some twin Beech Association get-togethers.

CHAMBERLAIN: The newspaper gal, is now retired. She never saw Barbie once she was flying. Weary Warriors still have some of her posters tucked away in a corner of the hanger.

MARK CLARK: Is still located at Rockford and still sells Warbirds as "Courtesy Aircraft." He has been in the same location doing the same thing, for twenty-five years plus. He is one of the best B-26 drivers around. Once again, Mark; thanks for all the help.

GENE: Our AI mechanic and landlord, gave up on the mechanic shop business and is now a corporate pilot, based in Rockford.

TIM MCCARTER: Of the Aero Plane Factory, has been the manager of Flight and Restoration Amphib, Inc., based at Kenosha, Wisconsin Regional Airport for ten years. His firm specializes in the management, sales, service and rebuilding of amphibian aircraft and warbirds. Always going places, Tim was recently involved in a trip to the Amazon in a twin-engined amphibian called an Albatross.

FIRST AIR COMMANDO REUNION: Moline, Illinois: Summer 1998. BARBIE III is there. Some fifty FAC veterans are there plus their wives, kids, and grandkids. Two of BARBIE III's original crew that was with her in Burma some fifty-five years ago are there. There are a lot of nostalgic tears. At last their wives, kids, and grandkids can see, touch, hear and explore the inside of a cannon-nose B-25. Many only saw pictures and heard mysterious tales of the cannoned-nose B-25's from the FAC veterans.

But it goes much further than see, touch, explore and listen. Whoever wants to go for a short trip around the patch in a fire-breathing smoke-belching lady named BARBIE III goes. Weary Warriors reach deep into their pockets to pay the tab. There are a lot of fly-bys. Weary Warriors lose count. But they fly till everyone who wants to go goes. The most noteworthy passenger is an eighty-seven year-old mother of an FAC veteran. With a lot of help and encouragement, up the hatch she goes. It is the most precious thing BARBIE III will ever carry. Barbie seems to understand and behaves herself. No cute tricks this time.

AIR SHOWS: There are many but only a few will be mentioned as they carry some significance. Our very first show is to MACDILL Air Force Base in in Tampa FL. In March of 1994, the place where #43-4106 spent most of her time during World War II. She is the hit of the show and gets a warm welcome. Every pilot stationed at MacDill gets to sit in her.

The second air show I will mention is also in the summer of 1994. I call it the sweet revenge show. You guessed it. BARBIE III is at the airfield where the failed museum used to be. It is the only show where Barbie is roped off at times. We remember the pilfering and how easy it would be for an unscrupulous person to cut a few wires or puncture a fuel or hydraulic line. There are many museum board members that drift by and former members at large. They view a pristine, cannon-nose B-25 and see what could have been. Those that were friends throughout the entire ordeal get inside.

BARBIE III never missed a warbird show held at Rockford. From a partial airframe towed to her spot for the first four Air Show years, she became the queen of the show. She always attracts a large crowd at Rockford and gets the loudest applause after her performance. Many patrons who attended The Rockford warbird show year after year and followed her progress consider her as theirs. They are not told she is based in Aurora, about forty-five miles away.

MAGAZINES: After many years, BARBIE III at long last makes it to the cover of the November 1996 AIR CLASSICS magazine. AIR CLASSICS is considered by many to be the premier warbird magazine in the World. She also has several full-page photos on the inside. Finally, one Michael O'Leary (the photographer) recognizes a warbird that looks like a warbird. He passes up many glamour gals with their unreal high gloss paint jobs. As always, FLY PAST carried 43-4106 throughout the eighties, nineties and into the twenty-first century. Many Weary Warriors consider being on the cover of AIR CLASSICS as one of the highlights of our restoration effort.

PROPS: You remember the props and the $9,000 overhaul from the shop that Fencel was close friends with and the AD that had to be complied with? The routine yearly inspection in 1996 revealed that one of the props would not feather. Feathering pump again? Not this time. A prop shop up in Minnesota is where the complete prop and hub end up and the news is bad: the three blade shafts are rusted, corroded, and pitted. There are no seals: the AD had not been complied with. We had been had again. Weary Warriors got a beautiful paint job with stenciling and no overhaul and no AD compliance for $9,000. Weary warriors are lucky they did not end up like the DC-3 did that threw a blade.

A complaint is filed with the FAA and Weary Warriors begins looking at litigation. The owner of the prop shop dies and the shop folds. His son opens a second prop shop —- Weary warriors cannot get to him. The son is the person that came to our hanger and hung our props and probably did the so-called overhaul. Weary Warriors are able to save some of the blades from the other prop.

ENGINES: The starboard engine has been changed so many times that Weary Warriors loses count. The port engine is the same engine that 43-4106 flew on out of Lambert's field twenty years ago. Every cylinder has been changed at least once; some twice and one three times.

LUMINAIR: who Weary Warriors rent the hanger from, kept their word. The rent is the same in the year 2002 as I negotiated in 1991. When Barbie, for about a three year period, spent some winter months with Tatelman down in Florida, the rent dropped to half price for the affected months. Weary Warriors was able to set up shop in a corner of the common hanger and Luminair still tows Barbie out and puts her back in with a phone call. Weary Warriors still receive a good fuel discount. AURORA now has more warbirds based there than any airport in the surrounding three states. The JU-52 group (the German transport from our first air show), still based at Gary, is considering a move to Aurora.

WINDSHIELD ARMOR: Is, at last, installed. February 2000 found Hillson, Charly Ramsden and I in the cockpit discussing that important omission along with the gun sight I had purchased some seventeen years ago. R.T. used to tell me that the windshield armor blocked his vision to such an extent that, when landing, he stuck his head out the side window to see where in the hell he was going. I could not help but think how good the closeup of BARBIE III would have looked on the front cover of AIR CLASSICS in 1996 if the armor plate were in place. Over many years, the turret pedestal has been completed and will be installed. Barbie at long last will have an operating top turret.

BARBIE III: Is going to Sun and Fun, considered the premier warbird show in the U.S., in a few months. She is going to the show with detachable armor plate for the windshield, which, for safety reasons, can be removed for flight. Parked on the flight line, the gun sight will be installed and the armor will be in place. (At the Sun and Fun Show, in Spring of 2000, Barbie missed the "Top Bomber" award by two points. Ironically, a highly polished B-25 with airline-type, upholstered seats took the top award. Weary Warriors had to admit, however, that it was a very nice bomber.)

OPERATING COSTS: Kids always ask how fast does it go and adults ask how much does it cost to operate. There are several ways to calculate cost and I have always liked to use hourly cost. Operating costs do not include restoration cost; they are what it costs to fly this thing.

From May 1992 to May 2000, Weary Warriors put 505 hours on her airframe. That is eight complete years of flying. It is nice to take an average over the years, as there are some fixed costs, like rent and insurance; and fluid costs like oil, fuel, and maintenance. It gives you a more honest hourly cost, as there are peaks and valleys. It is a better balance of how much per hour. To determine her hourly cost, we have to crunch some numbers.

Hanger rent has remained the same from day one and that is $483 a month. This number goes down cost-wise as Luminair is nice enough to charge half rent when Barbie is gone a full month. This would apply when Barbie was down in Florida with Tatelman for three short winters. The total hanger rent is $44,195 which, divided by 505 hours, equals $88 an hour.

Insurance is a big nut to crack but it clicks into the cost. One million liability, half million hull coverage, and one hundred thousand per seat costs $13,000 a year times eight years comes to $104,000 divided by 505 hours equals $206 per hour.

Fuel cost is a little bit more problematical. Fuel, at times, cost over three dollars a gallon and consumption can vary by power settings. Some fuel is donated as part of an air show contract but it costs somebody. Looking at fuel cost, an honest $2.50 a gallon is a good average, including discounts. Fuel consumption will average out at 140 gallons an hour. So, at that, fuel consumption per hour Barbie has burned, 70,700 gallons of fuel (ouch). The $176,750 in fuel cost divided by 505 hours is $350 an hour.

Oil is next on the list as Barbie does use oil. The more power, the more oil. It does not matter whether she burns it or leaks it: she consumes oil. Weary Warriors do not change the oil. At four gallons an hour (some swear it is five gallons an hour), Weary Warriors just keep adding. Oil is purchased in fifty-gallon drums at a discount price of $305 a drum, which works out to $5.55 a gallon. Average consumption is four and a half gallons an hour, which makes the cost of oil $25 an hour.

The above cost factors add up to $669 an hour but there is more.

Weary Warriors do most of their own labor and no number is clicked in for that. But there are parts and some labor. Small items like cleaning rags, rust inhibitors in spray cans, paint, and all those small odds and ends needed to support machinery must be considered. Freight for all those expensive cylinders must also be considered. This is where the long years smooth out the big dollar bites. We will not consider the hanger phone bill and such things as postage. Add the maintenance number in and Barbie costs $1034 an hour to fly. That adds up to one big expensive piece of iron to drive around. As of 2003, a tire is $1900. An exchanged, rebuilt cylinder is $800 (compared to $350 in 1987).

TWENTY YEARS: It would take just about that long to get BARBIE III fitted out properly. Individual exhaust stacks, the low profile air intakes, operating top turret, windshield armor, bombs in the bomb bay and the gun sight at long last come together. We also have the ring and post gun sight that can be mounted on the hood. It is a holdover from World War II. SMITH'S Warhawk over in China had one of these sighting systems in case the modern gun sight failed.

Now; where can Weary Warriors get a real 75MM cannon? I drop a suggestion to some of the more outgoing thinking Weary Warriors. A lot of American Legion and Veterans of Foreign Wars halls have 75MM cannons sitting out in front of them. Perhaps with a donation, there may be just one that may loan Weary Warriors one. It's worth a try.

THE CRESCENT-SHAPED DENTS: If you get a chance to see Barbie at an air show, look on the forward bomb bay sheeting bulkhead wall. You will see the dents caused by the 75MM casings striking the bulkhead as they were ejected from the breech. They are still there and can easily be seen and touched while standing in the bomb bay.

TAIGH RAINEY: The young man who found the top half of our cannon nose went on to become a pilot and owns a nicely restored AT-11. He saw Barbie at Oshkosh in 1997 and we had a nice long talk after the Fly-In. Like a lot of us, he had gotten married and was going to sell his AT-11.

SPRING 2000: While R.T. SMITH never got into the air in our BARBIE III, his son Brad did. On a nice spring day, Brad sat up front in the B-25 named after his mother and went for the ride of a lifetime.

About the Author :

In his middle teens, during the years of World War II, the author developed an interest in military aircraft and over several summers worked at a small airport for flying lessons. At age sixteen, before learning to drive, he soloed in a light trainer.

In 1950 during the early months of the Korean War, while in his freshman year of college, he enlisted in the Air Force serving in Europe and the Far East. He relates the experience as a Korean combat veteran and the place where he grew up in a hurry. Honorably discharged in 1953 he came home with four medals that he describes as insignificant. He returned to school and in December 1955 began a career in law enforcement.

Most of his twenty-six years in law enforcement were spent on the street as a Detective Sergeant and he retired as a Deputy Chief. He became a private detective licensed in four states and dabbled in investigations to the age of seventy-one. He has written a book about his private detective experiences (Poke, Phobe, Pry, and Peek: Detecting the Detectable).

He has owned several aircraft from a 175 HP cabin Fairchild, (The R46 and Little Louie) up to a 3400 HP twin engine B-25, (Barbie III and Company). His latest book, (Giants Over Korea: A Sky Too Far) takes the reader to the B-29 air war over North Korea with frightening detail.

He and his wife have four children and four grandchildren.